Beverly Nye's
Everyone's a Homemaker

Over 150 Delectable New Recipes • Best
Buys at the Supermarket • Canning,
Freezing, Drying and Storing Food •
Cooking and Sewing Tips •
Quick and Easy Housekeeping Hints •
Party Games • Family Activities •
Hundreds of Moneysaving Ideas

One of America's leading homemaking
authorities helps you
with loving ways to care for
a happy, healthy family

EVERYONE'S
A HOMEMAKER

Bantam Books by Beverly K. Nye
  Everyone's a Homemaker
  A Family Raised on Rainbows
  A Family Raised on Sunshine

EVERYONE'S A HOMEMAKER

by Beverly K. Nye

Illustrations by Tom Dusterberg

BANTAM BOOKS
TORONTO · NEW YORK · LONDON · SYDNEY

EVERYONE'S A HOMEMAKER
A Bantam Book / July 1982

All rights reserved.
Copyright © 1982 by Beverly Nye.
Cover art copyright © 1982 by Bantam Books, Inc.
Illustrations copyright © 1982 by Bantam Books, Inc.
This book may not be reproduced in whole or in part, by
mineograph or any other means, without permission.
For information address: Bantam Books, Inc.

Library of Congress Cataloging in Publication Data

Nye, Beverly K., 1934-
Everyone's a homemaker.

Includes index.
1. Home economics.   I. Dusterberg, Tom.   II. Title.
TX145.N89   640   81-17558
ISBN   O-553-01382-3 (pbk.)   AACR2

Published simultaneously in the United States and Canada

Bantam Books are published by Bantam Books, Inc. Its trade-
mark, consisting of the words "Bantam Books" and the por-
trayal of a rooster, is Registered in U.S. Patent and Trade-
mark Office and in other countries. Marca Registrada. Bantam
Books, Inc., 666 Fifth Avenue, New York, New York 10103.

PRINTED IN THE UNITED STATES OF AMERICA

0 9 8 7 6 5 4 3 2 1

Dedicated to our
seven sweet grandbabies—
Emily
Nathan
Mary
Jacob
Jessica
Travis
and Keri
Families truly
bring sunbeams from heaven.

ACKNOWLEDGMENTS

My father in heaven has certainly filled the windows of my life with sunbeams. Roy is the brightest spot in my life, and he makes every day a rich experience. My family certainly deserves a pat on the back for enduring my many experiemnts and showing me love and support when I needed them most. An extra special thanks to Kristen, who has been my right hand during this endeavor and without whose help my "dutchy" way of thinking may have never made its way onto these printed pages. She's been a "gem!" I love her very much.

Many, many thanks to my sister Donna, who worked long, hard hours to help and support me. She is one in a million.

I would also like to thank Bob Braun. Because of his willingness to give me a good foundation in TV, I have met many new, special friends, and enjoyed many other opportunities. I will always value the things I have learned from him. He's a real "pro" in my book.

And to you, my friends and family, who have kept me going with your love, support, and caring. Thanks, everyone! I love you!

CONTENTS

1
WHO IS A HOMEMAKER?

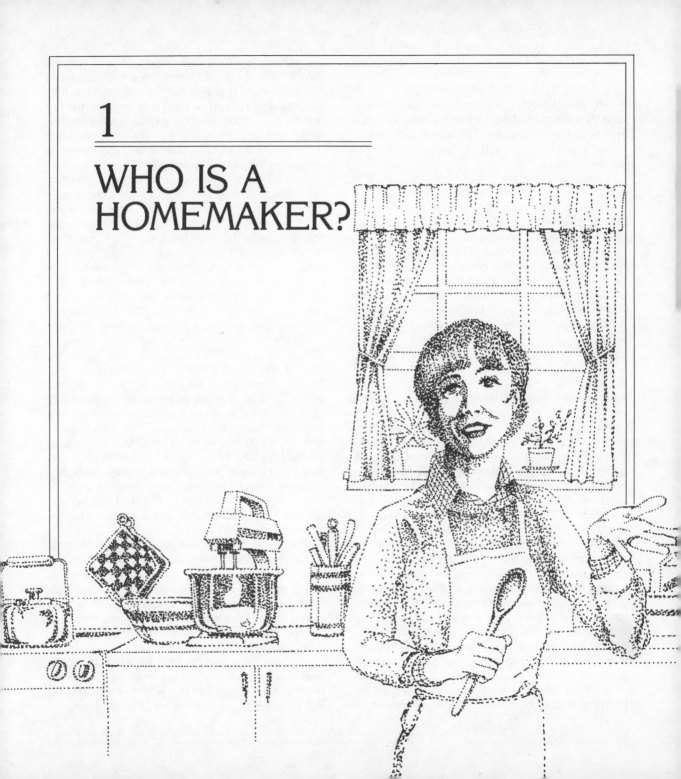

Hi, friends! After visiting with you through *Sunshine* and *Rainbows,* I feel as though you're my next-door neighbors. The world is full of so many special people, and I'm proud to have you as my friends.

I have so many more fun ideas to share with you. I'm really looking forward to our third visit. Here's hoping you come away from our chat feeling happier to be "you" and more excited about your challenge as a homemaker.

If we are asked, "Who is a homemaker?" I think the standard image that comes into our minds is of a 40-year-old woman wearing an apron and stirring up her chocolate chip cookies. This just is not a complete picture. A homemaker can also be a 20-year-old bachelor, an 80-year-old widow, or a 35-year-old single career woman. Each one maintains and "creates" a home for himself and, consequently, becomes a home*maker.* Each one must prepare meals, make the bed, and clean the bathroom, as well as establish the atmosphere of "their" home.

All the recipes and ideas I hope to share with you on these pages will help you accomplish all of these things more easily and with more enthusiasm. Get out those smiles and positive attitudes and add to them the determination to be the best "you" in the world. Remember, when you find someone at the top of the mountain, you know he didn't "fall" there. So if you want to reach the top and be the best, you must start climbing *today.*

I hope you realize what a choice individual you are. There is no other person in this world with the same combination of talents that you have, and you are the only one who can use these abilities. If you don't put them to work, they are worthless. Don't envy someone else; enjoy being you. As a friend of mine once said, "You may make a lousy someone else, but you can be an outstanding you!"

We have 24 hours a day, and how we start the morning and approach each day determines how we will approach life. Why not do it with enthusiasm? Even if you don't feel like smiling or being cheerful, work at it, assume the role, and you'll be surprised by noon how it will stay with you the rest of the day. Think of each day as a mini-life and enjoy it. Any habit is like a heavy cord, and each time we act, we weave a thread, and soon the cord becomes too strong to break.

I heard a story once about an unhappy little boy who became angry at his mother, shouting, "I hate you, I hate you." He ran out of the house and up the hillside shouting these words and soon came running back to tell his mother that there was a mean little boy across the valley shouting, "I hate you," back at him. His mother convinced him to go out and call across the valley, "I love you," and to the little boy's surprise, the voice also called back, "I love you." Like the little boy, we can create any environment for ourselves that we wish.

Too often, we have a tendency to develop a disease that Zig Ziglar discusses in his book *See You at the Top.* It's called "hardening of the attitudes." Do you ever find yourself planting negative seeds by criticizing, complaining, or nagging? Life is like cooking; whatever ingredients you stir in the bowl determines the end result. If you stir ingredients for a pie, you won't get a cake. Choose your ingredients carefully. Give it all you've got and you'll end up with beautiful and satisfying results.

Developing a happy attitude is also very contagious. Again, it's just like food. If you are hungry, go to where the food is; if you want to be happy, surround yourself with "up" people.

Practice thinking *only* happy thoughts. My husband, Roy, and I have a habit that adds a special touch to our lives. Right before we go to sleep at night, we each share the nicest thing that happened to us that day. It makes each of us feel good, keeps us aware of nice things throughout the day, and helps us realize things that are important to the other one.

Enjoying living can become a way of life. Some people are always looking for an excuse to have a miserable existence, but that is all it is—an excuse. We may depend on others for what we have, but what we are depends on us. We don't enjoy life less because we're getting old or tired; we are getting old and tired because we enjoy life less. Why not change that right now?

There is no excitement or real satisfaction in just "keeping up," doing our duty, or being mediocre. Instead we should make the most of our roles as special people and *homemakers.* Instead of just cooking breakfast, create atmosphere and put a flower on the table; instead of just cleaning up the living room, toss a bright pillow on the sofa. Duty brings a feeling of drudgery, but caring brings contentment.

In addition, we need to set our sights high. I'll never forget the story about a young boy who was

mountain climbing in a rugged range near his home when he discovered an eagle's nest with several eggs. He took one of the eggs home with him very carefully and placed it under one of the hens who was sitting on a nest of her own. Soon the eggs hatched, and there was a baby eaglet along with the other little chicks. This baby eaglet scratched for food in the barnyard right alongside the baby chicks. He grew with them and soon became full sized, but he never flew.

One day, the boy, concerned about the eagle, took it up on top of the barn, set the bird on his arm, and said, "You are an eagle, so fly!" But the eagle looked down at the chicks and fluttered down to them and began scratching for his food.

The boy grew more anxious about the bird, and so early in the morning, just as the sun was coming up, he took the eagle again. This time he climbed up the rugged mountain, stood out on a ledge, perched the bird on his arm, and said, "You are an eagle, so fly!" Just then, the eagle looked up at the sky. His eye caught another eagle in the morning sun through the cool, fresh air. Suddenly, the eaglet's wings spread wide, and the boy could feel the power sweep through the entire body of this magnificent bird. It lifted high into the air, sweeping across the mountain peaks, seeing more in an instant than those little earthbound chickens would ever see. Never again would he be content to be a barnyard chicken.

Are we reaching out constantly with an eagerness and anticipation for life, meeting new people, learning new skills, broadening our education, and making the most of who we are, or are we content to be barnyard chickens?

Many homemakers today feel that the solution to their boredom or problems can only come from outside, but "look inside yourself before you look outside." Contentment can only come from within.

Recently, while traveling on a plane, I had a conversation with a stewardess, whose profession many think is exciting. She told me she often feels "taken for granted" when people demand attention and things from her, obviously not caring or thinking of her as a person. She must always smile and "be there." I couldn't help thinking that some mothers should hear her express these things. No position in life is without trying times, and being a successful homemaker, whether you are working or not, is worth every sacrifice. The blessings came back a hundredfold.

A few years ago, a stamp was issued with a picture of a woman and child that read, "A nation is no greater than its homes." Think of the opportunity that you have of creating a peaceful home and thus a stronger nation!

Of course, there are mothers who must work to support their families. To you, I take my hat off because it is a *big* job to wear two hats raising a family. May I counsel you, however, to keep your priorities in the proper perspective. By making your home a "heaven on earth" full of love and caring, you will be blessed and get the added help and support you need to carry forth. Every child deserves a happy home.

To those of you who are single, your role as a homemaker is just as vital. You are creating an atmosphere for a very important person—yourself. The food, the decor, the budget, all shape the person that you are. The attitude with which you go into the world will ultimately affect thousands. You owe it to them *and* to yourself to be the best you can. Enjoy the haven that you create for yourself; take pride in your accomplishments and surroundings. I thoroughly enjoy talking to bachelors when I do an autograph party or lecture and see the joy and enthusiasm on their faces as they describe a particular dish they fixed the night before or tell me of their success canning or dehydrating food. Life is to enjoy, and everyone has much to offer. By filling our homes with love, we have more to share with the world.

Grandparents, don't overlook your roles in homemaking. Just because your children are raised does not mean you haven't anything more to create. Grandparents are blessed with an abundance of affection, and no little child can have too much love. How treasured are those extra hugs, the cuddling, the storytelling, and the patient, listening

ear. You also provide a link to the past, a feeling of belonging, and a sense of continuity. You can extend your four walls to encompass your children's families by helping to meet emergencies, providing an occasional "break" for busy parents, and sharing your wisdom and knowledge.

Joy and happiness are not limited to a certain age group. Everyone has the right and privilege to enjoy these things.

David O. McKay, in *Secrets of a Happy Life,* lists the following sources of happiness:

1. A sense of being free. Free agency is the greatest gift to mankind.
2. A sense of self-mastery. He is a slave who would be led by his appetites.
3. The privilege of work. Idleness does not bring happiness. The right to work is a blessing.
4. The possession of health. Clean and wholesome bodies bring joy. Debauch them and we lose happiness.
5. The ability to see God's beauty about us.
6. The harboring of upbuilding thoughts. What you think about when you do not have to think shows what you really are.
7. Being true to those who trust you.
8. Making friends. True friends enrich life. If you would have a friend, be one.
9. Doing best this hour and you will do better the next.
10. Developing faith. Faith is the foundation of all things—including happiness.

If we could all incorporate these things into our lives, the world would have to be a better place.

We can! With the determination to "make" the best home possible, all it takes is a goal and a willingness to emulate the traits that can make us great.

As a teenager, my favorite story in literature was the "Great Stone Face" by Nathaniel Hawthorne. I read and reread that story many times; even today, just the mention of it gives me a warm feeling. However, after so many years, I couldn't remember why I liked the story so much. When I pulled it down off the shelf recently and reread it, I suddenly realized why it had always touched me so. It taught me that a life of goodness comes with effort, self-discipline, and determination to do right and often not through the ways we would expect at all.

It is a story about a boy named Ernest. He lived in a mountain village. On one of these mountains was a form that from a distance, as the sunset fell across it, resembled a human face. It was a very kindly face.

One night, as Ernest and his mother sat looking at the mountain, she told him of the old Indian legend that someday a child would be born who would grow noble and great and whose face would resemble the man on the mountain. Ernest hoped with all his heart to live to see him. The legend was always in his mind. As he grew up, he was very dutiful to his mother, helping and assisting in any way he could, showing love and kindness to everyone. He had no teachers, only the Great Stone Face. After he finished his work at night, he would sit for hours studying the kind face on the mountain that always seemed to smile at him with encouragement.

Soon there was a rumor in the valley that a man was coming who was the image of the Great Stone Face. His name was Mr. Gathergold, and he was a very rich man, obsessed with his wealth. When he arrived in the village, it was obvious that he was not the man of the legend. Ernest was disappointed, but the Great Stone Face seemed to say, "Fear not, Ernest. He will come!"

Ernest was a young man now, and he went about his work, neglecting no duty and serving with love and humility. He could never commit an unkind act or think unkind things with the Great Stone Face smiling down on him, trusting and encouraging him in every deed.

Soon another man, Old Blood and Thunder, an illustrious commander who was rumored to be the image, came into the village. But Ernest immediately knew with his stern countenance and bloody sword, that he was not the man.

The years flew by, and Ernest became known throughout the valley for his widsom and gentle manner. Many came to visit and counsel with him. "Not a day passed that the world was not better because this man, humble as he was, had lived."

Old Stony Phiz was the next figure that entered the valley. Although called the fulfillment of the legend, once again he did not have the likeness of the Great Stone Face. Ernest grew old, and wrinkles and furrows were inscribed on his kind, gentle face. People traveled for miles just to bask in his knowledge and wisdom. His face would shine on them like an evening light.

One day, a great poet came to see him. They visited together and then went to the mountainside where Ernest was to speak. As the evening sun set on Ernest's face and he spoke the words from his heart, the poet's eyes filled with tears, and he threw his arms up and shouted, "Ernest's face is the image of the Great Stone Face!"

He had become the legend because his goal in life was what he saw in the face on the mountain. He wasn't wealthy, a great military leader, or a politician, but he became great because he served others, and his goals were righteous ones.

Every one of us as homemakers can achieve these goals with our sights set in the right direction. I'm determined to fill my home with sunbeams and be proud that I'm a *homemaker*. How about you?

2
SUNSHINE
IN THE
SUPERMARKET

Lots of people really dislike going to the supermarket, and I agree it can really be a challenge. Life was much easier when the homemaker could send the "man of the house" out to shoot a wild bird while she gathered a pan of potatoes and vegetables from the root cellar, but it wasn't nearly as exciting then. With a little determination and ingenuity, you can save money, provide healthy meals, and have fun doing it as well.

Here are a few beginning hints that will help.

1. Always shop with a list but be flexible to adjust to unexpected specials.
2. Make a map of your supermarket (at least a mental one) so your list is in the right order as you go through the store.
3. Clean out the refrigerator and food shelves before shopping to avoid buying what you don't need or overlooking something you *do* need. (It saves another trip back a day or two later.)
4. Study the grocery ads *before* leaving home.
5. Save coupons only for healthy items you need. Avoid impulse or junk food items. We buy too many things just because we have a coupon.
6. Get acquainted with your butcher. He can give you lots of friendly and valuable advice. Don't be afraid to seek his help.
7. As you wheel your cart into the check-out line, look over your items and see if you can eliminate anything. Often, there are several things you really could do without. Run them back to their places on the shelves. It will save you money, the exercise will be good for you, and you'll feel righteous for having managed your money better.
8. As you place items on the check-out counter, place the prices up. It helps speed up the process.
9. Help the bagger place all the frozen food together in a bag, all perishables together,

and so on. You're just standing there waiting, anyway, and it sure saves time when you get home.

10. If you must shop with children, utilize the experience as a learning tool for them and as a help to you. You can furnish each one with a little list of their own. If they are small, pictures will help. It's a great time to teach them comparison of brands, types, cost, size of package, and so forth. Don't ever feel you don't have time for this. They will always remember the experience, and it will be a big help to them later in their lives. It will also be a big help to you when they, as teenagers, run to the store for you—their choices will be good ones. You couldn't be spending your time more wisely.
11. Be aware of the tricks of the trade to entice you to spend more than you planned to spend. You will be tempted from the minute you walk in the door by those pretty little shortcakes right next to the bright, fresh strawberries, or those snack crackers in a cute little barrel right by the cheese packets, or the bags of caramels which are right beside the apple display. Of course, the lighting and relaxing music puts you in a pretty good spending mood, also. Watch out for the big meat-sale signs when the sale price per pound doesn't coincide with the price on the individual packages. Learn where all the bargains or special sale items are kept and get acquainted with that produce scale. It really pays to weigh those bags that are *supposed* to contain 1 pound of carrots or 5 pounds of potatoes. I've found many to be a half to a full pound off.

Why don't we grab a grocery cart and do some shopping together. The produce department is a good place to start since it is usually right up front in most stores. Let's just discuss each item as we come to it.

PRODUCE

Apples—peak bargain month, October
    3 medium apples to 1 pound
    Rome Beauty and Jonathan for
    baking and cooking
    Delicious for eating

Don't be tempted by those huge beauties; the smaller ones are more tasty. Watch for bruised and soft ones in prepackaged bags. Keep refrigerated.

Artichokes—peak month, April

Look for tight heads; spreading leaves indicate age, and they may be bitter and tough. Artichokes are low in calories and high in nutrition and have a very mild flavor. They are really simple to prepare. Wash well, snip the points with scissors, stand upright in a saucepan (don't use aluminum or cast iron), add 2–3 inches of boiling water, and simmer 45 minutes. Lift out; turn upside down to drain. To eat, pull off leaves one at a time, dip in sauce or butter, and with teeth, scrape off the edible bottom of leaf. Continue until all the leaves are eaten. Then remove the fuzzy core and enjoy the "heart" or tender bottom with a fork.

Asparagus—peak month, April

This vegetable loses sugar quickly, so use it up soon after purchasing. Keep in a plastic bag for no more than 3–4 days. Look for firm stalks and compact tips. Asparagus spears will automatically snap in the right place to remove the woody ends. Cook in a *small* amount of water.

Avocados—peak months, November
    and December

The skin should be smooth and shiny and free from any bruises or brown spots. Avocados are usually very firm in the grocery store; when ripe, however, they will yield to slight pressure with your thumb. Take the firm ones home and place in a brown paper sack on your counter. When they yield to pressure, keep them in the refrigerator until using. If you are only going to use half, leave the pit in the other half and it will keep better. When an avocado is ripe, cut it in half; the skin should peel off each half in a whole piece.

Avocados can also be mashed (add 1 tablespoon lemon juice and a dash of salt to each one) and frozen. They are great on salads or topping a baked potato.

Bananas—peak month, March

These are also low in calories—only 85 per average banana. There are usually about 3 bananas per pound. They are one of the easiest fruits to digest—great for babies or someone with stomach problems. They are best for you when they are flecked with brown spots. This means the starch has converted to sugar. Buy them when they are green or green tipped and allow them to ripen in a paper bag on your counter. When they reach the right stage of ripeness, store in the refrigerator. The skins will turn black, but the banana will keep fine. If you discover a good buy on ripe bananas, you can also mash and freeze them to use in cakes or cookies. We like to slice them on a cookie sheet covered with plastic wrap, freeze, then, when frozen, place the slices in a plastic bag. One handful of frozen slices tossed in the blender with a cup of milk and a few drops of vanilla makes a delicious milkshake, or two handfuls with a cup of milk and vanilla will make a terrific bowl of lo-cal, sugar-free ice cream. A real treat!

Beets—peek month, year round

These are usually a better buy from the farmer's market or, of course, your own garden. If they are priced quite high in the store, I would recommend the canned variety. However, in buying fresh beets, look for firm ones, not too large, with good tops still intact. The tops are delicious steamed in a little water until tender and served with butter. In cooking whole beets, leave the root and a bit of stem on and cook unpeeled. This maintains most of the nutrition and keeps them from "bleeding." After they are fork tender, the skins will slip off. Then serve the beets with a little butter and salt and pepper.

Broccoli—peak month, March

Look for firm, dark-green, almost purplish buds.

The buds that are yellowed and open indicate age. Broccoli is low in sodium and loaded with nutrients. The lower, heavy stems can also be used if you peel away the tough, outer layer. I like to use the tougher ends to make cream of broccoli soup. Don't overcook this vegetable and use a small amount of water. It is good served hot with butter or cheese sauce, raw with a dip, or cooked, chilled, and marinated in an Italian dressing.

Brussels Sprouts—peak month, November
Look for firm, compact little heads. Avoid yellow leaves. Cut a tiny "X" in the core of each one to speed up the cooking. Again, use only a small amount of water and don't overcook. A small piece of celery added to the cooking water will help eliminate the strong cooking odor.

Cabbage—peak, fall and winter
Look for firm, tight heads with no worm holes or yellow, wilting leaves. Cabbage is very high in vitamin C and iron and is a good roughage food. Add it to lettuce salads or use in place of lettuce when lettuce is expensive. A head of cabbage goes a long way. It is delicious steamed as a vegetable, served in a cream or cheese sauce, cooked with sausage, and, of course, in coleslaw. Be sure and try the red cabbage, too. It's just as tasty and *so* pretty. Keep both wrapped in a plastic bag in the refrigerator.

Carrots—peak, spring and fall
Look for carrots with the tops on if you can find them—they will be fresher. Remove the tops as soon as you get home so they don't continue to sop the nutrition and sweetness from the carrots. Store the carrots in a plastic bag. Avoid carrots that are too large; they won't be as nutritious. When preparing cooked carrots or raw carrot sticks, please don't peel them; just scrub them well. Most of the nutrition in vegetables is either in the skin or right under it. If you must peel, do it *thinly*! For a taste treat, try shredding some carrots and mixing with peanut butter and maybe a few raisins. Then spread on fresh whole wheat bread. This is really good!

Cauliflower—peak month, October
Look for firm white heads; avoid brown spots or molding on the head. Clean the head as soon as you get it home and cut or break it into cauliflowerettes. Keep in a plastic bag in the refrigerator and you're always ready with a fresh snack with a dip if you like or with a ready-to-cook vegetable. Don't overcook; use just a little water. Then serve with a cheese sauce or plain with a dab of butter.

Celery—peak, all year
Celery has very few calories. In fact, they say you burn up more calories eating it than you consume through the celery. Isn't that nice? Look for firm, tightly packed bunches. The wide, light-colored stalks are usually most tender. Avoid the yellowing or limp stalks. Clean the celery as soon as you get home. Holding the whole bunch on the cutting board, cut off the end and you will separate and trim the whole bunch at once. Then cut into sticks and store in a plastic bag, washed and ready to eat. Be sure and save all the leaves—the excess can be dried on a paper towel or grocery sack on top of the refrigerator, then kept in a little jar for seasonings.

By keeping celery, cauliflowerettes, broccoli, and some carrot sticks cleaned in bags, you will always have fresh snacks available. Then, after a week or so, if there are any left and they are starting to age, I chop them up together to add to soup or a casserole, or I fix steamed or stir-fried fresh vegetables. Nothing goes to waste!

Coconuts—peak month, December
I hope you don't pass up this taste treat, as well as added nutrition and bulk for your system. Choose a coconut that feels heavy and that you can hear the liquid in when you shake it. To use the coconut, pierce holes in the end eyeholes and drain out the milk. Then place the coconut in a 300° oven for about 1 hour. Then, with a sharp knife, cut the meat from the shell. Store pieces in a plastic bag in the refrigerator and enjoy as a snack. It is also really a good idea to pare slices with a

vegetable parer, toast in a 350° oven for a few minutes (stirring often), and then sprinkle with a little salt. You can shred the pieces, also, to use in cooking. Give these a try!

Corn—peak months, July and August

I can't think of anything that makes my mouth water more than hot corn on the cob dripping with butter. Always eat corn on the cob as soon after picking as possible because the sugars turn quickly to starch. Remember, "freshest is sweetest." If you must store it a day or two, put it in a plastic bag with the husk intact and keep it refrigerated.

When buying corn, look for fresh, green husks with no drying. Never buy corn that has been prehusked if you value flavor. The kernels should be well filled out and never dented or shriveled. The silk should be fresh and attached, never dry. (Did you know there is a strand of silk attached to *each* kernel on the ear? This is the way pollination and development take place.)

Never add salt to the water when cooking your corn. It toughens it as well as leaching nutrients from the vegetable. I always add a smidgen of honey and a couple of the tender light green husks to the water. Have your water boiling, drop in your ears, return to boiling with a lid on your kettle, then let stand for 5–8 minutes. If you overcook corn, it will be very tough. It only takes a short time. As my mom used to say, "You don't have to cook the *cob!*"

Cucumbers—peak months, May and June

Look for firm cucumbers with no shriveling on the ends. Remember that most supermarket cucumbers are waxed to help hold their moisture and shiny appearance. Be sure you don't use the peelings on these.

Eggplant—peak, all year

Look for firm, bright, and shiny plants. Some people avoid these because they don't know how to prepare them. They are really good for you. The smaller ones have a sweeter flavor, and you should pick a heavy one even if it's smaller. Peel the egg-plant, cube it, and toss with Italian dressing—it's terrific raw. Or to cook it, just peel, slice, dip in flour and egg, and then fry in hot oil for about 5 minutes on each side until it's nice and brown. It's also delicious to fry it like this and then layer with mozzarella cheese and cover with spaghetti sauce; bake at 350° for about half an hour. This vegetable can add some real variety to your menu.

Garlic—peak months, July and August

Personally, I don't think any kitchen should be without garlic. It's a little powerhouse of health and flavor. Buy unbroken bulbs with paper-thin skin, free from brown spots. Don't keep the garlic in the refrigerator. It should be out, exposed to the air. To peel the cloves easily, just drop them in hot water.

Grapes—peak months, August and September

Grapes are low in sodium and very high in vitamin A. Avoid any grapes that are shriveled and soft. Green or seedless grapes should be slightly on the yellow side to be real sweet; the red grapes should be dark red. For a fun taste, try freezing a few grapes and then eating them slightly frozen. The kids love them!

Grapefruit—peak season, November through March

Look for heavy fruit that has a smooth, thin skin. A bumpy-type skin indicates thickness. Store in a plastic bag in the refrigerator and they will keep a month or so.

Greens and Spinach—peak month, March

There are all sorts of "greens," from mustard greens to collard greens to turnip greens. They are very rich in vitamin A and are a high-bulk, low-calorie food. Avoid limp, yellowing leaves. Don't leave the greens in a plastic bag in the refrigerator; wrap in a paper towel and use soon. Wash only as you use it. Don't forget to serve some raw by combining them with lettuce in your salads. When cooking, use a very small amount of water and *no* salt. Spinach cooked in *salted* water loses 50 percent of its iron. Salt and butter it when serving. Try a few drops of vinegar or lemon juice on cooked spinach. It's delicious!

Lemons—peak months, June and July

Look for heavy fruit. There are about 3 lemons per pound. One lemon will give you about 3 tablespoons juice and 1 tablespoon grated rind. If you only need a bit of juice, just prick the end and squeeze out what you need. The lemon will keep longer if it's uncut. Lemons are sodium-free, so use the juice instead of salt on your vegetables and salads.

Lettuce—available all year

The leaf-type lettuce comes on the market in early spring. In head lettuce, look for a head that is not too heavy (it will be all core) and one that has a good green color. Avoid any with rust on the core. Don't get in a rut, though, and only buy head lettuce. Try Boston lettuce; it has a rich buttery flavor and is reasonably priced. Endive and escarole are, too, and their curly leaves look so pretty in a salad. Romaine has a long, narrow head and is great on sandwiches. It's a little crisper and has bigger leaves, so it is easy to work with when making sandwiches. Bibb lettuce is usually quite expensive but a real taste treat.

Limes—peak month, July

Again look for heavy fruit. This fruit goes from dark green to light green and then turns yellow. It is flavorful and juicy at all stages. A little wedge of lime really enhances a serving of melon.

Mushrooms—available all year

Look for caps that are closed underneath near the stem. If they are wide open, they will be spongy. Brown soft spots indicate spoiling. Mushrooms are very low in calories but rich in vitamins and minerals and especially high in protein. There are about 6 cups in a pound, so they really aren't as expensive as they may seem. Don't wash the mushrooms until you are ready to use them and never let them stand in water. Just rinse well and trim off the ends. They are delicious raw in salads. They also freeze well—just slice and freeze on cookie sheets and then store in plastic bags.

Onions—available all year

Avoid any onions that are sprouting or wet—they should be firm and dry. Yellow onions are used primarily in cooking, white onions are more delicate in flavor, and the red onions are sweeter and really good for slicing on hamburgers. We like sliced red onions or onions and cucumbers combined in a glass jar and covered with vinegar and lots of salt and coarse-ground pepper. Let stand in the refrigerator overnight. They're delicious. Don't store onions with potatoes. The potatoes give off moisture and will hasten spoilage. Also don't throw those tops away from the green onions. Chop them, dry on a paper towel, and store for seasoning.

Oranges—peak season, December through March

Look for firm and heavy fruit. The thin, smooth skin indicates a juice orange, and the coarser skin is a good eating orange. However, if the skin is *too* coarse, it will be very thick. If you find an extra-good buy on oranges, buy a bunch, peel, slice, and freeze on cookie sheets covered with plastic wrap. Then store in plastic bags. They make a great snack, taste just like a popsicle, are terrific for teething toddlers to chew on, and can be put on a pretty plate for a breakfast treat. They thaw quickly.

Parsley—peak months, November and December

This is one of the least expensive, most nutritious vegetables you can buy. Look for fresh green bunches. Avoid any yellowing or mushy stems. Wash the parsley well (picking out any bad sections) and pat dry with paper towels. Then pack tightly into a clean glass jar, cover, and refrigerate. You'll be surprised how nicely it keeps. Cut it up in salads, chop in other vegetable dishes, or even serve it on sandwiches in place of lettuce. Parsley was meant to be eaten, not just used as decoration! Learn to enjoy its flavor. It's also a great bit of chlorophyll. Eat a little after a spicy meal for nice clean breath!

Parsnips—peak month, January

This is another vegetable often avoided because people don't know how to fix it. They really are so good. Avoid the extra large ones and the ones that feel wilted. Parsnips are nearly always coated with wax, so they do need to be peeled. Then just cut in chunks and cook in a small amount of water until tender. I like to sprinkle a little nutmeg over them with some butter, and our family thinks they're great.

Peaches—peak months, July and August

It's really sad that you can very rarely find good peaches in the supermarket. Avoid the green, hard fruit; they hardly ever ripen to satisfaction. Judge a good peach by its smell; and for the best flavor, always serve at room temperature.

Pears—peak months, September and October

Pears are usually sold green because they don't keep well after ripening. However, they do ripen at home quite nicely. Just put them in a brown paper sack and check often. Once they have ripened to your taste, keep them in the refrigerator but bring them out a while before serving so that they warm to room temperature. The Bartlett variety is the well-known, autumn, eating pear. The Bosc pear, also known as the homely pear because of its brown, fuzzy appearance, is a winter pear. It's good for baking but is usually quite expensive.

Peppers—peak month, June

A good pepper should feel heavy and be free from soft, shriveled spots. Peppers are rich in vitamin C and low in calories. A red bell pepper is simply a "ripe" green bell pepper.

Pineapple—peak months, May and June

Avoid any with soft spots. They should have a pleasant pineapple smell and a slight yellow tinge. When a pineapple is ripe, the leaves will pull out easily from the top. Remember, never use fresh pineapple in gelatin; the gelatin will not "set up."

Potatoes and Yams—regular potatoes (white and red) available all year
—Yams, peak month, November

Watch for decay spots, sprouting, or large green areas. Some red potatoes and yams are dyed. The white, or Idaho, potato is a dry, mealy type; the red, round potato is moister and holds its shape after cooking. I prefer the white for baking and the red for potato salad, scalloped potatoes, mashed, and so on. Don't overlook the small, "new" red potatoes in the spring. They are delicious cooked in their skins and served with butter and parsley or creamed with peas. All potatoes are rich in vitamin C and are a good source of fiber in the diet. When possible, cook with the skins on—there is a powerhouse of nutrition in and just below the potato peel. All potatoes should be kept in a dark, cool, *dry* place. Light causes them to turn green, and refrigeration causes the starch to turn to sugar.

A yam has rich, dark-orange meat and is very moist. A sweet potato is lighter yellow and is quite dry in comparison to a yam. Also, its shape is a little more round than a yam's. Please don't mask the delicious flavor of a baked yam with lots of sweet toppings and syrups. They are so very good just baked in their skins and served with a generous dab of butter.

Radishes—peak months, April and May

Radishes should feel firm and crisp. The bunches with tops still intact will be fresher than those packaged in the cellophane bags. White radishes usually have a little more "bite" than the red ones. For a change of pace, try winter or Oriental white radishes, which are about a foot long. These are really terrific. Slice them thinly on some fresh bread and butter and sprinkle with a little salt, shred and marinate them in Italian dressing, or shred them up in a salad. They are even good sautéed and served as a vegetable. Believe me, you'll get your money's worth!

Summer Squash and Zucchini—peak months, July and October

They should be heavy for their size and firm

and crisp. Avoid those that are real big, as they will be seedy. Watch out for shriveling on the ends. This is a sign of aging.

Winter Squash
(Acorn, Butternut, Hubbard)—
peak month, October

These also should be heavy for their size and show no bruising or decay spots. I prefer to cut them in large pieces, bake in a 375° oven until tender, and just serve with butter and salt and pepper. Since the acorn squash tends to have a little drier-type meat, I invert the halves on a cookie sheet or pie pan with a little water in the bottom of the pan. These are also good baked with a stuffing in the cavity. A little browned sausage added to the stuffing mixture is good. It adds moisture and flavor to the squash. All squash is rich in vitamin A.

Turnips and Rutabagas—
peak season, November to March

These vegetables should feel heavy for their size. They are usually waxed to help preserve moisture, so be sure and peel them. They are delicious and crunchy and make a nice accompaniment to a sandwich. (Serve raw in strips or sliced.) They are also very tasty boiled, mashed, and sprinkled with a little nutmeg and a dab of butter. Rutabagas are very rich in vitamin C, and one serving gives you half the daily requirement of this vitamin.

Tomatoes—peak season, May, June, and July

Tomatoes should feel firm and have a good color and a fragrant tomato smell. I feel they are a waste of money out of season. They are a pretty addition to a salad but very expensive and don't have much flavor or nutrition. When slicing tomatoes, slice them up and down instead of crosswise and you will have less juice in your salad or on your sandwich.

Remember, with all vegetables, don't overcook, serve raw when possible, don't peel any more than necessary, don't *soak* in water, and never add salt to the small amount of cooking water. (It leaches out vitamins.) Salt when serving. Be adventurous and try them all.

Think twice before passing up all that beautiful fruit at 89¢ a pound, thinking it's too expensive, and then go and pay $2–$3 a *pound* for a package of cookies!

BAKERY AISLE—
BREAD, CRACKERS, ROLLS, COOKIES

There are many types of crackers available, but they are very expensive. Soda crackers are about the only type I consider buying, as they are cheaper than you could make at home. For a change of pace, you might like to try the oyster crackers. They taste the same, but the shape adds some interest to your meals. The cost is the same.

When picking up that loaf of bread, remember it is at least 50 percent water and air. When we realize how little nutrition and how many chemicals we are getting, it is easy to see why a slice of bread has been described as an edible napkin or presliced Styrofoam, as my husband, Roy, calls it. Some breads boast of "no preservatives," but what they aren't saying is that there are about ninety chemicals that they can add without listing them on the label. Be aware of words like "natural," "old-fashioned," and "health." They can be very misleading. Always read the labels. You'll find most "wheat" bread contains nearly all white flour and some coloring. A wheat grinder can be a very wise investment. Those wheat kernels are so inexpensive and so good for us; it's a shame to miss out on so much with commercial products. I always smile when a label says "enriched" because in this process twenty-five known nutrients are destroyed and five are added back. That makes as much sense as withdrawing $100 from our savings and putting back $20. We can't build our savings or our bodies and health with that type of logic. Baking is so easy now. It takes very little time and is so worth the effort, so think twice before you spend $1.29 for a loaf of "health" bread or $3 for that starchy, sweet pie. You can also bake a lot of good, nutritious cookies for that same $2 that will

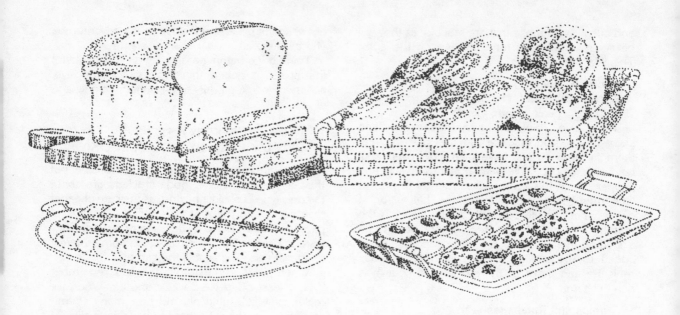

only buy you a bag of chemicals, preservatives, coloring, and sugar off the shelf.

DRIED FRUITS

Raisins are usually a fairly good buy. However, don't pay for all that extra packaging and "convenience" by buying individual packets. Raisins should be kept in a tightly covered glass jar or plastic container with a tight top. Raisins contain no fat, no cholesterol, and are very low in sodium. I usually buy currants instead of raisins. They are not quite as sweet but very similar in flavor and much smaller than raisins. We find that we enjoy them more in cookies, cakes, and so on, than the "big" raisin. Also, our son is allergic to grapes, so this is a way he can have raisin-type recipes.

Prunes also can be a good buy. A few stewed for breakfast with a little lemon juice and grated rind or cut up in a cake or pudding are tasty and very good for you.

Dates are another natural snack that are worth the money. Because of their natural sweetness,

they go a long way and can be used in many ways. Try a few dates instead of a candy bar. You'll feel better.

Apricots, apples, and peaches are usually very expensive and can be dried easily at home. See chapter 4 for directions.

Nuts are also on this aisle, and we shouldn't overlook their goodness. Nuts keep better in the shells. When they are shelled, they should be kept in the refrigerator or freezer. Their natural oils go rancid very easily, and the vitamins and minerals do deteriorate. A bowl of peanuts in the shell can be as tempting as a dish of candy and are a great source of protein to those who don't eat much meat.

Popcorn is an outstanding buy. This is one snack food that is really good for you. It can even be a diet food. If you don't drown it in butter, it's so low in calories you can eat all you want. Dentists recommend popcorn as a snack for children, too. It's actually good for their teeth. Keep a supply on hand always. Just don't make the costly mistake of buying all the gimmick-type bags, pop-in pouches, artificially colored kernels, special oils, or seasonings. That simple, bulk popcorn pops just as well.

CANNED FRUITS AND VEGETABLES

The average life of canned food, unopened, is one year. However, watch for bulged lids, which indicate spoiling, and discard immediately. I try never to buy dented cans because this can cause an air pocket and lead to spoilage.

Learn to be a label reader so that you know what you are eating. Labels can be very interesting and helpful things.

The following is my advice on canned goods: canned potatoes are a waste of money—it is so simple to cook a few at home. Canned pumpkin is considerably cheaper than prepared pumpkin pie filling. I completely avoid any canned fruit pie filling. You are paying for cornstarch, and you usually end up with more thickener than fruit. When buying canned pimentos, freeze any left over. Since they are expensive, we need to eliminate any waste. Get acquainted with canned white corn as well as yellow. It comes in the creamed style, also, and is delicious. There usually is no price difference. Canned carrots lose a lot of nutrients and are no saving over fresh or frozen.

Keep a can of beets on hand to drain and add to your leftover pickle juice. Let stand in the refrigerator a couple of days and you'll have delicious pickled beets. Watch the cost on green beans. These can really vary a lot according to brand and cut or style.

Keep a glass jar in your freezer to accumulate scraps of leftover vegetables; this will eliminate buying mixed vegetables.

Don't overlook the institutional-sized cans. These things can be opened and repackaged. I have recanned pickles, especially hamburger slices, and relishes in pint jars and have frozen smaller containers of nearly all the fruits—pineapple, applesauce, pears, and so on.

Be sure and check the type of syrup on canned fruits. Peaches in light syrup are much tastier and better for you than the ones in heavy syrup. Be careful also of the so-called "lite" brands. Often they are full of additives and artificial flavors, and you are not saving many calories.

GELATINS AND PUDDINGS

Bear in mind here that gelatins are mostly sugar and artificial coloring. You may want to get some Knox gelatin and make your own with real fruit juices at home. (See chapter 3.) It's just as easy. Instant puddings are nice to have on hand, but they can be made simply at home, also.

Tapioca is nutritious and great to have on hand. It is inexpensive and can be used in many ways. Buy a box and give it a try. There are lots of ideas on the package. I prefer the quick-cooking variety.

Please pass up the custard mixes, cheesecake mixes, canned puddings, and nondairy whipped cream powders. Just reading the labels makes me feel ill. Nothing can compare to real whipped cream, and if you are concerned with calories, just eat a small amount. You'll be better off than eating that long list of chemicals.

DRIED BEANS, PEAS

Canned beans are convenient to have on your shelf, but you pay for the convenience. The dry varieties are easy to cook, and you can freeze containers of them to use later. Dry beans can be soaked overnight and then cooked until tender. Or you can cover them with hot water, bring to a boil, boil 2 minutes, and remove from heat and let stand, covered, for 1 hour. Then cook until tender. I prefer to soak them overnight. Any acid ingredient toughens beans and slows down the cooking, so never add tomatoes, vinegar, and so on, until the beans are tender. Beans also take longer to cook in high altitudes. There are so many delicious varieties, and they are such an important source of vitamins and minerals, as well as being inexpensive, so cook some type of bean every week. Be sure and try split peas, lentils, limas, and garbanzo varieties.

Rice is also a tremendous buy on this counter.

Avoid the packaged mixes and instant types, as the long-grain, regular rice is better than the instant variety. Brown rice is the richest in nutrition because the bran or hull is left on.

JUICES

Stick with the 100 percent juices in this aisle. Check the label to make sure you aren't paying for a lot of water and sugar. Watch for words like "natural style," "old-fashioned," and "healthful." These can be really misleading; 100 percent juice is your best bet! The powdered "juice" mixes are simply sugar, citric acid, and chemicals. You might as well take a sugar-coated vitamin C tablet.

Try some of the more unusual juices. You may discover a real treat for your family to take the place of all that soda pop. How about apricot nectar, red or white grape juice, papaya, cranberry (great for the kidneys), or even prune juice. (With a wedge of lemon, it's a delicious ice-cold drink.)

PREPARED FOODS—SPECIALTIES

All of the canned fishes are a good buy nutritionally in this aisle. Tuna is very rich in vitamin B_{12} and iodine. It also is easily digested, as the oil contains no cholesterol and the fish is high in polyunsaturates. There is no waste in any of the canned fishes, so considering this, they are a good choice for lunches and even main-dish meals. Even the bones in a can of salmon are good for you and provide needed calcium. Introduce your family to sardines, herring, kippered snacks, even canned mackerel. With a little mustard, these make delicious sandwiches.

Do avoid the canned chicken, ham, beef, and so on, though. They are very overpriced and can be easily duplicated with fresh cuts. I also pass up all the canned stews, chili, macaroni and cheese, spaghetti, boxed pizza mixes, supper helpers, and so on. The amount of actual nutritious food you get for your dollar is ridiculous. None of these things are difficult to make and are so much more reasonable. I could not believe it when I studied a package of instant soup "helper." You had to add

your own beef and cook for 90 minutes; the package contained a very few dried vegetables, seasonings, and a lot of chemicals—all for $1.20. By using my own meat and water, I can add my leftover vegetables and seasonings for practically nothing and still make soup in 90 minutes. "Convenience foods" aren't what they're cracked up to be!

Canned soups are very high in salt content, so I usually avoid them, too. However, occasionally, a can makes an easy addition to a casserole without a great expense. Soup is such a joy to make, though; so don't always rely on cans. Make up a homemade batch and see how satisfying it can be.

In the Mexican and Chinese section, try to purchase only the basic ingredients. The mixtures, combinations, and ready-prepared items are very much overpriced. Can you believe 79¢ for four taco shells that are preshaped when you can get a dozen for 59¢ and fry your own in 1 minute?

BAKING NEEDS

Usually, the larger-sized bags of flour and sugar are more reasonable, but this isn't always true, so compare bag prices.

Both dark and light brown sugar are available. Brown sugar is *not* raw sugar. It is simply white sugar with a molasses-type syrup stirred into it.

Flour comes in whole wheat (the germ is usually removed because it would turn rancid on the shelf), "enriched," white, unbleached, self-rising (this usually contains salt and baking powder and/or soda), rye, graham (a coarse pumpernickel type), and bread flour. Bread flour is relatively new on the market and is made from a hard wheat, giving it more gluten, which works to rise with the yeast in bread.

Cornmeal, both yellow and white, is something we should always have on hand. It's a great source of protein and so versatile.

Look for the pinhead oatmeal (also called pin oats or steel-cut oats) near the flour section. It is very economical and a real taste treat.

When buying oils and shortening, again be sure you read your label. Most oils are soybean oil. Peanut oil is more expensive but gives a very good flavor and has many nutrients. Neither olive oil nor safflower oil contains any cholesterol. I avoid the "spray-on" oils because they are so expensive. I don't like the chemicals, and a tiny dab of my regular oil works just as well and gives me no more calories.

I can't believe all the expensive chocolate mixes and flavorings. It's so easy to make your own hot chocolate mix. (See *A Family Raised on Sunshine*, page 12.) Even cocoa is expensive now. I suggest you buy a bag of carob powder at the health food store and mix it half and half with your can of cocoa. It's much cheaper, tastes the same, and is better for you.

You can also make your own sweetened condensed milk. (See *A Family Raised on Sunshine*, page 13.) Powdered milk is always a good buy and should be kept on the shelf at all times. Canned milk comes in several varieties. "Evaporated" milk (milk with some of the water removed) comes in low-fat, skim, and whole. "Sweetened

condensed" milk is very sweet and thick. It also has some of the water removed, but large amounts of sugar are also added. Buttermilk is available now in powdered form and is a great advantage to the shopper because you don't have to worry about spoilage and it will keep for months.

All of the pasta products are a good buy. Be sure and try a variety. Rigatoni and shell shapes are fun, and the many types of noodles can add excitement to your meals. Try the spinach noodles or whole wheat pasta if you can find it. Avoid the canned, bottled, and packaged sauces, though. A can of tomatoes or tomato sauce and a few seasonings from your kitchen shelf will taste much better and save you many cents.

The price of spices is absolutely ridiculous, and we'll discuss that more in chapter 4, but you can save a great deal just by avoiding the flavored salts (celery, garlic, seasoning). A crushed garlic clove or two in a box of salt works great and costs only pennies. When buying vanilla, be sure and buy pure vanilla and then use much less. The flavor is so much better. Vanilla can actually be left out of many recipes (such as chocolate chip cookies,

and so on) when its flavor should not dominate in any way. Save the vanilla for sauces or delicate things where the flavor counts.

No use wasting your grocery money on baking crumbs, croutons, or bread crumbs. You can accumulate your own in a bag in the freezer from that leftover toast, heel of bread, and so on, and season them as you wish. The blender is great for making bread crumbs; just throw in about ½ cup of pieces and in a few seconds you have beautiful bread crumbs!

Be sure and watch for expiration dates on baking powder. It can be real disheartening to have poor baking results because it was too old.

Now zip right by the candy aisle. We get enough sugar in our other foods, and for a special treat we can enjoy that delicious fruit or make some wholesome goodies at home!

SALAD DRESSINGS

Salad dressings are another item that we purchase for so much money and from which we get so little food value. Don't be misled by those fancy big bottles; just look and see how few ounces they really hold. We can make a quart of dressing for so much less at home. (See recipes in chapter 3.)

I like to look for ideas on all the crouton and salad-fixing packages and then go home and make my own from leftover bread and a few seasonings. Some combinations we like are:

Homemade croutons, crumbled bacon, and grated American cheese
Homemade croutons, diced pepperoni, and Parmesan cheese
Homemade croutons, garlic, onion, and parsley, toasted with a little melted butter

FROZEN FOODS

I just whiz on by the convenience frozen food section. Nothing here tastes as good, is nearly as reasonable, or keeps us as healthy as the things we can make and freeze at home.

The best buys in the frozen food section are the large bags of vegetables. With these, you can cook just what you need without waste. We can all add a dab of butter or make a cream sauce, so don't pay them to do this simple task for you.

COSMETICS

This is usually a good aisle to avoid, also, because most of your purchases here will be impulse items. They will probably be cheaper at your discount drug store, so make a separate list for these things.

JAMS, JELLIES, SPREADS, AND CEREALS

Jams and jellies are a personal preference but very expensive. We'll discuss making your own in chapter 4.

Peanut butter is very high in protein and vitamins, but look for the kinds that say peanuts and salt and that's all! Some of the leading brands are loaded with dextrose (sugar) and lots of additives. Check those labels.

The cereal counter is one of the most misleading in the whole grocery store. The boxes and packages just sing out to us about all the goodness they contain, but the nutritionists tell us that "never before have we bought such a small amount of food in such big boxes." By the time they "crack" and "shred" and "puff" and "pop" the ingredients together and add all the colors and sugar coatings, we'd probably be better off eating the box. Did you realize that if you eat an average-sized bowl of any cereal that is 50 percent sugar, and there are many, you get the equivalent of *18 teaspoons* of sugar. Even the cooked cereals are becoming the victim of additives and "dressing up." Stick with the basics—oatmeal, cream of wheat, cracked wheat, and so forth—and dress them up at home with raisins, dried apples, or whatever your family likes. Try making your own cocoa wheat cereal with some finely cracked wheat or cream of wheat, a bit of white cornmeal (farina), and a sprinkling of cocoa. The toaster pastries and granola bars are about as good for you as a candy bar, so don't waste your money. A piece of whole wheat toast and some fruit are just as simple and much better for your health.

CLEANSERS AND SOAPS

This section of the store is mind boggling. It seems as if there is a cleaner for every item made. If we bought everything that it is claimed we need, we wouldn't have room for anything else in our cupboards.

A few basic products can accomplish as much as all of these put together. A good all-purpose detergent, a jug of bleach, a dishwashing liquid (this doubles for hand washables), and a large can of cleanser are about all you need to tackle any job. I make my own window cleaner by combining 1 pint water, 4 tablespoons alcohol, 4 tablespoons sudsy ammonia, and coloring if desired—and put the contents in a squirt bottle. A soft cloth (wring out in vinegar and let dry) makes a great dust cloth that the dust will cling to. Next time you shop, ask yourself how many of these items you can do without (more hints in chapter 8).

SOFT DRINKS AND SNACKS

Save your money and try some of the good recipes that are included in the next chapter.

PAPER PRODUCTS

When shopping this section of the supermarket, there are two major things to remember. First, many of these disposable products can be done without; second, those that you use regularly can be purchased from wholesalers at a big savings. Buying larger rolls and packages designed for commercial use is much more economical, and they are often stronger. Remember that facial tissues are usually on sale at a bargain price in the summer months since we don't have many colds then and the demand is not so great. Large rolls of foil, waxed paper, and plastic wrap are good things to purchase (the larger the roll, the better) but should be used sparingly. Foil can be wiped off and used again. Start thinking twice before you tear off yards and yards of these products and ask yourself if it's really necessary. I completely pass by the paper napkins. Cloth ones can be made from scraps of fabric (even flannel works nicely), and it sure saves a lot of waste. Besides, cloth ones are nicer to use. Paper towels can also be eliminated or cut back on. A hand towel hung near the sink works fine, and an old rag or sponge can be used to wipe up spills, rinsed well, and used over and over. Brown paper grocery bags are very absorbent and work great for draining bacon, French fries, and so on. Besides, you get them free with your groceries.

I do buy the large boxes of plastic sandwich bags and food storage bags. These can also be washed out and used over and over. I usually wash mine out in clean dish water before I start washing dishes; then my water is free from any grease and will leave the bags sparkly clean. I also save any other plastic bags that items come in, wash them, and use them over and over. We could learn a great lesson from the Europeans, who always carry a cloth bag or basket with them to eliminate the need for extra packaging. A good share of what we pay for our food products goes for the material it is wrapped in. Let's help our environment and our purses by cutting down on all these disposables.

Paper cups and plates can be passed by, also, except for those rare occasions of large picnics and similar events. Ordinary dishes are much more pleasant to eat from, and dishwashing *can* be a choice time either to get better acquainted with your mate or child or, if you are alone, to contemplate or plan ideas.

Don't waste your money on plastic wastebasket liners. A brown grocery bag works just as well, and if the garbage you'll be using it for is damp, put a Styrofoam meat tray in the bottom of the sack to protect it from the moisture. Don't throw money away on throwaways!

MEATS

Be wise in this department. Meat is one of the biggest money makers in the store, so the store will be trying to tempt you to spend a lot. Take advantage of the meat specials; they are often cheaper than wholesale. Look for dry packages of meat. Avoid the ones with a lot of liquid in the trays. A lot of flavor, nutrition, and tenderness are lost through this liquid, and the longer the meat lies in the liquid, the more it deteriorates. Beef should be bright red; pork, a grayish pink; veal, pink; and smoked meats, a rosy color. Ham will have a grayish cast when exposed to the light. This is why the packages of ham are always turned upside down in the meat case. Learn to think in terms of cost per serving. Often, a well-trimmed, boneless piece will cost less to serve than a cheaper cut even if initially it is more per pound. *Always* check the *price per pound.*

Be sure and save the Styrofoam trays. Wash them well and use them to cook in your microwave, to freeze cookies or baked goods, or as a small cutting board to chop onions or garlic.

When buying beef, look for the large cuts; then compare price per pound. Look at the piece and determine how you can cut it in smaller pieces for a variety of meals. The round bone or arm roast is a good example. The oblong lean part can be cut away, partially frozen for easier handling, and then sliced horizontally to make individual Swiss or country-fried steak. The round lean section makes a nice little pot roast with vegetables, and the other sections can be cut up for a stew, stroganoff, chili, or spaghetti. It can also be used with the bone and trimmings for a big pot of soup. You'll find you get much better meat this way and at a far better price than buying individual packages of stew meat, roast, steaks, and so on. Get out of the habit of thinking individual packages per meal. This is especially a good idea for a couple or singles because you save so much money and have a variety, too. I always keep a package of suet in my freezer. (This is a rich, flavorful fat; just ask your butcher for some.) It is so nice to use to brown the lean steaks or roast you have cut yourself. Just put a few pieces of the suet in a hot skillet and fry out enough fat to brown the meat well. It really gives a good, rich flavor.

The ground sirloin patties or ground chuck or round are often a better buy than hamburger. Since you won't end up with so much grease and water, you can get by with a smaller package. The amount of ground beef in chili, spaghetti sauce, or casseroles can nearly always be cut down without affecting the recipe. You receive all the necessary proteins and amino acids with the combination of meat and beans or grains such as wheat, rice, or corn-meal. I've often made a big batch of chili from just one or two sirloin patties because they are all meat and not fat and water. You'll be surprised how far a piece of beef can go when you start cutting it up yourself and using your imagination.

Veal is the meat of a very young calf (usually under three months), so it is always tender. How-ever, because it is so young, it has very little fat on it. Therefore, it will dry in cooking unless you use some suet on it. It has a delicate flavor and is quite expensive, so avoid it in your daily menus if you are watching your budget.

Pork has really been improved over the years and is a very versatile as well as economical meat. Pork should always be cooked done and never served rare.

By the way, I cook all my beef and pork roasts as well as Swiss steak, pork and sauerkraut, and so on, *on top* of the stove. Just heat your pan well, brown meat on all sides, add desired vegetables or other ingredients, cover, and cook over low heat until done. It saves so much electricity or gas, is very easy, and the meat is absolutely delicious and tender. Try it!

I feel the best buys in pork are pork chops and the loin. You get the most meat for your money. The thinly cut breakfast chops can be misleading, however. They are usually so thin they dry out in cooking. Buy a whole loin and cut up the chops yourself. It's very simple.

Ham is always a good buy, and you have such a large selection. A whole ham is the hip and leg section of the pig. It is often cut in half with a large slice out of the center (called a ham roast). The top round or meaty half is called the butt end, and the lower half is called the shank end and includes the tapering leg end. The butt end will usually cost a few cents more per pound but is worth it because it is meatier. If the ham is labeled butt or shank *halves,* it means the center slice has not been removed; if it is referred to as ends, it has been. I like to buy the whole ham (it's cheaper per pound that way) and have the butcher cut it for me. These pieces of ham are so full of delicious varieties of meals.

First, I roast one of the halves in a 325° oven for a couple of hours and serve it sliced for dinner. Then I cut off a few more slices for sandwiches or to fry with eggs for breakfast. (It's so much cheaper than bacon, more practical because it doesn't shrink down like bacon, and you get much more food value.) Then I cover the rest with water and sim-mer for an hour or so. After simmering, I cool it slightly and pick all the meat from the bones. In the liquid, I cook up some "great northern" or "lima" beans with a few sliced carrots and celery for a delicious soup, adding a little of the cut-up ham. I package the rest of the pieces of ham I picked from the bone in bags and freeze. They're great to add to a casserole or scalloped potatoes or even to grind up and add a little mayonnaise and pickle relish for a delicious ham salad sand-wich. This way you won't waste a scrap.

A country ham is salted and cured by smoking and needs to be soaked before cooking to remove some of the salt. It has a much stronger flavor than regular city ham, and they are often com-bined to be served together. City ham is cured with a liquid or pickling solution. Smoked Boston butts and cottage or picnic hams are also avail-able and reasonable. These will be a little fattier than regular ham and have a more irregular bone structure. The boneless hams are always a good buy, also. I never buy canned hams because I prefer the other types where I can see what I'm buying. But if you buy them, remember they must be refrigerated.

Include more pork in your menus. It is higher in thiamine than any other food and is rich in protein and iron.

Turkey and chicken are good choices in the meat counter, also. They are priced reasonably, are low in calories and good for you, and provide countless choices in preparing meals. I prefer tur-key to chicken because it contains more meat and less bone, but you can use the two meats inter-changeably in all recipes. Be sure and cut up your own fryers. Then you can accumulate bags of white meat for fried chicken, wings and backs for stock, and so on. Don't forget to save the chicken livers in a bag in the freezer until you have enough to fry for a yummy supper. I like to have chicken broth on hand in the freezer at all times, so I even simmer my chicken in a pot to make stock before I fry it. Then I fry it in the oven. (See *A Family Raised on Sunshine*, page 21.) If it has been presimmered, it fries in half the time, with half the margarine needed, is so juicy and tender, and I have the benefit of a nice kettle of stock or broth.

As you know, I try to avoid frankfurters and luncheon meats because of all the additives and fillers as well as the outrageous price per pound for the amount of meat we are getting. Stop and think: if you pay $1 for a little 4 ounce packet of that wafer-thin, chopped, pressed beef, you are paying $4 a *pound*. You could have a delicious ham or roast beef sandwich for much less than that. Give some thought to the sandwiches you are making for your family.

If pork sausage is expensive, I just watch for a sale on pork loins. Then I cut the meat off the bone and grind up my own. It's so good and you can add any seasonings you desire. In addition, you *know* what type of meats are in it. I always smile when sausage or frankfurters say "all-meat." They should say "all kinds of meat" because they can put in lips, snouts, tails, and so on, according to government standards!

When you cook your meat, don't forget to save *all* bones and trimmings in a plastic bag in the freezer. They are terrific for soup stock.

But meat is one item we can stand to cut down on in the grocery store. Let's be more creative and economical when it comes to this section of our shopping.

THE DAIRY CASE

Watch for the date stamped on the top of milk cartons. It is the last day recommended for sale, but it will usually be good for a few days after that. The older dates are usually pushed to the front of the case, so be careful. The higher the cream content, the longer the milk will keep, so skim milk will sour before whole milk. Also, don't ever pour a little leftover milk from one carton into another. Milk perishes gradually, and this could cause the new carton to spoil. You can keep leftover milk in a dark-colored glass jar or covered container. Exposure to the light will cause some vitamin loss, and waxed cartons do allow some flavors and smells to penetrate.

Milk continues to climb in price. Two percent milk is just as nutritious for us and has less fat, so teach your family to enjoy it.

Also, did you know that milk is a primary source of calcium and that chocolate inhibits calcium absorption by the body? So it seems silly to drink chocolate milk, doesn't it? Carob, banana, or strawberry would be much wiser choices to flavor milk for drinking.

Commercial buttermilk is not the by-product of churning cream into butter as it used to be. It is made from skim milk or stale, pasteurized, whole milk with a fermenting culture added. It doesn't have all the nutrients the old type did, but it still is a good food product because of its lactic acid. It is also low in calories and easy to digest. You can make your own buttermilk to drink according to the recipe on the side of the powdered milk package or use the powdered buttermilk for cooking to save money.

The only types of cream generally found in the dairy cases are half-and-half and whipping cream. Half-and-half is a mixture of milk and cream and must contain 10–12 percent milk fat. I use it in all recipes calling for light cream. Whipping cream must have at least 30 percent milk fat. Although it's a far cry from the heavy, rich whipping cream we knew on the farm, it's still the best when a recipe calls for whipped cream. There is no taste comparison to the nondairy whipped toppings despite what the commercials tells us. Even their labels make me feel a little ill—sugar, hydrogenated coconut and soybean oil, sodium caseinate, sodium silico aluminate, propylene glycol monostearate, acetylated monoglycerides, and so on!

Yogurt is a very healthy food. It is excellent for soothing indigestion and contains lactic acid, which helps assimilate iron, protein, and calcium. It also attacks the harmful bacteria in the digestive system and manufactures vitamin B. It can be enjoyed plain, or you can add your own fruit (avoiding the sugar that the commercial fruited kinds contain). Use it in puddings, ice creams, dressings, and sauces. Also with a few seasonings, it's great on baked potatoes and has less calories than sour cream.

CHEESES

Cheese can be a great meat substitute and used in many ways. If you want to get the full protein benefit from your cheese dollar, always buy packages with "cheese" as the last word on the label—not cheese food, cheese spread, or cheese product. All of these have extenders, additives, gelatins, and often lots of water added. You get much more food value for your money with just straight, ordinary cheese. Cheese is rich in calcium and protein and is a very concentrated way to get milk in our diet. It takes 1 gallon of milk to make 1 pound of cheese.

When buying cheese, like meat, be sure and check the price per pound, not just the cost of the package. This way you can compare for the best buy. Avoid the shredded and cubed packages. It's very simple and much cheaper to shred or cube cheese yourself. In fact, when I see a good buy on several types of cheese, I buy them, cube them, and freeze them in plastic bags. They thaw quickly and are ready for a quick snack or lunch. Be sure and try several varieties. They each have their own personality and provide you and your family with a good supply of nourishment.

Blue—is a white, semisoft cheese streaked with veins of blue mold. Quite strong in flavor, blue cheese is used in salad dressing or appetizers and resembles Roquefort but is more reasonable. Roquefort comes from a specific locale in the world and is quite expensive. These two cheese names are often mistakenly used interchangeably.

Brick—is a cream-colored cheese often with a brown covering. It is semisoft and is delicious grilled in sandwiches. Its flavor is mild.

Brie—is a smooth, soft cheese and is very good served with fruit as a dessert.

Camembert—has a delicious tangy taste. It is very smooth and soft. It is also good with fruit (especially apples).

Cheddar—is an American cheese that comes in varieties from mild to very sharp, depending on the length of aging. Sharp cheese is stored much longer, which accounts for the higher price. However, less of the "sharp" cheese is needed to develop a rich cheese flavor in cooking a cheese dish such as macaroni and cheese. Cheddar is good served almost any way—in cooking, sandwiches, appetizers, or desserts.

Colby—is a little softer than cheddar and is quite crumbly after freezing. It is also milder in flavor than cheddar.

Edam—is the cheese that is packaged in a red ball of wax. It has a mild, nutty taste and a rubbery texture. It is delicious as a snack.

Gouda—is very similar to Edam but has a higher fat content. It also comes in a red ball of wax and has a mild, nutty taste.

Gruyère—is classified as a dessert cheese, tasting a little salty. It is a light yellow in color.

Limburger and **Liederkranz**—are cheeses that are very similar. They have a strong taste and aroma and are smooth and creamy. They are delicious served on crackers with fruit for a snack.

Monterey Jack—is used in most Mexican recipes. It is a smooth, semisoft cheese and has a very pleasant, mild flavor. It melts beautifully in cooking.

Mozzarella—is used in Italian dishes. It is a firm cheese and has a very mild flavor. Like Monterey Jack, it melts well for pizzas, lasagna, and so on.

Muenster—is one of our favorites. It has a delicious mild flavor and is a semisoft cheese, creamy white with a tan or reddish covering. It freezes very well.

Neufchâtel—is very similar to cream cheese but has less calories.

Parmesan—is a very hard cream-colored cheese with a very sharp flavor. It is used mostly grated for Italian cooking. For a real taste treat, try buying a small chunk and grating your own. There is no comparison in taste to the kind you buy in a shaker can. Wrap it well, though, because it has quite a strong aroma that will fill the refrigerator if not tightly covered.

Ricotta—is very similar to cottage cheese but has a sweeter, nutty flavor and is used in Italian dishes such as lasagna and manicotti.

Swiss—is a firm cheese with a nutlike but very mild taste. It is creamy white with large eyes (or holes). For another taste treat, try the baby Swiss. It has such a delicate flavor and is terrific with ham on rye bread.

All cheeses should be kept tightly wrapped in the refrigerator. I use plastic bags sealed with a twisty. Most cheeses freeze well. Just remember to store small pieces (less than one pound) for successful results. I always let it thaw at room temperature and, when completely thawed, store in the refrigerator. This helps to prevent crumbling. If it is a crumbly-type cheese, you may want to cube or shred it before freezing it.

BUTTER AND MARGARINE

I'm surprised that so few people have done their homework on butter and margarine. Most people buy margarine over butter for economy, but it really is a false type of savings. Our bodies need a certain amount of fat to function properly, and this can be obtained best from the natural fats in butter. Margarines have become such a conglomerate of additives and chemicals, and many of the types of oils used are not the best. For instance, cottonseed is not grown specifically as a food, and so it is often sprayed with harmful chemicals. Some margarines actually contain very little food value at all and could be termed a "plastic food." We would be so much better off using a high-quality shortening or oil for cooking, and then use real butter sparingly for spreading and to flavor vegetables.

When buying butter, always choose the sweet cream, unsalted butter. The other butters may be made from soured or stale milk and cream with lots of salt added to mask the taste and inhibit mold growth. That salt is also a preserver, so salted butter may be much older than the unsalted type, which is always handled much more carefully and will be fresh. Butter is sensitive to light, air, and temperature, so keep it well wrapped and refrigerated or frozen. If you feel the cost of butter is prohibitive, you can alternate spreads on bread. Try using yogurt or a mashed avocado (which has a very buttery taste and is very healthful). As far as good health and nutrition go, I'd rather eat my bread plain than waste my food dollars on the "plastic" margarine.

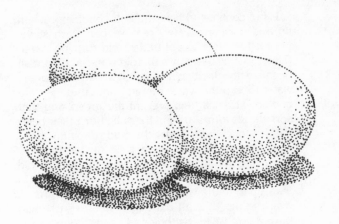

EGGS

Eggs are a terrific food value. In fact, they really are nature's complete food, containing everything except vitamin C. They are the best source of protein and also contain high amounts of vitamin A, iron, riboflavin, and natural vitamin D. They are low in calories, containing about 80 calories per egg. If you are concerned about the cholesterol, you would be wise to watch your animal fat intake instead of eliminating eggs from your diet. In fact, egg yolk is a rich source of lecithin, which is a natural cholesterol inhibitor. It breaks up the fats into tiny bits so they don't clog the arteries and veins.

In purchasing eggs, remember the 7¢ spread that we discussed in *A Family Raised on Sunshine*. Always buy the bigger size if it's less than 7¢ more than the smaller ones.

Never buy or use cracked eggs, as they can be the cause of food poisoning and especially never use them in anything uncooked such as egg nog. Keep all eggs refrigerated. (This goes for hard-boiled ones, too.) Refrigerated raw eggs will keep several weeks. Avoid high temperature when cooking eggs, as it will toughen them.

To successfully hard-boil eggs, cover with cold water, bring to a boil (as soon as boiling begins, set timer for 10 minutes), and turn heat down a

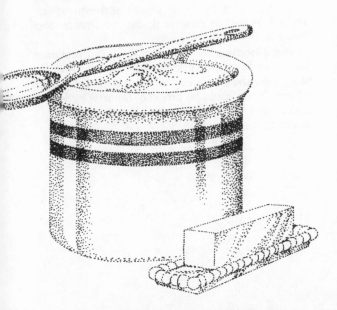

little but continue to have the water bubbling. When time is up, immediately remove pan from stove, pour off water, and put under cold running water. (Don't just fill the pan with cold water and let it sit because the heat in the eggs will warm up the water.) Keep the water running until the eggs are cooled. This will help prevent the green ring that sometimes forms around the yolk. For easier peeling, just peel them under the cold running water.

A little tip I learned as a child on the farm—a fresh egg will float in water, while a stale or old one will sink. Also, when cracking an egg into a frying pan, if the white is very watery and runs all over the pan, it is an old egg. A fresh egg should have a firm white that holds its shape. If your eggs are consistently old, you may want to purchase them elsewhere.

ICE CREAM

We end our trip through the supermarket at the ice cream case; frankly, we'd be better off if we saved our food dollar and created our own ice cream concoctions at home. Commercial ice cream is one of the most adulterated products in the grocery store today. Legally, there are at least 1,200 chemicals and artificial flavors and colors that can be added to ice cream. Did you know that sawdust has even been used as a "filler" in cheaper ice creams? Some of the chemicals used in common flavors are:

Piperonal—used in vanilla and is a chemical used to treat lice. It can cause depression of the nervous system.

Aldehyde C17—used in cherry-flavored ice cream and is an inflammable liquid used in plastic and rubber.

Amyl Acetate—used for banana flavor and also as an oil paint solvent. It can cause headaches, irritate the mucous membranes, and cause fatigue.

But chocolate ice cream is the worst. This flavor, even though chocolate itself is a natural ingredient, is often "reworked." This means that returned, old ice cream or batches that are beginning to spoil are recycled into chocolate because the dark color covers the off-taste and color of the old.

Commercial ice cream is also the victim of the same trick that manufacturers use with commercial white bread. They are both pumped full of a lot of air to get a lot of volume with very few ingredients. Check the scale; good-quality ice cream will be much, much heavier. Be aware of that word *natural*, however. There are lots of natural things, even sawdust, right? Even some poisons are "natural." Learn to read labels carefully and write letters to manufacturers if you are in doubt.

Homemade ice cream is such a delicious treat and can be made very easily and inexpensively without a lot of fancy gimmicks and equipment. Try the recipes in chapter 3 and see what a treat they can be.

Hurry home now with all the good purchases we've made in the grocery store and be sure to store everything properly to get the most for your money. You should be proud of the money you've saved and think how much better everyone is going to feel, too!

3

BETTER MEALS
FOR LESS
MONEY

Planning three meals a day can be a real challenge to you whether you're single or have a large, hungry family to feed. Some nutritionists tell us to eliminate all refined sugar and flour; others, to eat only high-fiber foods; and still others, all vegetables and no meats. Then there are all the faddist-type diets featuring specific foods only and others advising little food consumption with a lot of vitamin pills. It all gets pretty confusing, doesn't it? I like to take a common-sense approach to all of this. I feel that our Heavenly Father gave us our bodies and provided a lot of good, basic, healthy food for us to eat, and if we use the common sense we have, a balanced diet is the best way to go. By doing this, we will save a lot of money (nothing is more economical than good staple food), have more interesting, creative, and fun meals (the varieties of good foods are endless), and feel good. (There is no comparison to the healthy, energetic way we can feel if we eat right.)

We need to learn about the daily basic food requirements, eat everything in moderation, exercise, and retain a happy frame of mind. (Never forget my two rules of wearing a smile and thinking positively!)

The four basic food groups are as follows:

Meats (2 servings daily)—includes pork, beef, lamb, poultry, veal, fish, and eggs. A substitute can be nuts, peanut butter, or dry beans and peas. When dried beans are combined with a small amount of meat, you get the full benefit of all the proteins for very little money.

Vegetable and Fruit Groups (4 servings daily) —is the most neglected category and can be the most exciting and fun.

Milk and Dairy Products (2–4 cups daily, depending on age, as teenagers and nursing mothers require more)—can include yogurt, cheese, ice cream, and buttermilk.

Breads and Cereals (4 servings daily)—includes crackers, pasta, rice, and all the grain products.

Don't overlook any of these groups because our bodies need them all to function properly. If you choose wisely, you will not need any vitamin supplements or have to worry about weight gain. Choose from *all* the groups. You'll find that if you eat the whole-grain products and plenty of fruits and vegetables as well as the dairy products and meats that are low in calories, you will not need a special reducing diet. You will be trim and feel well naturally. It's the junk food and "large" servings that get us in trouble. Wholesome foods are much more filling and give you stamina much longer than the calorie-loaded snacks.

Some rules to remember:

1. Plan three balanced meals a day around these requirements.
2. Create a tempting meal—we eat with our eyes first, so make the meal attractive. Use garnishes for color; it only takes a minute. You don't need to sculpt a rose from a radish—simply use a lemon slice, an apple wedge, a lettuce leaf, a spring of parsley, watercress, or a few grapes. You can combine flavors; always have a spicy or tangy food with a bland one. Learn to tease the taste buds with pleasant combinations. Mix textures—a crunchy or crisp food with a soft one—sizes, and shapes of food. Be sure you serve hot things hot and cold things cold. It is well to have a contrast at each meal to make the meal more enjoyable.
3. Learn to shop in quantity, utilizing one purchase for several meals. (That ham or chicken can do wonders if you use it properly.)
4. Learn to ask questions. Your butcher can be a wealth of information, as can the produce dealer at the fruit stand.
5. Avoid commercial, starchy, and sugar-laden foods. An occasional home-baked goodie is much more satisfying, and there is no comparison to the amount of sugars that are poured into commercial things as well as

chemicals and preservatives. If there are 18 teaspoons of sugar in a bowlful of some commercial cereals, think how many there are in a twinkie or other snack food!

Please don't let the term *leftover* become a bad word at your house. It is simply food that can be served in many different ways, and by cooking in quantity, you save on utilities as well as on your labor. You'll eat better, too, because those things prepared ahead will become your nutritious "convenience" foods!

Have you noticed how nearly all recipes call for a "can" of this and a "box" of that or are full of nonessential, nonnutritious, sweet, and expensive ingredients that we don't have on hand, anyway? Eating well and spending less are my goals in the kitchen, and I hope they're yours, also. I've gathered some of my special favorite recipes that I know you'll enjoy, and they'll help you accomplish your goals, also.

Many of my recipes have chicken or beef broth as a base. Broth is valuable to have on hand not only for the flavor it gives but also for the added nutrition. Never waste a scrap of meat or a bone and remember to add a tablespoon of vinegar when cooking the broth to draw the calcium out of the bones into the broth.

CHICKEN OR TURKEY BROTH

Whenever you have some bony parts of poultry, cover them with water, a little carrot, celery, and onion, 1 tbsp. vinegar, and salt and pepper to taste and simmer for at least 1 hr.

Strain and you have delicious broth ready to use. I always keep quart jars of it in my freezer. Just don't fill the jar too full; leave about 2 in. expansion head space so the bottle doesn't break.

Beef stock is made the same way except the beef and bones should be browned well first either in a hot pan on the stove or in the oven. Beef stock should simmer at least 2 hr.

Country potato cheese soup is absolutely delicious. It's so easy *and* economical, you'll serve it often. A steaming hot bowl of this with a tossed salad and whole wheat rolls is a great summer-evening meal. An apple dumpling makes a delicious topper for this meal in the fall.

COUNTRY POTATO CHEESE SOUP

In a saucepan, melt 2 tbsp. margarine or butter.

Add: 6 large potatoes, diced
2 medium onions, chopped
3 stalks celery, chopped
½ tsp. salt
pepper to taste

Sauté about 5 min., stirring often.

Add 2 cups chicken broth.

Cover and simmer until vegetables are tender.

Put mixture in blender and blend smooth.

Return to heat and stir in 1 cup half-and-half.

Add 2 cups cheese. (Colby or American is good.) Heat until cheese is melted.

Serves 4 nicely.

A yummy, quick way to serve chicken is this casserole. A Jell-O salad with strawberries and bananas and some hot muffins, with a piece of "Sunshine Cake" for dessert, round out the menu. If you're feeding a hungry man, a baked potato could also be added to the menu.

CLASSIC CHICKEN AND BROCCOLI

(For two people—
can be doubled or tripled as needed.)

Cook a 10 oz. pkg. of frozen broccoli.

Drain and place broccoli in a buttered pie plate. Sprinkle with ½ cup shredded cheese.

In a saucepan, melt 1 tbsp. butter.

Stir in 1 tbsp. flour and blend well.

Stir in: ¾ cup chicken broth
¼ cup milk (or half-and-half)
salt and pepper to taste

Cook and stir until thickened.

Place two chicken breasts, skin side down, on top of broccoli.

Pour sauce over chicken.

Bake at 350° for 30 min.

Turn chicken over and sprinkle lightly with Parmesan cheese and paprika.

Bake another 30 min.

We like soups so well, and if you enjoy the "peppery" bite of watercress, you have to try this soup. It makes a great appetizer.

PERKY WATERCRESS SOUP

In a saucepan, melt 2 tbsp. margarine or butter.

Stir in 2 tbsp. flour.

Slowly add 3 cups chicken broth, stirring constantly.

Simmer for about 5 min.

Add: 1 cup half-and-half
1 large bunch watercress, chopped

Put mixture in blender and blend well.

Heat thoroughly and season with salt and pepper to taste.

If you want to be real fancy for a party, when you serve this as an appetizer, put a small dab of whipped cream on top of each serving.

This will make 4 bowls full.

By the way, this same recipe can be used for any delicious creamed vegetable soup. Just use about 1–1½ cups cooked vegetable in place of the watercress.

I always feel that leftover ham is a gold mine. There are so many uses even if you only have a tiny bit.

This casserole is so good but must be eaten *immediately* after baking. It goes well with a tossed salad and hot biscuits. Pineapple cream pudding and black walnut cookies are a nice ending to this menu.

CHEESY HAM POOF

Beat 6 eggs.

Stir in: ½ cup flour
1½ tsp. baking powder

Gradually add 1 cup milk.

Then add: 1 cup ham, chopped finely
2 tbsp. soft margarine
1–3 oz. pkg. cream cheese (broken up)
2 cups shredded cheese (any kind)
1 cup cottage cheese
3 green onions, chopped
1 tsp. dried parsley
¼ tsp. paprika

Beat with electric mixer until blended.

Bake in a greased 2 qt. casserole at 350° for 45–50 min.

Serve immediately. Serves 6.

This recipe is good with coleslaw, cornbread or biscuits, and ice cream for dessert.

LOUISIANA JAMBALAYA

In a saucepan, melt 1 tbsp. butter or margarine.

Sauté 2 medium onions, chopped.

Stir in: 1 clove garlic, minced
2 tsp. dried parsley
½ tsp. thyme
¼ tsp. cayenne pepper
1 bay leaf
1½ cups canned tomatoes
1½ cups water
1 bag (8 oz.) frozen tiny shrimp (or whatever you have)
1 cup finely chopped ham (or whatever you have)
½ cup uncooked regular rice

Cover, bring to a boil, turn down heat, and let simmer ½ hr.

Add salt, pepper, and Tabasco sauce as you desire.

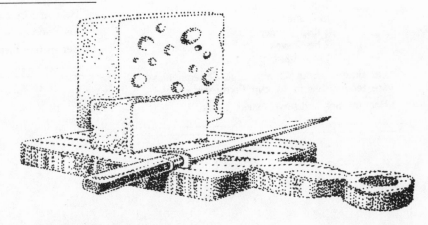

You can vary the vegetables in this Hearty Minestrone soup according to your tastes, but this is absolutely the best minestrone ever made. It's a terrific way to use up those bits of things in the refrigerator, and the soup is even better each time it's reheated. We like it with slices of my "English Toastin' Bread" and pie for dessert. Ooh! I could eat a bowl right now.

HEARTY MINESTRONE

Into a large, heated kettle place 2 slices bacon, a cup or so of leftover ham scraps, and some beef trimmings and bones that you've cut off a roast or round steak before cooking. (I always trim my meats and keep the trimmings in a bag in the freezer.) Use any scraps you have.

Cook these *well* together until nicely browned.

Add 2 qt. *hot* water.

Cover and simmer about 2 hr.

Strain the broth and pick off any meaty beef or ham pieces and add back to the stock.

Then add: 2 carrots, sliced
1 small onion, chopped
2 cups tomatoes, canned or fresh
1 cup lima beans (or green beans)
1 celery stalk, chopped
2 potatoes, peeled and diced
1 zucchini, chopped
1 cup cut-up cabbage
1 cup broken-up spaghetti or macaroni, uncooked
1 tbsp. parsley
2 bay leaves
½ tsp. basil

Let simmer about 45 min. until all vegetables are tender. Stir in ¼ cup Parmesan cheese.

Heat through and serve. Makes 2½ qt.

Canned salmon is really versatile, too, and can make a very inexpensive main dish. Try it with my "Five-Cup Fruit Salad" and hot rolls and maybe chocolate cake for dessert.

JACOB'S HE-MAN SALMON

Drain 1 can (15 oz.) of pink salmon.

Mash salmon with a fork and combine with:
1 beaten egg
1 cup shredded cheese
2 tbsp. wheat germ

In a saucepan, melt 1 tbsp. margarine.

Sauté: 1 small onion, chopped
2 stalks celery, chopped
1 clove garlic, minced

When onion is tender, add: 1 can (8 oz.) tomato sauce
½ tsp. oregano

Simmer together about 10 min.

Meanwhile, cook 3 oz. green (or spinach) noodles until tender.

Toss noodles with: ½ cup cottage cheese
½ cup shredded cheese

Stir tomato mixture into salmon mixture.

Spread half of combined mixture in a greased 9 in. × 5 in. bread pan.

Spoon noodle mixture on and then cover with the other half of the salmon mixture.

Bake at 375° for about 35–40 min.

Let stand a few minutes before serving.

Serves 6 (if they aren't too hungry).

With this, you'll want my big Mexican tossed salad, lemon sherbet and homemade cookies for dessert.

SOUTH OF
THE BORDER SALMON

Into a large mixing bowl, combine:
- 1 can (15 oz.) undrained salmon
- 1 can cream of chicken soup
- 1 can chopped green chilies
- 1 can (6 oz.) tomato paste
- 1½ cups shredded cheese
- 2 garlic cloves, minced
- 2 green onions, chopped
- 1 cup corn chips, lightly broken but not crumbs

Mix well and add 4 well-beaten eggs.

Pour into a greased 2 qt. casserole and sprinkle with more crushed corn chips.

Bake at 350° for 1 hr.

Serves 4–6.

That good old basic hamburger is a never-ending source of meals. I know you'll like these.

There isn't a sloppy Joe that compares to this, and it tastes better each time it's reheated. Serve on hot buns with coleslaw. You'll want to keep some of this on hand in the freezer for a quick lunch or picnic.

REHER'S BARBEQUED
BEEF SANDWICHES

Brown: 1½ lb. ground beef
      ½ lb. pork sausage
      1 chopped onion

Add: 1 can tomato soup
- ¾ cup water
- ½ cup vinegar
- 2 tbsp. sugar
- 1 tsp. salt
- 1 tsp. chili powder
- 1 tsp. Worcestershire sauce
- 1 clove garlic
- 1 bay leaf

Mix well and simmer for 1 hr.

I couldn't share all our favorite recipes with you without including the famous Cincinnati-type chili. Everyone loves this, and no one comes to Cincinnati without visiting a popular Cincinnati chili parlor. (Our kids could eat this several times a week. Even the grandbabies love it.) It is not chili in the traditional sense but a dish you'll serve over and over. Don't be overwhelmed at the list of spices. They are common ones you have on your shelf, and the dish is really simple to make.

CINCINNATI CHILI

Combine: 2 lb. hamburger (*don't* brown first.)
           2 chopped onions
           1 qt. water

Simmer together for 30 min.

Add: 2 cans (8 oz.) tomato sauce
     ½ tsp. allspice
     ¼ tsp. garlic powder
     4 tbsp. chili powder
     1 tsp. cumin
     ½ tsp. red pepper
     ¼ tsp. cloves
     ½ oz. unsweetened chocolate (That's right!)
     2 tbsp. vinegar
     1 bay leaf
     2 tsp. Worcestershire sauce
     2 tsp. cinnamon
     1½ tsp. salt
     4 drops Tabasco sauce

Simmer uncovered for 2 to 3 hr. until thickened.

Refrigerate overnight.

Cook *thin* spaghetti as directed. To serve, put spaghetti on each plate. Cover with heated Cincinnati chili. Sprinkle with *lots* of shredded cheddar cheese. This forms a traditional "3 way."

If you want a "4 way," add a layer of hot beans under the cheese.

For a "5 way," add a layer of hot beans and fresh, chopped onions under the cheese.

Serve with bowls of oyster crackers.

On a cold winter evening, I like to stick this casserole in the oven. It can even be prepared in the morning so it's ready to heat. I usually make this in two 9 in. × 9 in. pans and freeze one before baking. Serve with a tossed salad and a piece of homemade cake and you will have a complete and satisfying meal.

SCALLOPED POTATOES WITH MEAT LOAF

Butter a 9 in. × 13 in. pan.

In the bottom of the pan, put:
        6 cups thinly sliced potatoes
        2 tbsp. chopped onion
        1½ tsp. salt
        dash of pepper

Dot with butter and pour in ½ cup milk.

Add a layer of 1 can (8 oz.) green beans, drained.

Then mix together: 1 large egg, beaten
                1 cup milk
                ⅓ cup catsup
                3 tbsp. chopped onion
                ¾ cup soda cracker crumbs
                1½ tsp. salt
                dash of pepper
                1½ lb. ground beef

Mix well and spread over potato and bean layers.

Combine a topping of: 4 tbsp. brown sugar
                ½ cup catsup
                ½ tsp. nutmeg
                1 tsp. mustard

Spread over meat mixture and bake at 350° for 1 hr.

Serves 8 nicely.

This "hurry-up" dish is a change of pace. It's delicious served with my spinach salad and fruit and cookies for dessert.

HAMBURGER STROGANOFF

Brown 1 lb. ground beef with 1 small onion.

Add: 2 cloves minced garlic
        1 can (8 oz.) mushrooms and liquid
        1 can cream of chicken soup
        ½ tsp. salt
        ½ tsp. coarse black pepper
        2 tbsp. minced dried parsley

Simmer together for about 5–10 min.

Stir in 1 cup sour cream.

Heat just through. Serve over hot cooked noodles. (I like to toss my noodles with 1 tbsp. butter and a little poppy seed before serving.)

Serves 4–6.

Of course, the standard meat loaf and meat balls can't be beat. I use the same mixture for both:

MEAT LOAF/MEAT BALLS

Beat 2 eggs well.

Add: ¾ cup milk
     1 small onion, chopped
     1 tsp. salt
     ¼ tsp. nutmeg
     ¼ tsp. sage
     dash of pepper
     1 lb. ground beef
     ½ lb. ground pork (or mild sausage)
     ¾ cup bread crumbs (I like French or Italian bread best, but it doesn't matter. Sometimes I use soda cracker crumbs and cut down on the salt, and sometimes I've even used rolled oats.)

Mix well with your hands, keeping it light.

Shape into a meat loaf and cover with:
     3 tbsp. brown sugar
     1 tsp. mustard
     ⅓ cup catsup
     a little garlic if desired

Bake at 350° for about 1 hr.

For meat balls, I just form the mixture into balls and put them in a baking dish raw and pour 1 can of undiluted tomato soup over them. Bake at 350° for about 1 hr.

This noodle dish goes real well with either of the above meat dishes. Just stick it in the oven when the meat is about half done.

NOODLES ROMANOFF

Cook 4 oz. fine noodles.

Drain and combine with a mixture of:
     3 oz. cream cheese
     ½ cup sour cream
     1 tbsp. minced onion
     ¼ tsp. Worcestershire sauce
     dash of garlic salt
     2 drops Tabasco sauce

Mix well and place in a small buttered casserole.

Cover with buttered crumbs.

Bake at 350° for about 20–25 min.

For a nice luncheon or a simple family supper, served with a fresh spinach salad and fruit cobbler, nothing is better than this:

WESTERN CHEESY ONION PIE

Prepare a pie shell; chill but don't bake.

Grate 2 cups cheese, any kind, and toss with 2 tbsp. flour.

Sauté 2 large onions, thinly sliced in 2 tbsp. butter.

Spread half of cheese in pie shell.

Cover with sautéed onion slices.

Cover with 2 large tomatoes, sliced.

Sprinkle with: 1 tsp. basil
                ½ tsp. oregano

Cover this with the rest of the cheese.

Beat 2 eggs and combine with ¾ cup half-and-half.

Pour this mixture over the pie.

Bake at 350° for 40–45 min.

Let sit a minute or two before cutting.

A different and tasty way to use up the rest of that turkey or chicken is this old-time recipe. The little ones really enjoy this.

PENNSYLVANIA DUTCH CHICKEN CASSEROLE

Melt 2 tbsp. butter and stir in 2 tbsp. flour.

Add: ½ cup apple juice
       1 cup half-and-half

Simmer and stir until it starts to thicken.

Then stir in: 1 medium onion, chopped
               2 small apples, chopped
               1 stalk celery, chopped
               3 cups diced chicken or turkey

Cover and simmer until vegetables are tender (10–15 min.).

Pour into a buttered casserole.

Cover with buttered crumbs and sprinkle with nutmeg.

Bake at 350° for about 20 min.

Serve with green beans, carrot and pineapple Jell-O, and cookies for dessert.

If you're feeling adventuresome and would really like to try a taste treat, make up some pickled chicken or pickled beef. It's a little bit of a procedure but well worth it and such a tasty dish for a picnic, family get-together, or an afternoon with friends watching the football game. Serve it with my potato salad (*A Family Raised on Rainbows*), some baked beans, and that easy "Boston Brown Bread."

GRANDMA HAACK'S
SOUR CHICKEN

Cover 2 cut-up chickens with water, add a little salt, onion, and celery, and cook, covered, until tender, about 1 hr.

Take the meaty pieces and 2½ cups broth and place in a heavy saucepan. (Use the remaining broth and bony pieces to make soup, etc.)

Add to the meat and broth: 1½ cups vinegar
½ cup sugar
1 tbsp. pickling spice

Bring to a boil and cook about 10 min.

Leave the meat in the broth mixture, cool, and refrigerate for about 24 hr. before eating. The liquid will become jellied.

Pickled beef makes the yummiest, best sandwiches you've ever tasted. It really isn't any work; it just takes time for the process. I buy about a 4 pound roast, preferably a bottom round, but whatever is on sale will do.

PICKLED BEEF

In a saucepan, combine: 1½ cups vinegar
1 cup water
2 tbsp. salt
2 tbsp. sugar
½ tsp. cloves
2 tbsp. pickling spice

Bring to a boil and simmer 15 min.

Cool thoroughly.

Put the roast in a plastic bag, set the bag in a large mixing bowl, then pour the cooled liquid into the plastic bag. Fasten the bag tightly with a twisty.

Leave the bag in the bowl and refrigerate for *3 days*, turning the bag over twice a day.

Put the meat and liquid in a large kettle (not aluminum) and bring to a boil.

Cover and simmer for 3—4 hr. until very tender.

Let cool completely and return the meat and broth to a plastic bag as before.

Refrigerate for several days for the flavors to blend well.

Slice thin and serve.

Clam chowder is one of the easiest soups to make and one of the most satisfying. Served with some hot bread or rolls and a relish tray, it's a complete meal. There are two kinds of chowder: Manhattan style, which has a tomato and stock base, and the New England style, which has a creamy base. We prefer the New England variety. This particular recipe freezes well and tastes even better reheated.

NYE'S CLAM CHOWDER

Into a large saucepan, put:
    4 cups diced potatoes
    1½ cups chopped celery
    1 cup chopped onions

Drain the juice off of 2 cans (6 oz.) of clams and pour it over the vegetable mixture, adding enough water to cover the vegetables.

Cover and simmer until tender.

Meanwhile, in a small saucepan, melt ½ cup margarine.

Stir in ½ cup flour.

Then add: 2 cups milk
            2 cups half-and-half
            1½ tsp. salt
            1 tsp. sugar

Cook until it starts to thicken.

Combine sauce with vegetables and liquid.

Stir in minced clams and 1 tsp. vinegar.

Heat through and serve.

The type of food that holds a favored place in our kitchen and fills the bill when it comes to economy *and* good nutrition is Mexican cooking. It is also very simple to prepare. It can be hot and spicy or very gentle to your taste buds. It can be high in calories or real lean cuisine! How can you ask for anything better than that, and besides, it tastes fabulous! Here are some of the recipes I fix most often. (Don't forget to begin the meal with some hot chips and *salsa*.)

Don't let the ingredients in this one startle you. It is really fantastic. It's a takeoff from a recipe of my friend Lupita, of Tucson. Since some ingredients of authentic *molé* are difficult to find, this recipe will enable you to make it regardless of the area you live in. It's a great family dish in one pot.

MEXICAN MOLÉ (STEW)

In a blender, combine:
    2 cups chicken broth
    2 tbsp. peanut butter
    1 tbsp. sugar
    2 tbsp. cocoa
    ¼ cup chopped onion
    1 small tomato
    1 small can chopped green chilies
    3 cloves garlic
    1 tsp. chili powder
    dash of coriander
    salt and pepper

Blend until smooth. Pour into large skillet.

Add 4–6 chicken pieces (legs, thighs, or breasts as desired).

Add: 3 celery stalks, cut up
      2 carrots, cut up
      1 zucchini, cut up
      1 small onion, cut up
      ⅔ cup uncooked long grain rice

Mix so that the sauce covers all.

Put lid on and simmer for 1 hr. Stir occasionally.

These refried beans are used in so many ways, so cook up a batch today and keep some containers full in the freezer for a quick snack.

REFRIED BEANS

Cover 1 lb. pinto beans with 7 cups hot water and let soak overnight.

In the morning, bring to a boil, cover, and let simmer 2–3 hr. until beans are tender. Drain.

Run the beans through the blender, a cup or two at a time, until almost smooth.

To bean puree, add a little chopped onion.

In a frying pan, heat 2 tbsp. oil or bacon drippings.

Add a few spoonfuls of beans at a time, frying and turning with a spatula until well heated.

To make *tostados,* fry tortilla in hot oil until crisp. Spread with refried beans, cover with browned hamburger, shredded cheese, diced onion, lettuce and tomato, and sprinkle with *salsa.*

To make *nachos,* spread tortilla or corn chips with refried beans, a slice of Jalapeño or green chili pepper, and grated cheese. Place under the broiler until cheese melts.

Refried beans are also good in tacos or enchiladas.

We enjoy this Mexican brunch on the patio on Saturday mornings: serve a large platter with scrambled eggs on one half and refried beans, heated, on the other half. Surround the platter with avocado slices, shredded cheese, and ripe olives on a bed of lettuce. (I usually add a little chopped green onion to my scrambled eggs.) Pass around plenty of *salsa* and serve with ice-cold glasses of milk and hot corn muffins. You'll have a real fiesta!

Another hearty dish is this casserole. It's great for covered-dish suppers since it's filling and inexpensive.

RANCHERO CASSEROLE

Brown: 1 lb. ground beef
       1 medium chopped onion

Add: 1 can (4 oz.) chopped green chilies
     1 can (8 oz.) tomato sauce
     1 cup whipping cream

Simmer together for 10 min.

Meanwhile, take a package of 12 corn tortillas, and after stacking them, cut them in thin strips.

Heat ⅓ cup oil in large frying pan and sauté the strips, stirring often.

Grease a 2 qt. casserole and place half the strips in the dish.

Cover with half the meat sauce.

Sprinkle with 1½ cups shredded cheese.

Add the rest of the strips, followed by the rest of the sauce and another 1½ cups shredded cheese.

Bake at 350° for about 25 min.

Serves 6.

Quesadillas (pronounced Keh-sah-dé-yas) are fun to make when you have a get-together, and everyone can assemble their own. These can be done ahead of time and kept hot on a platter if you like. Have a big bowl of Mexican salad and plenty of chips and *salsa* along the side. For a real south-of-the-border meal, finish it off with my "Mexican Sundaes—Upside Down."

QUESADILLAS

Set out bowls of: grated Monterey Jack cheese
chopped green chilies
avocado slices
salsa
a saucepan of cut-up (chopped) chicken or turkey sautéed with a little chopped onion

In a frying pan or griddle, melt 1 tbsp. butter.

Place 1 large *flour* tortilla on the griddle.

While it's heating, pile on a little chicken, cheese, green chilies, avocado, and a spoonful of *salsa* in the center.

Fold in each end of tortilla and fold over each side, forming a package. (The tortilla should be a little crisp at this stage.)

Hold the folded edge in place for a few seconds to form, and then eat the quesadilla "out of hand" with more sauce if desired.

Nothing is simpler to make than your own enchilada sauce, and you'll be astonished at how much you save compared to the cans of commercial brands.

ENCHILADA SAUCE

Heat together: 1 qt. cold water
½ cup chili powder
½ cup paprika
1 tsp. salt

Bring to a boil, then stir in a mixture of:
2 tbsp. oil
4 tbsp. flour

Stir and heat until well mixed.

Store in a jar in the refrigerator.

ENCHILADAS

Heat tortilla in hot oil until lightly crisp, then dip in a pan of enchilada sauce. Lay tortilla on a plate, add filling across center and roll up, and place in a baking pan. Make as many as desired, then pour additional sauce over. Bake at 350° for about 20 min. until heated through. Fillings can be simply grated cheese and onion or a meat filling:

Brown together: 1 lb. hamburger
1 medium onion, chopped

Add: 1 can (8 oz.) tomato sauce
1 tbsp. vinegar
½ tsp. salt
1 clove garlic, minced
½ tsp. cinnamon
¼ tsp. cumin

Simmer together for 15–20 min.

Another recipe that's a meal in a dish and absolutely delicious is Beans Olé. Serve it with corn chips and desired toppings: grated cheese, chopped tomato, chopped avocado, chopped onion, shredded lettuce, and *salsa*. It can be made ahead of time and reheated. It also freezes well.

BEANS OLÉ

Soak 1 lb. pinto beans in 7–8 cups water overnight.

In the morning, add:
2–3 lb. pork loin roast, uncooked
½ cup chopped onion
2 cloves garlic, minced
1 tbsp. salt
2 tbsp. chili powder
1 tbsp. cumin
1 tsp. oregano
1 can (4 oz.) chopped green chilies

Combine all in a large Dutch oven, cover, and simmer for 5 hr. (or longer).

Take out roast and pick all meat from the bones.

Add meat back to the pot, discarding the bones and fat.

Cook another ½ hr. or so, uncovered, until desired thickness.

FRUITS AND VEGETABLES

Today, we are lucky that no matter what part of the country we live in, we have fresh fruits and vegetables available all year. However, these foods are still seasonal, and it's wisest for both economy and good nutrition to buy them at their peak. With so many varieties to choose from, learn to plan your menus with this in mind and realize you don't need fresh strawberries in December. Moreover, isn't it exciting to anticipate that first cool bite of cantaloupe in the summer or those juicy, sweet, mouth-watering pears in the early fall? Another beauty of all these fresh things is that whether you are a bachelor living alone or a mother of twelve children, you can buy exactly the quantity to serve you best.

For planning your menus and saving food dollars, here is a guideline for fresh fruit and vegetable availability:

Winter

citrus fruits   avocados
   (lemons, grapefruit,   pineapples
   oranges, and limes)   coconuts
bananas

Spring

starwberries   parsley
artichokes   radishes
spinach and   asparagus
   other greens   potatoes
rhubarb

Summer

peaches   cucumbers
apricots   eggplant
melons   berries
green beans   plums
beets   celery
mushrooms   summer squash
peas   peppers
tomatoes   cherries
corn

Fall

carrots	broccoli
cabbage	brussels sprouts
yams	pumpkin
potatoes	squash
apples	turnips and
pears	rutabagas
grapes	parsnips
cauliflower	

Remember that for a balanced diet each day, we should eat 4 or more servings of fruits and vegetables. At least 1 serving should be something high in vitamin C such as orange juice, tomatoes or tomato juice, cabbage, grapefruit, berries, or green peppers. One of the other servings should be a fresh, green, leafy vegetable or one rich in vitamin A, such as apricots, carrots, broccoli, cantaloupe, or sweet potatoes or winter squash.

Here are some of our family's favorite ideas and recipes. Bear in mind, we don't waste a thing. Fruits and vegetables are areas where many people have a tendency to throw away more than they use; so after purchasing carefully and storing wisely, let's cook them economically. I'll try to include little hints that I have found to help.

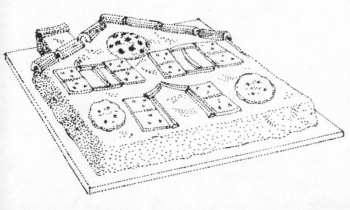

SALAD IDEAS

We often enjoy finger foods as a fresh salad. I put a mound or dish of dip on a plate and then circle it with carrot sticks, celery sticks, fresh broccoli, cauliflowerettes, tomato wedges or cherry tomatoes, cucumber sticks, zucchini sticks, radishes, fresh mushrooms, green pepper wedges, and even turnip slices, depending on what's in season. Sometimes, I serve fruits like this to be eaten with dip: apple wedges, orange wedges, pineapple chunks, coconut chunks, strawberries, pear slices, grapes, or banana chunks—whatever is in season.

My favorite dip recipes are "McCroby's Vegetable Dip" in *A Family Raised on Rainbows* or a carton of sour cream with 2 tablespoons dry onion soup mix (not the whole package) and a dash of garlic powder. For fruits, plain yogurt makes a good dip, or if you like it sweetened a little, blend in 2 tablespoons honey to an 8 ounce container of yogurt.

Youngsters enjoy salads like this, and adults will find themselves nibbling on them more and eating *less* calorie-laden foods.

Little ones always enjoy things they can eat with their hands; so if you find your children are not eating as many fruits and vegetables as they should, try giving them apple slices or banana wedges with a dab of peanut butter spread on them. Another fun little treat is a carrot stick spread with peanut butter and wrapped in a ruffly lettuce leaf!

By the way, when you are fixing your finger-food salads, you can even put your artistic talents to use. I cover a sturdy cardboard square or rectangle with heavy-duty (or 2 layers) aluminum foil. Then I spread my dip in a design such as a wreath, a Christmas tree, an initial, a house, or a flower. Have the dip about ¾ inch deep. Then I cover the dip with vegetable wedges to create my picture, using snack crackers where needed (tree trunks, roofs, etc.). Then, when the guests pick up a vegetable or cracker, it is already "dipped."

Fresh spinach is a tasty green to form the basis of a salad. The two combinations we like best are (1) fresh spinach leaves, thinly sliced onion rings, 1 can drained mandarin orange slices (use the juice in Jell-O, add it to fruit punch, or thicken it and use as a fruit sauce over lemon or yellow cake), dressing, and then sprinkle with chow mein noodles; (2) fresh spinach leaves, fresh sliced mushrooms, and dressing, sprinkled with bacon crisps.

DRESSING FOR SPINACH SALADS

6 tbsp. olive oil
4 tbsp. wine vinegar
⅓ tsp. French mustard
¼ tsp. minced garlic
salt and coarse ground pepper to taste

Shake well.

We love coleslaw at our house. I always make it in my blender. Just fill the blender with 3 cups of water, and after washing and trimming as necessary, add a large head of cabbage. (Cut it into wedges and add a few at a time, turning the blender off and on until the cabbage is as fine as you like it. It will take about 4 blendersfull to do a whole head of cabbage.)

Drain *very* well and toss with dressing:

DRESSING FOR COLESLAW

1 cup Miracle Whip
4 tbsp. vinegar
½ cup sugar
pinch of salt
1 cup half-and-half
Optional: chopped onions or celery seed

Mix well.

Roy loves onions, and one of his special treats is to slice onions into a jar (red onions are delicious this way) and cover with vinegar and lots of salt and pepper. Cover jar and let stand at least overnight. Cucumber slices are good added, also. After these marinate for a day or two, they are delicious served on a plate arranged with sliced tomatoes on a leaf of lettuce. You'll love them!

A summer fruit salad that's a yummy change of pace is my standard "Five Cup Salad."

FIVE CUP SALAD

1 cup pineapple chunks
1 cup mandarin orange slices
1 cup coconut
1 cup green grapes (I usually put more.)
1 cup sour cream
pinch of salt

Toss all together and chill until serving.

Since we eat a lot of Mexican food, this recipe gets used often.

MEXICALI SALAD

Toss together: cut-up lettuce
slice cucumbers
diced tomatoes (added last)
a little onion
chopped green pepper
radishes
some sliced ripe olives

Serve with my spinach salad dressing to which I add ½ tsp. of my taco seasoning.

Two tablespoons of this mix is equal to 1 package of commercial taco seasoning and is much, much cheaper. This dressing is also good over a salad of sliced tomatoes and onions on shredded lettuce.

TACO SEASONING MIX

Mix together well: ¼ cup dried onion flakes
3 tsp. red pepper flakes
3 tbsp. salt
2 tsp. beef bouillon powder
4 tsp. cornstarch
4 tbsp. chili powder
3 tsp. minced garlic
1½ tsp. oregano

Store in airtight container.

Roy and I really enjoyed the type of salad we were served in Europe. On a bed of lettuce, we were served individual mounds of several fresh vegetables that had been shredded and marinated (carrots, celery root, and huge radishes, about 8–10 inches long). These radishes look almost like a parsnip and are available in supermarkets here. Please give them a try. We like to slice them on bread, also.

In the summer, I often cook up a quarter of a turkey to have broth on hand; then I freeze the meat for salad. We love chicken (or turkey) salad served in a tomato cup or on a slice of cantaloupe. I mix chopped meat with chopped celery (we like lots) and chopped walnuts, and mix with a little Miracle Whip, salt and pepper, and a dash of onion salt. If I am going to stuff tomato cups, I use the pulp I scoop out of the tomatoes and stir it in with the meat mixture. To serve it with cantaloupe, I often stir some pineapple and green grapes into the meat mixture. Then I slice through the whole cantaloupe, forming rings. Clean out the seeds and serve a ring on each plate filled with salad. This looks so pretty.

If you have never tried marinated vegetables served cold, give them a try. This is a great way to serve leftover cooked vegetables and is a terrific wintertime salad served on a lettuce leaf. We especially like green beans, brussels sprouts, or asparagus marinated in my basic spinach salad dressing mixture. Let stand in the refrigerator overnight and serve cold. I often use the dressing several times.

Jell-O salads are good additions to a winter meal. Some of our favorite combinations are: (1) One package (6 ounces) lemon Jell-O prepared as directed. Stir in 4 grated carrots and a can of crushed pineapple. I use the liquid as part of the cold water in the Jell-O mixture. (2) One package (any size) strawberry Jell-O with strawberries and banana slices. (3) One package (any size) lime Jell-O with some cottage cheese, pineapple, and some cut-up canned pears, if I have any. A few maraschino cherries are pretty in this.

The kids always enjoyed it when I made a package of any flavor Jell-O, using only half the water recommended, and then stirred in some vanilla ice cream when the mixture had cooled some. Fruits (fruit cocktail, bananas, berries, peaches, even miniature marshmallows, and nuts) are good added to this.

We also like a Jell-O fluff salad. Prepare Jell-O as directed using a little less water. When partially set up, blend well with the electric mixer and then whip in ½ pint whipped cream (already whipped). I add fruit to this, also.

VEGETABLE IDEAS

Vegetables add color, nutrition, and variety to meals. Be adventuresome and expose your family to lots of types. Don't get in a rut. I know you'll like these recipes.

CHEESY VEGETABLE BAKE

In saucepan, melt 1 tbsp. margarine or butter.

Add: 1 tbsp. soy sauce
¼ tsp. minced garlic
¼ tsp. dill seed

Mix and add: 1 stalk chopped celery
2 cups fresh broccoli flowerets (Use the stems for soup.)
3 sliced carrots
2 chopped green onions (Use green tops, also.)
salt and coarse ground pepper to taste

Mix with sauce in pan, cover, and simmer about 10–15 min., stirring occasionally.

Meanwhile, beat 3 eggs.

Add: ⅔ cup milk
1½ cups Swiss, mozzarella, or Monterey Jack cheese

Mix with cooked vegetables and pour into a buttered 2 qt. casserole or 9 in. × 9 in. baking dish.

Set on a cooking sheet filled with water.

Bake at 350° for about 50–60 min.

Serves 4–6.

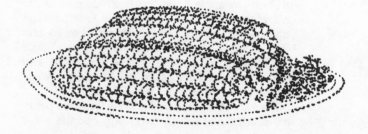

Everyone is always requesting the recipe for "Kristen's Yummy Potatoes," so here it is!

KRISTEN'S YUMMY POTATOES

Cook 8 medium potatoes in salted water with a bay leaf.

When cold, peel and grate coarsely. Put potatoes in a greased 9 in. × 13 in. pan.

Mix together and pour over potatoes:
1 can cream of chicken soup
¼ cup melted margarine
1½ cups sour cream
1½ tsp. salt and pepper
1 finely chopped small onion
1½ cups grated cheese

Cover and bake at 350° for 30–35 min.

Sprinkle top with: ½ cup grated cheese
½ cup crushed potato chips

Bake a few minutes more.

With all the surplus of zucchini in our gardens and at the market, be sure you give these a try. They are so good.

ZUCCHINI CASSEROLE

In a saucepan, melt 1 tbsp. butter.

Sauté 1 small onion (chopped) until tender.

Add: 2 chopped or sliced zucchini
2 chopped or sliced tomatoes

Cover and simmer until tender.

Sprinkle with 1 cup grated cheese (any type) and a little dill seed.

Cover again for a couple of minutes until cheese melts and serve hot. Serves 4.

SUNFLOWER ZUCCHINI

In a large frying pan, heat 2 tbsp. oil.

Arrange slices of 4–6 zucchini in a circular pattern in the pan, completely covering the bottom of the pan.

Add 1 tbsp. water and sprinkle with salt, pepper, and a little oregano.

Cover and cook about 5 min. until almost tender.

Sprinkle with Parmesan cheese and a little melted butter.

Place under the broiler until lightly browned.

Serves 4–6.

GREEN BEANS À LA ITALY

Melt 2 tbsp. margarine or butter.

Add 4 green onions and cook slightly.

Stir in: 1 chopped tomato
½ cup chopped leftover ham
¼ tsp. minced garlic
¼ tsp. basil

Heat well.

Add 3 cups cooked green beans.

Sprinkle with salt and pepper.

Serves 6.

This dish makes a pleasant change of pace and is so good on a cold winter night with meat loaf.

SCALLOPED CELERY

Clean 1 large bunch of celery. (Save the leaves and trimmings for your soup stocks.)

Cut stalks into diagonal bite-sized pieces.

Put in a saucepan and add ½ cup chicken broth.

Cover and simmer about 10 min. until tender.

Pour celery into a 9 in. × 9 in. baking dish.

In the saucepan, melt 3 tbsp. butter or margarine.

Add: ¼ tsp. nutmeg
     salt and pepper

Remove from heat and stir in 2 cups bread crumbs. (Tear up slices of bread and put ½ cup or so in the blender at a time. Whir it up and you'll have crumbs in a jiffy with no mess!)

Stir in 1 cup shredded cheese (any kind).

Spoon this mixture over the celery.

Bake uncovered at 375° for 15–20 min. Serves 6.

One of the most enjoyable vegetables we were served in Denmark was sautéed cucumbers. I know it sounds different, and I'm really not an avid cucumber fan, but we *loved* these! Peel and slice cucumbers and soak in ice water for an hour or two. Drain and pat dry. Melt a little *butter* in a fry pan and just sauté the slices until tender. Sprinkle with salt and pepper. Boy, are they good! You can serve a wedge of lemon with them to squeeze over if you like.

To really please Roy in the spring, all I have to do is serve him creamed peas and carrots or little, boiled new potatoes and peas. I just make the medium white sauce on page 55 and stir in the cooked vegetables. For a different taste treat, use half milk and half chicken broth in making the white sauce. Sometimes I add a bit of onion, too.

Speaking of this, we also enjoy creamed onions served with baked potatoes, roast chicken, and tossed salad in the winter. Clean and cut into chunks 3 cups of large sweet onions. Cover with ½ cup water. Cover and simmer until tender (about 10 minutes). Meanwhile, in a little saucepan, melt 1 tablespoon butter. Stir in 1 tablespoon flour. Mix well, then pour the liquid from the onions into a cup and add enough milk to make 1 cup. Add this to the flour and butter and cook until thickened. Then add ½ cup grated cheese. Mix sauce with onions and pour into a casserole. Cover with some buttered crumbs and heat at 375° for about 20–25 minutes.

Vegetables *are* exciting. Serve a different one tonight!

MISCELLANEOUS

I have so many good old, tried and true recipes that don't really come under a main dish, vegetable/salad, or dessert category, so we'll just call them miscellaneous. These are recipes that you've really *got* to try, not just because they are delicious but because they'll save you lots of money at the grocery store, too.

An absolutely terrific meat spread for sandwiches is our family's old Danish liver spread. It's called "Pluckmah."

PLUCKMAH

Ask your butcher for ½ of a whole pork liver. (It's very reasonable.)

In a heavy saucepan, cover the liver with water and add about 1 tsp. salt.

Cook for 1½–2 hr. Reserve liquid.

Grind the liver in a meat grinder with 6–8 apples and 2–3 onions.

Put the ground mixture back in a saucepan and add a little of the liquid.

Cook, stirring occasionally, for 2 hr. adding a little more liquid if necessary. Salt and pepper to taste.

Serve this *warm,* spread on rye or pumpernickel bread with sweet pickles. I put it in meal-sized containers and freeze it. It heats up quickly for a lunch or snack.

Speaking of snacks, I hope you'll all try your hand at making your own Mexican chips and *salsa.* You'll really save money here, also.

To make your own hot, fresh chips, take a stack of corn tortillas and cut in quarters. Separate the pieces and fry in hot oil (375°–400°), turning or stirring a few at a time until they are crispy. *Don't let them brown.* Drain on a brown paper bag and sprinkle with salt. Serve in a basket to dip in *salsa.*

This sauce is also good on tacos, enchiladas, meats, eggs, or even a Mexican salad. It's better after it's been refrigerated for a few hours.

SALSA

Combine: 2 cups chopped tomatoes (fresh or canned)
1 medium onion (chopped)
1 4 oz. can chopped green chilies
½ tsp. salt
¼ tsp. coarse black pepper
½ tsp. sugar
1 tbsp. vinegar

Blend in the blender for just a second. It should still be a little chunky, not smooth.

Keep covered and refrigerated.

It seems that you like to make breads as much as I do. Doing so is rewarding and economical. Breads are "musts" for your recipe file, and whether you're a bachelor, older couple, or have a large family, you'll rave about them. They never fail to satisfy!

"THE BEST" BOSTON BROWN BREAD

Combine: 3 cups whole wheat flour
2 tsp. soda
1 tbsp. salt

Add: 2 cups brown sugar
2 egg yolks
2 cups buttermilk or soured milk

Stir in ½ cup currants or raisins.

Gently fold in 2 beaten egg whites.

Bake at 350° for about 45 min. (I bake mine in vegetable cans, *well greased* and half full. They make such nice, little round loaves for slicing.)

Let cool slightly, remove from cans, and then cool on racks.

Delicious with cream cheese!

Everyone should make their own English muffins. There's nothing to it! You can make any variety you choose, they cost less than one-fourth the commercial types, and nothing compares to them toasted for breakfast.

They freeze well. Just split them and package in plastic bags and they'll be ready to pop in the toaster! For variation, you can use part whole wheat flour and add cinnamon and raisins, onion flakes, or any seasonings you like. We even use them for sandwiches or "hurry-up" pizzas with some of these variations.

ENGLISH MUFFINS

Dissolve 1 pkg. yeast in ½ cup lukewarm water.

Sprinkle with 1 tbsp. sugar and let stand a few minutes.

Scald 1¼ cups milk.

Add 1 tbsp. shortening and 2 tsp. salt.

Let cool to lukewarm.

Combine: milk mixture
yeast mixture
2 cups flour

Beat well with a portable mixer for 3 min.

Add 1 cup flour and stir in well.

Cover and let rise in a warm place until double. Stir down.

On a lightly floured board, pat the dough to about ½ in. thick.

Cut in circles. (I use a "wide-mouth" jar ring.)

Place circles on a cookie sheet that has been sprinkled with cornmeal.

Cover and let rise until almost double.

Cook on a lightly greased griddle or electric fry pan at 375° for 15 min. on each side (as you would pancakes). Only turn once. Don't cover pan.

Let cool. Split with a fork and toast.

Now, if you like English muffins, you'll love my "English Toastin' Bread," and this freezes well, too. It's easier to make and can be varied like my muffins. It really makes good toast, too.

ENGLISH TOASTIN' BREAD

Dissolve 2 pkg. yeast in ½ cup lukewarm water.

Sprinkle with 1 tbsp. sugar.

Scald: 2 cups milk
       2 tsp. salt

Cool to lukewarm.

Combine: milk mixture
         yeast mixture
         3¼ cups flour
         pinch of soda

Beat well with electric mixer for 3 min.

Add 3 cups flour.

Stir in well with a wooden spoon.

Spoon into 2 greased loaf pans (8 in. × 4 in.) that have been sprinkled with cornmeal.

With lightly floured hands, pat the top of each loaf to smooth. Sprinkle with cornmeal.

Cover and let rise until almost double.

Bake at 400° for 25 min.

Take right out of pans and cool on a rack.

We love biscuits, and these are straight from heaven! They are so light and fluffy and truly melt in your mouth. They have both yeast and baking powder, which accounts for their lightness, yet they don't require any rising time. This recipe originated in the South where biscuits are a way of life and where many families have their version of this specialty. Biscuits are also delicious served as a base for creamed chicken. The dough keeps well in the refrigerator for a week or so, so you can enjoy biscuits in several ways. The biscuits can also be baked and frozen and then rewarmed in the oven.

SOUTHERN
HIGH RISE BISCUITS

Dissolve 2 tbsp. yeast in ¼ cup warm water.

In a large mixing bowl, combine:
    5½ cups flour
    ⅓ cup sugar
    3 tsp. baking powder
    1 tsp. soda

Cut in 1 cup Crisco, as you would for pie crust, until mixture forms coarse crumbs.

Stir in 2 cups buttermilk and yeast mixture.

Mix well with a fork.

Knead lightly a few times on a floured board.

Pat dough out to about ½ in. thickness and cut out biscuits with a small round cutter. (I use a juice glass.)

Place on a lightly greased cookie sheet and bake at 425° until nicely browned (about 10–12 min.).

This will make about 48 biscuits.

In *A Family Raised on Rainbows*, I told you about "sourdough starter" and gave you that delicious recipe for my sourdough pancakes. This is a way of cooking that grew out of necessity when the early settlers needed to make bread to survive but yeast was not always available. As they traveled from camp to camp, their sourdough starter was the last thing they packed and the first thing they unpacked. The "starter" was a prized possession and was shared many, many times. When you try these fabulous recipes, you'll see why pioneers often walked miles to get a "start" from someone for baking. It really does wonders and gets better with age as long as you replenish it about once a week. It will last for months and months, even years.

The night before, make a "sponge" of a package of yeast in 2 cups warm water, stirring in 2 cups flour. (Always use a glass or plastic bowl. Never use metal or allow a metal spoon to stand for any length of time in the mixture.) Cover and let sit on a counter overnight. In the morning, remove ½ cup for your "starter" and place it in a clean, covered jar and refrigerate for next time. Proceed with the rest of the "sponge" to make the recipe.

If you already have ½ cup starter in the refrigerator, the night before, take out the ½ cup starter and add 2 cups milk (or water) and 2 cups flour. Stir well and let stand on your kitchen counter, covered, overnight. Remove ½ cup for your starter to refrigerator and use the rest for the "sponge" for the recipe.

This bread is crisp and crusty and chewy inside. It is good with a soup and salad.

SOURDOUGH BREAD

Into a large mixing bowl, combine:
    4 cups flour
    1 tsp. salt
    2 tbsp. sugar

Stir 2 tbsp. shortening into sourdough sponge.

Form a well in the center of dry mixture and pour into well:
    sourdough mixture
    1 beaten egg

Mix together and knead for about 10 min. (This is great therapy for tense nerves. It's also great exercise for those upper arms *and* bust line.)

Place the dough in a greased bowl, cover, and put in a warm place to rise. (This bread is a little slow rising; it may take about 3 hr.) Let rise until double.

Dissolve ¼ tsp. soda in 1 tbsp. warm water. Knead this into the dough.

Form the dough into 2 loaves in 8 in. × 4 in. greased bread pans. Cover and let rise until double.

Bake at 375° for 50–60 min.

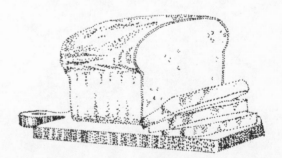

You really have to try this cake. It is so easy to put together and is as light as a feather and tender. To make it, I set my sponge at night; in the morning, I remove ½ cup for my starter to put back in the refrigerator, use ½ cup to make the cake, and use the rest for muffins at the same time.

SOURDOUGH CHOCOLATE CAKE

Mix together: ½ cup starter
              1 cup milk
              1½ cups flour

Stir well and let stand for 2 hr. or so until foamy and bubbly.

Cream together: ½ cup shortening
              1 cup sugar
              1 tsp. vanilla
              ½ tsp. salt
              1½ tsp. soda
              1 tsp. cinnamon

Add 2 eggs, beating after each one.

Then stir in the sourdough mixture and 3 squares of melted chocolate.

Mix just until blended.

Bake in a greased 9 in. × 13 in. pan or 2 layer pans at 350° for about 30 min. or until well done.

Frost as desired.

I promise you, these are the best muffins you will ever eat. If you don't make the cake, you can just use your sponge as usual, and it still works fine.

SOURDOUGH MUFFINS

Mix together: 1½ cups whole wheat flour
              ½ cup sugar
              1 tsp. soda
              1 tsp. salt

Make a well in the center and add:
              ½ cup Mazola oil
              2 beaten eggs
              remaining sponge (from cake)

Stir only to moisten.

Add ½ cup raisins or currants if desired.

Bake in muffin pans at 375° for about 30 min. or until done. Makes 16 muffins.

For variety on my pancake recipe in *A Family Raised on Rainbows*, try adding some shredded apple. To make waffles, use the pancake recipe and add a little more flour (about ½ cup) when adding the other ingredients to the sponge.

Give sourdough a try. You'll be so pleasantly surprised, and soon others will be asking for a "start."

Commercial sauces are so expensive and usually full of a lot of additives. Here are three favorites that you'll want to keep on hand all the time.

BEV'S BARBEQUE SAUCE

Mix in a saucepan: 1¾ cups tomato juice
¼ cup cider vinegar
1 medium onion, finely chopped
2 tbsp. brown sugar
1½ tsp. paprika
1 tsp. liquid smoke
½ tsp. celery seed
8 drops Tabasco

Simmer 15–20 min.

Store in refrigerator.

COCKTAIL SAUCE

Mix well: 1 bottle (14 oz.) of catsup
2 tbsp. vinegar
dash of salt
4 tbsp. horseradish
2 drops Tabasco
juice of 1 lemon
1 tbsp. Worcestershire sauce
3 stalks of celery, finely chopped

Keep refrigerated.

You got Mrs. Lauria's fantastic pizza dough recipe in *A Family Raised on Rainbows*. Now here is the sauce! A tip from Mrs. Lauria: for a nice crust, grease the pan and sprinkle with cornmeal before putting the crust in the pan.

MRS. LAURIA'S PIZZA SAUCE

Mix together in saucepan:
1 fat can (28 oz.) Italian/plum tomatoes
1 can (6 oz.) tomato paste
2 cloves of garlic, minced
1 tsp. oregano
salt and pepper to taste
½ cup olive oil (Do use olive oil, not salad oil.)

Simmer together 5–10 min.
(I crush the tomatoes with a fork.)

Many recipes call for a can of chow mein noodles, but the price charged for a few of those crispy noodles is outrageous. Why not make your own for a fraction of the cost, as we do?

To make "oodles and oodles" of Chinese noodles, cook 1 pound of spaghetti as directed on the package. Rinse *very* well with cold water, drain, and pat dry with paper towels. Put part of the cooked spaghetti into a plastic bag with a tablespoon or two of cornstarch. Shake to lightly dust cornstarch onto the spaghetti. Drop a few noodles at a time into hot oil and fry to a crispy brown. I cook up a big batch and then store it in a tightly covered container. Try it; you'll be so proud!

Since white sauce is such a basic recipe and so versatile and economical, let me tell you how I make mine. The proportions to remember are as follows:

WHITE SAUCE

for *thin* sauce: 1 tbsp. margarine
1 tbsp. flour
1 cup milk

medium sauce: 2 tbsp. margarine
2 tbsp. flour
1 cup milk

thick sauce: 3 tbsp. margarine
3 tbsp. flour
1 cup milk

In a saucepan, melt the margarine. Then stir in the flour, stirring well for a few minutes over medium heat to thoroughly dissolve and cook the flour. Slowly add the milk, stirring constantly for 2–3 minutes more until sauce thickens. Season with salt and pepper. You are now ready to make scalloped potatoes, au gratin potatoes by adding cheese, or a cheese sauce for macaroni and cheese or a cheese sauce to serve over vegetables. Let your imagination be your guide. This is the same technique I use in making any kind of sauce. I use the thin sauce for soups, cream gravies, and creamed vegetables such as new potatoes and peas. The medium sauce has a good consistency for scalloped potatoes or macaroni and cheese-type dishes.

Another standard recipe I use as a base for most types of frostings is as follows:

FROSTING

2 cups powdered sugar
2–3 tbsp. butter or margarine
dash of salt
hot water to make frosting consistency

For chocolate, add about ½ cup cocoa. For lemon, add 2 tablespoons lemon juice and 1 teaspoon grated rind or ½ teaspoon lemon extract. A few strawberries can be beaten into this mixture or try a little pineapple juice or any of the extracts. A little mint or rum extract with the chocolate is good.

One of my family's favorites is French toast for breakfast or a Saturday night supper. I always like to serve it with sausage, applesauce, and milk.

FRENCH TOAST

Put into the blender: 3 eggs
½–¾ cup milk
salt and pepper
dash of nutmeg

Blend well and pour into a shallow dish.

Dip bread slices into mixture, on both sides, and fry in a little hot oil in a frying pan until golden brown on each side.

Use French or Italian bread sliced thick.

Serve with butter and hot maple syrup.

DESERTS

Desserts are the "crowning touch" to a home-cooked meal. They can be light and fluffy to "top off" a heavy main dish or filling and hearty to compensate for a light meal. They can be fruity and nutritious, high in protein with lots of milk, butter, and eggs, or just rich and yummy to satisfy that occasional desire. I have found that by providing my family with satisfying desserts and treats now and then, they eat very little, if any, candy or commercial sweet things. Goodies from our kitchens made with wholesome ingredients are much tastier. Just remember to maintain a balance and include a variety in your diets. I know you'll enjoy these recipes. Pick and choose what will go best with *your* meals.

Everyone loves cookies. Here are some more of our family favorites that will be kind to your budget and pleasant in your tummies!

KRISTEN'S CHERRY CHOCOLATES

Mix together: 1 stick margarine
              ¾ cup sugar
              1 egg

Add: 1¼ cups flour
     5 tbsp. cocoa
     ½ tsp. soda
     dash of salt

Mix well.

Stir in: about 30 chopped maraschino cherries
        ½ cup chopped nuts

Drop by spoonfuls on ungreased cookie sheet.

Bake at 350° for about 10–12 min.

Makes 2½ dozen. (I usually double this. They freeze just great.)

Pineapple cookies really are *so* soft and tender. The nutmeg gives that added touch. (I usually open a 15 ounce can of pineapple and use the rest to make a carrot and pineapple Jell-O salad.)

TENDER PINEAPPLE COOKIES

Cream together: ½ cup shortening (I use Crisco.)
                1 cup sugar
                1 egg and then add ½ cup drained pineapple

Add: 2 cups flour
     1 tsp. baking powder
     1 tsp. soda
     1 tsp. salt
     ½ tsp. nutmeg

Drop by spoonfuls on an ungreased cookie sheet.

Bake at 350° for about 10 min.

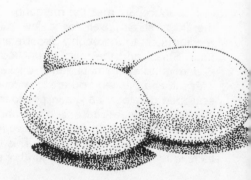

I like to keep some rolls of refrigerator cookie dough on hand in the freezer or refrigerator. What a nice touch it is to serve "drop in" friends some fresh cookies warm from the oven. This is one of my favorites.

BLACK WALNUT ICE BOX COOKIES

Beat together: 2 cups brown sugar
                2 sticks margarine
                2 eggs

Add: 4 cups flour
      1 tsp. baking soda
      1 tsp. cream of tartar

Stir in: 1 cup chopped black walnuts
         1 tsp. vanilla

Mix well and form into 2 long rolls on sheets of plastic wrap.

Roll up the rolls in the plastic and refrigerate overnight.

Slice and bake on a lightly greased cookie sheet at 375° for about 6–8 min.

These bar-type cookies are easy to make and taste so good in the fall with a glass of cider or cold milk.

APPLE DREAM BARS

Mix together: 1¾ cups flour
               ⅔ cup sugar
               ⅔ cup margarine

Put mixture into a 9 in. × 13 in. ungreased pan.

Cover with 4 cups of apple slices. (Any variety but tart ones are best.)

Sprinkle with a mixture of: ¼ cup sugar
                         ½ tsp. cinnamon

Bake at 375° for 30 min.

While that is baking, mix together:
    1¼ cups brown sugar
    2½ tbsp. flour
    3 eggs
    dash of salt

Then add: ¾ cup coconut
           ½ cup chopped nuts

Spread on top of first mixture while it's hot.

Return to oven and bake another 20 min.

Cool and cut into bars.

Of course, one of our family's favorite desserts is ice cream. When all the kids were home to help "crank," we loved the old-fashioned kind, but now that they are gone, Roy and I have invested in one of those little counter-top ice-cream makers and we love it. It uses regular ice cubes and a carton of table salt. It's so handy, quick—and we can make it as "fat" or "skinny" as we want. I highly recommend it. It's so simple to use and makes a half gallon.

Here are a couple of our favorite recipes. This one is so simple, we all love it:

LAZY DAY ICE CREAM

1 qt. of half and half
1 cup sugar
a dash of salt
2 cups of fruit (mashed).

Our favorites are strawberries, peaches or bananas (and be sure they are *real* ripe). I always add some chopped nuts. It is absolutely out of this world. You can even use just milk but it will have a little different texture. It makes about a half gallon.

LEMON CUSTARD ICE CREAM

Beat two eggs well. Gradually add 1½ cups sugar. *Slowly* stir in 2 cups of scalded milk. Cook this together over low heat until it's thickened. Stir constantly. Let cool. Then stir in

2 cups half and half
dash of salt
1½ tsp. grated lemon rind
½ tsp. lemon extract
1 tsp. vanilla

You can leave out the lemon in this and add other flavors of fruits. But any way you do it, it's sure super delicious.

ORANGE SHERBET

We also make a delicious orange sherbet using just

3 cups milk
2 cups orange juice
1¼ cups sugar
dash of salt

People are always asking me for a good zucchini bread recipe, and this one is absolutely fabulous. It's an easy and yummy way to use those squash in the garden.

PARA LEE'S
ZUCCHINI BREAD

Beat 3 egg yolks and add: 1 cup Mazola oil
                               2 cups sugar
                               2 cups grated zucchini
                               2 tsp. vanilla

Mix well, then add: 3 cups flour
                       1 tsp. soda
                       ½ tsp. baking powder
                       1 tsp. salt
                       1 tsp. cinnamon

Then stir in 1 cup chopped nuts.

At last, fold in 3 beaten egg whites.

Spoon gently into 2 greased and floured loaf pans.

Bake at 325° for 1 hr.

Cool slightly, turn out of pans, and cool on a rack.

Who doesn't like hot apple strudel with a scoop of ice cream or whipped cream? Here's an easy version of a very delicious recipe.

SIMPLE GERMAN STRUDEL

Butter a 9 in. × 9 in. baking dish.

In a bowl, combine: ¾ cup sugar
                          1 cup flour
                          1 tsp. baking powder
                          ½ tsp. salt

Break 1 egg into the dry mixture and add 1 tbsp. vinegar (a hint I learned in Germany).

Mix well until crumbly. (I use my hands.)

Sprinkle over apples and bake at 350° for about 45 min.

Serve warm with cream or ice cream.

Homemade cakes are so tasty, you can't miss with these recipes for dessert.

This chiffon-type cake is so light and fluffy, yet moist. It's a great dessert to take on a summer picnic. After that fried chicken and potato salad, it will really hit the spot. The texture also makes it easy to eat out of hand. I bake mine in a 10 inch tube pan and frost it right in the pan. I still use mom's old pan from the farm, and I have floods of memories whenever I cut a piece of that cake.

SUNSHINY ORANGE CAKE

Beat together: 4 egg yolks
1¼ cups sugar

Then add alternately: 1½ cups flour
dash of salt
½ cup orange juice
grated rind of 1 orange

Beat 4 egg whites and ½ tsp. baking powder until stiff.

Fold the egg whites gently into the creamed mixture with a rubber spatula.

Spoon batter into an ungreased tube or angel food cake pan. (If you plan to remove the cake from the pan to frost for serving, cut a piece of waxed paper to fit into the bottom of the pan before pouring in the batter.)

Bake at 325° for about 1 hr.

Invert the pan while cooling the cake. Then, for easy removal, run a knife around the edge.

This frosting is out of this world!

ORANGE FROSTING

Beat to spreading consistency:
2 cups powdered sugar
juice of 1 orange
dash of salt
2 tbsp. butter (I prefer real butter.)

You may need a little more sugar or juice.

This will frost the cake top and sides.

By the way, since I have several recipes in this chapter that call for beaten egg whites, let me remind you that if you get any yolk at all into the white when separating the egg, it will not beat up to full volume. Even a speck of yolk will make a difference, so be careful not to break the yolk. It is also wise to use a glass bowl in which to beat the egg whites so that there is no trace of grease. Sometimes there may be some on a plastic bowl that you don't see, and that will hinder the volume of your egg white, also. Egg whites, beaten stiff, are beaten to such a point that when you draw your beaters up, they will form little peaks that will hold their shape. Then you just cut the whites into the other mixture in the recipe with a rubber spatula in a folding motion.

Sheet cakes are a favorite of mine because, with very little work, I can provide lots of servings either for entertaining or to fill my freezer.

This recipe comes from my sister-in-law, Dolores Scheel, and is at least 1,000 calories a bite but worth every one!

DOLORES'S
TEXAS SHEET CAKE

Combine: 2 cups flour
2 cups sugar

In a saucepan, mix together:
1 cup water
1 stick margarine
½ cup Crisco
3 tbsp. cocoa

Bring to a boil and pour over the flour and sugar mixture.

Mix well.

Stir in: ½ cup buttermilk or soured milk
1 tsp. soda
1 tsp. cinnamon
2 eggs

Beat well and pour into a greased 10 in. × 15 in. cookie sheet with sides.

Bake at 400° for 20 min.

While cake is still warm, frost with this icing:

Bring to a boil: ½ cup margarine
3 tbsp. cocoa
5 tbsp. milk

Remove from heat and add:
1 package (1 lb.) powdered sugar
1 cup chopped nuts

Beat until smooth and spread carefully on warm cake.

This cake is *so* moist and tender!

PINEAPPLE SHEET CAKE

Combine: 2 cups flour
1 tsp. baking soda
dash of salt
2 cups sugar

Add: 2 eggs
1 cup salad oil (I use Crisco Oil.)

Then add: 1 can (15 oz.) crushed pineapple, undrained.

Pour into a large (10 in. × 15 in.) greased sheet cake pan.

Bake at 350° for about 25–30 min.

In a saucepan, mix: ⅔ cup evaporated milk
¾ cup sugar
1 stick margarine

Bring to a boil and simmer 9 min., stirring constantly.

Then add: 1 cup chopped nuts
1 cup coconut

Spread on warm cake.

One of my all-time favorites is this nut cake. It's so simple to make and gets raves every time. I usually frost this with the orange frosting on page 60.

LUNCH BOX NUT CAKE

In a large bowl, combine:
       2 sticks margarine
       1 cup brown sugar
       ½ cup sugar
       3 eggs
       1 cup orange juice
       1 tbsp. grated orange peel

Then add: 2 cups flour
       1 cup graham cracker crumbs
       1 tsp. salt
       1 tsp. baking powder
       1 tsp. soda
       ½ tsp. cinnamon

Beat together for 3 min.

Sitr in 1 cup chopped nuts.

Pour into a greased 10 in. tube pan.

Bake at 350° for 45–50 min.

Cool upright for 30 min. Frost in pan or run a knife around the edge of cake and invert on a serving plate.

These lemon cups are another lunch box treat.

LEMON CUPS

Cream together: 1 stick margarine
             1 cup sugar

Add: 2 eggs
     grated rind of 1 lemon
     juice of 1 lemon and enough water to make 1 cup liquid

Then add: 2 cups flour
          2 tsp. baking powder

Beat well.

Pour into paper-lined muffin cups or a 9 in. × 9 in. greased pan.

Sprinkle with a mixture of: ½ cup chopped pecans
                     ½ cup coconut

Press gently into batter.

Bake at: 375° for about 20 min. for cupcakes
       350° for 50–60 min. for a 9 in. × 9 in. pan (or until it tests done)

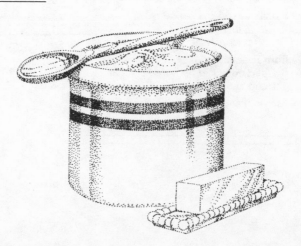

Puddings are one of the easiest and most satisfying types of desserts. They are quick to fix and really hit the spot after any meal or for a treat in the evening.

Those fruits in the freezer really come in handy for this delicious light dessert.

STRAWBERRY-RHUBARB FLUFF

In a saucepan, combine: 4 cups frozen rhubarb
           ¼ cup sugar
           ¼ cup water

Cook together, stirring often until tender and saucy (about 10 min.)

Remove from heat and stir in 2–3 oz. pkg. strawberry Jell-O.

Stir well for about 2 min. until Jell-O is well dissolved.

Stir in 1 pkg. (about 1½ cups) frozen strawberries.

Chill in refrigerator until partially set.

Whip 1 cup whipping cream and fold into pudding.

Chill until set. Serves 8.

This airy, refreshing pudding is an old recipe from the South Sea Islands. It is so good.

PINEAPPLE CREAM

Drain the juice from a 15½ oz. can of pineapple chunks. Add water to juice to make 1 cup.

In saucepan, combine: 1 cup juice
          ¼ cup sugar mixed with
          1 tbsp. cornstarch
          1 tbsp. butter (Use real butter if possible.)
          2 beaten egg yolks

Bring to a boil over medium heat and simmer 2 min.

Stir in drained pineapple chunks.

Set in refrigerator to cool.

Beat 2 egg whites until stiff and fold gently into completely cooled pudding with a rubber spatula.

Chill well. Serves 4–6.

This is absolutely delicious and so simple and inexpensive. You'll never want a "box" pudding again!

LUSCIOUS CREAM PUDDING OR PIE FILLING

In a 2 qt. saucepan, combine: ¾ cup sugar
5 tbsp. cornstarch
dash of salt

Add 3¼ cups milk. (I use a little half-and-half in place of some of the milk if I have some on hand.)

Cook over medium heat, stirring constantly, until it's smooth and thickened.

In a small bowl, mix up 3 egg yolks with a fork.

Stir a little of the hot mixture into the egg yolks, stirring well.

Add the egg yolk mixture back into the pudding mixture and cook another 2–3 min.

Stir in 2 tbsp. butter and 1 tsp. vanilla.

Spoon into bowls or pie shell.

This makes a great coconut or banana cream pie. For chocolate pie, just stir in ½ cup chocolate chips at the end of cooking; mix well until melted.

If you really want to "splurge" the calories, try this yummy ending to a meal of Mexican food. It's truly heaven!

MEXICAN SUNDAES— UPSIDE DOWN

Melt: 3 squares baking chocolate (unsweetened)
⅓ cup margarine

Beat 4 eggs and add: 1 cup sugar
1 cup white corn syrup
chocolate mixture

Add 1 cup chopped pecans.

Pour into a greased 9 in. × 9 in. pan.

Set on a cookie sheet filled with water.

Bake at 350° for 40 min.

Serve a small dish of warm pudding with a scoop of vanilla ice cream on top.

Makes 8 servings.

This pudding cake is a delightful ending to a soup and salad supper.

COUNTRY CARAMEL PUDDING

Mix and bring to a boil: 3 cups water
$\qquad$ 1½ cups brown sugar
$\qquad$ 3 tbsp. butter

Cream together: 1 cup sugar
$\qquad$ ¼ cup margarine

Add: 1½ cups chopped apples
$\qquad$ 1 cup milk

Then add: 2 cups flour
$\qquad$ 2½ tsp. baking powder
$\qquad$ 1½ tsp. soda
$\qquad$ ½ tsp. salt
$\qquad$ 1 tsp. cinnamon
$\qquad$ 1 tsp. nutmeg

Mix well and add: 1 cup raisins or currants
$\qquad$ ½ cup chopped nuts

Spread the batter in a 9 in. × 13 in. pan (greased).

Pour hot syrup mixture over the batter.

Bake at 375° for 45 min.

Serve warm with ice cream or whipped cream.

(Note: the cake rises to the top, and sauce will be in the bottom).

Don't let apple season come and go without making a pan of apple dumplings. These are absolutely the best you'll ever eat. Why not make up a batch and take to some older people or those friends living alone? They'll love you for it.

BEV'S FARM-STYLE APPLE DUMPLINGS

Make pastry for a two-crust pie. (See *A Family Raised on Sunshine*.)

Roll out and cut into 6 7-in. squares.

Peel and core 6 apples.

Set each apple on the center of a square of pastry.

Fill core cavities with a mixture of:
$\qquad$ ½ cup sugar
$\qquad$ 1½ tsp. cinnamon
$\qquad$ 1½ tsp. nutmeg

Put a dab of butter on the top of each apple.

Bring the four corners of the square of pastry up over the top of the apple and overlap.

Place the dumplings in a baking dish with a little room between them.

Make a hot syrup of: 1 cup sugar
$\qquad$ 2 cups water
$\qquad$ 3 tbsp. butter
$\qquad$ ¼ tsp. cinnamon
$\qquad$ ¼ tsp. nutmeg

Pour 1 cup of syrup into pan.

Bake at 425° for 45 min. Save the rest of the syrup and pour over the dumplings just before serving. Serve with cream.

So many of you have written to tell me how much you like the sweet roll dough recipe in *A Family Raised on Sunshine.* I have a couple of variations that we really like. I thought you might want to try them.

To make the big, flat, chewy "elephant ears" you see in the bakeries, I just make the dough as usual, roll out, and shape for cinnamon rolls. Place the rolls on cookie sheets, flatten with your hand, cover with a towel, and let rise until double. Cover the rolls with waxed paper and flatten them with your hand to ⅛ inch thick. Brush the roll tops with melted butter; sprinkle with cinnamon and sugar mixture and chopped nuts. Cover again with waxed paper and press mixture slightly into dough. Bake immediately at 400° for 10–12 minutes. Cool on a rack. You'll love them.

We also enjoy the old German cream-filled coffee cake. It's so easy to make. Just mix up the sweet roll dough, let rise until double, stir down, and then pat dough into greased cake pans one-half the depth of the pan. Let rise until double. Bake at 375° until done (about 20 minutes for an 8 in. × 8 in. pan). Let cool, then split coffee cake in half horizontally. Fill with this delicious cream filling:

GERMAN CREAM-FILLED COFFEE CAKE

Cook over low heat until thick:
  ¼ cup flour
  ½ tsp. salt
  1 cup milk

Cool completely.

Cream together: ⅔ cup margarine
  1 cup sugar

Add cold flour mixture and beat until light and fluffy.

Blend in 1 tsp. vanilla.

Frost the top of the coffee cake with a powdered sugar frosting or glaze and sprinkle with chopped pecans.

By the way, if you want fresh rolls for breakfast, prepare dough, shape your rolls, and freeze before letting them rise. The night before, set them out in the kitchen, cover with a towel, and in the morning, they'll be ready to bake fresh for breakfast!

Never forget that mealtime should be a happy time, and the attitude with which we serve our food is as important as the food we bring to the table. We *can* serve nourishing meals, enjoy doing it, and save on our budgets, too. Let's start today!

4
SUNSHINE
FOR A
RAINY DAY

No one ever hopes for a rainy day, and I would like to wish a sunny day, every day to all of you. However, in these economically tense times, it wouldn't take much—a flood, a job loss, a strike, an earthquake, or an illness—to put a real strain on our purses and our peace of mind. More and more people are beginning to realize the benefits of a preparedness program of a year's supply of basic necessities. In addition to the feeling of security it brings, it's also just plain good common sense. By buying in quantity, storing in season, and learning to eat more healthful, economical foods, you will be able to accomplish much more on the same amount of, or even less, money. A food storage program should not be something separate from your normal meal shopping. It should become a way of life.

The first requirement for a successful storage program is desire. Desire to save money, to feed your family well *every day*, and to have a feeling of security and contentment. Remember, a successful program involves everyone in the household. Include everyone in the planning *and* doing. You'll find a lot of excitement and enthusiasm when everyone works together for a common goal, and there is no better way to build happy memories and a secure feeling for your family. Hard times have no respect for people's needs, so let's begin today!

It may seem overwhelming or even mind boggling to envision a year's supply of basics, but believe me, it can be done, and what a terrific feeling! It will take time, dedication, effort, persistence, and yes, patience, but the secret is to begin *now* by:

1. Shopping specials
2. Buying bulk where possible
3. Raising a garden
4. Doing all the canning, freezing, and dehydrating possible
5. Eating less meat

6. Setting up a budget and allocating whatever possible for stock-up buying
7. Establishing a plan for your family

Friends are always asking me what they should store, and the best answer I can give them is "What *you* need." For instance, if your family likes tuna and noodles once a week, be sure you plan so that you can prepare this without running to the store. Bear in mind that eventually you and your family will be eating everything you store, so be sure you consider any special dietary needs, the size and ages of your family, the availability of foods in your area, and things that store best in your climate. Also be sure you have a pleasant *variety* as well as foods that provide good, balanced nutrition.

It is always best to begin with the basics:

1. Wheat and grains
2. Powdered milk
3. Sugar and/or honey
4. Salt
5. Water
6. Fats or oil
7. Dried legumes

Then determine your family needs by keeping a diary of your menus for 2 weeks. This will give you a guideline to start building a supply of those things necessary to your particular tastes. Be specific with your diary, For example:

	Monday	Tuesday
Bread	6 slices	4 slices
Salt	2 tsp.	½ tsp.

This experience can be very helpful and enlightening. You may want to have two final lists to help you start storing: a list of essentials and a list of "nice to have" foods.

Be careful to avoid the "stockpiling" habit. It will cost you money in the long run because you will end up throwing away off-color, spoiled, and inedible food. Always plan to rotate *everything* on your shelves. Nothing should be over 2 years old. Store only what you need!

In storing, the four worst enemies of food storage are heat, light, air, and moisture.

To provide long shelf life, you should store canned fruits and vegetables at a temperature less than 70°. Near 50° is ideal. If these foods are stored at high temperatures, the food will become soft and mushy, will change in flavor and color, and, more importantly, will lose much of its nutritional value.

Attics are nearly always too warm for storage. Basements provide ideal space as long as the area is dry. Be careful never to store foods next to heating vents.

Use glass, metal, or rigid plastic containers and avoid paper or cardboard. This is especially true if there is a problem with moisture, insects, or rodents. Keep your storage area clean and dry to help eliminate these problems. Our favorite containers for large bulk storage are metal garbage cans. If these are new and clean and dry, there is no need to line them with a plastic bag. (Some types of plastic bags may give off harmful chemicals when used in food storage.) Large cans with tight-fitting lids are also available from restaurants, bakeries, and so on that purchase such things as shortening in them and often sell them reasonably. Just scrub them well and dry thoroughly. We have also gotten many large heavy plastic bucket containers with tight-fitting lids from hamburger chains. Sometimes pickle slices come in these, but the pickle odor can be removed with a little work. Just scrub the containers well in hot, soapy water; rinse and dry; stuff them tightly with wadded-up newspapers; and then secure the lid and leave it for several days. The paper will absorb the pickle odor.

Never set any of your storage containers directly on a cement or dirt floor. Always place a piece of wood under them to provide ventilation and protection against moisture.

Some foods (sugar, gelatins, crackers, and so on) don't require cool temperature but do need a dry atmosphere, so you can utilize other areas to store these things.

Be sure you label all containers with date and contents so that you can have an inventory for rotating.

I never throw away any glass jars or containers. I wash them well, and they are great for beans, rice, cornmeal, and so on, after the original container or bag is opened.

There are so many creative ways of storing things that space never needs to be a problem.

1. Store boxes of food under beds, cribs, and tables with a pretty dust ruffle as a coverup. When we lived in Texas and had no basement for storage and a garage that got to be 175°, we stored a different variety of food in each bedroom: fruit in Heidi's room, vegetables in Kristen's, and pasta and bean items in the boys' room. This eliminated hunting all over the house for a certain type of food. It was a challenge but fun.
2. Fill 1–5 gallon cans with dried foods and stack with boards to form book shelves. The

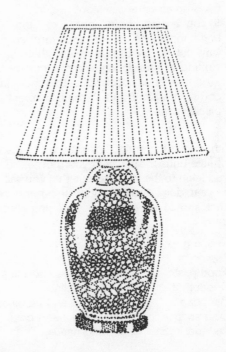

cans can be covered with attractive contact paper.

3. Build shelves for storage and hang a pretty curtain or drape in front of them. This will fit into any room.

4. Add an extra shelf above the one in that bedroom closet. It is just wasted space, anyway.

5. Fill a large garbage can with wheat, cartons of powdered milk, and so on, put the lid on upside down and tape it, then cut a large circle of fiberboard or plywood, set it on top, and cover it all with a pretty print table cover made from a colorful sheet. Presto, a beautiful table!

6. A friend of mine even stored food in her lamps (beans, dried peas, and so on). She filled a large glass water bottle with layers of colorful legumes, purchased an inexpensive light fixture to place in it, and added a pretty little shade.

7. A little can with a padded top added to it can become an attractive stool.

8. If you are short on spaces to store extra bedding, sheets, pillow cases, and so forth, why not do as I did and use them as the stuffing or foundation to make pillows for a window seat or couch? Just fold them into a compact square and slip into a bright-print pillow cover.

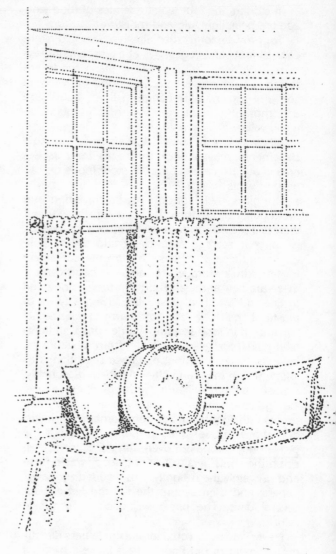

With a little ingenuity, I'm sure you'll discover lots of little unused spaces in your home.

In addition to the food storage that you will plan for the year, don't overlook all those other necessities that should be a part of your preparedness program:

Rubbing alcohol	Paper towels	Bleach	Toilet tissue
Aspirin	Candles	Baby needs	Hot water bottle
Toothpaste	Paper plates and cups	Matches	Feminine hygiene needs
Deodorant	Extra bedding	A Coleman stove, fuel, and lantern	
Bar soap	Flashlight and batteries		
Dish soap	First-aid kit and book		
Laundry soap	Sewing needs		

A fireplace or Franklin or free-standing stove is a good investment. These can be used for heat as well as cooking. During a bad ice storm in Kansas City one winter, nearly all homes were without electricity for several days, and many of our friends would have frozen if it hadn't been for their fireplaces and a good supply of wood.

When buying wood, keep in mind it is sold by units of measurement. A full cord is a stack 8 feet long, 4 feet high, and 4 feet wide. Be cautious in just buying a truckload. This amount can vary greatly. Woods with the highest energy level are live oak, hickory, black locust, dogwood, slash pine, apple, white oak, black birch, rock elm, sugar maple, ash, and black walnut. Some woods low in energy level are black spruce, hemlock, red fir, large-tooth aspen, ponderosa pine, redwood, sugar and white pine, and cottonwood.

Why not put those old newspapers to good use and make your own logs? Fold the paper in half, having it no more than ½ inch thick, soak it overnight in 1 gallon of water and 1 tablespoon of detergent, roll the wet segment out onto a rod, squeeze out the water, and smooth the surface edges. Slide the rod out and let the roll stand on end until thoroughly dry. These burn great, and you'll accumulate a lot in a hurry.

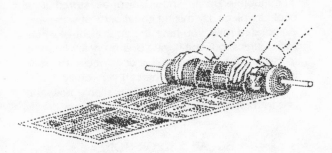

Coal can also be stored; just be sure you check with your city council so that you purchase the right variety. You are not allowed to burn some kinds within certain areas.

Together with your family, itemize all the things you would need in an emergency.

Now let's discuss, thoroughly, the food basics.

GRAIN
(wheat, rice, corn, etc.)

Average yearly need per person: 250–300 pounds

Grains have been one of mankind's staples since ancient times. They are a tremendous source of body-building energy at a low cost. They provide us with B vitamins, protein, iron, and carbohydrates and should be used jointly with protein in milk, meat, and eggs. If your family hasn't been exposed to many of the grains, now is the time to have some fun using them as a cereal, in place of potatoes, mixed in a soup or casserole, or sprouted. In *A Family Raised on Sunshine*, I introduced you to wheat and gave you a few recipes and uses to get started. I hope by now it's a regular part of your diet. There are also some of my favorite wheat recipes in *A Family Raised on Rainbows* and in the "special diets" chapter of this book. Here are a couple more that you'll have to try that are lots of fun and really good.

WHEAT TREATS

Soak wheat overnight (24 hr.) in cold water. (Rinse and re-cover with water once during this time.)

Rinse and pat dry in paper towels.

Heat oil in a deep fryer to 375°.

Fry a small amount of wheat kernels at a time in a strainer.

Drain on paper towels and sprinkle with salt. For a fun variety, try garlic salt, seasoning salt, or Parmesan cheese.

These are terrific with our homemade tomato soup.

CHEEZY WHEAT CRACKERS

Combine: 1 cup cornmeal
          1 cup whole wheat flour
          dash of salt

Stir in: 1 cup water
       4 tbsp. salad oil

Stir in ½ cup finely grated cheese (any kind).

Divide dough in half.

Lightly grease the "bottom side" of a large cookie sheet. Place half the dough on the pan, cover with Handiwrap, and roll out as thin as possible. Be sure it's an even thickness so it will bake evenly.

Score into cracker size, prick with a fork all over, and sprinkle with salt.

Repeat with the other half of dough.

Bake at 300° for about 30 min. or until crisp. If not totally crisp when cooled, set back in warm oven a few minutes.

Enjoy wheat and all the grains each day in your diet.

POWDERED MILK

Average yearly need per person: 75 pounds

Milk is a vital item to have on hand. Because of convenience of storing, powdered or canned milk is the wisest for storage. In its powdered form, it has all the nutrients except fat, which has been removed. It is also the most economical type available. It comes in many sizes and is also available in instant and noninstant forms. Noninstant stores better and retains its flavor more so than instant; however, it is harder to reconstitute smoothly. It can be reconstituted and used in any recipe. (One-third cup milk powder and 1 cup water equals a cup of milk.)

In an emergency, you can also use it as a whipped topping. Just combine equal amounts of powdered milk and ice water in a chilled bowl and whip. Then add a little sweetener and flavoring. Eat immediately.

Powdered milk should be stored in air-tight containers in a cool, dry place because it tends to absorb moisture and other flavors easily. Stored in a cool, dry place, it has a shelf life of about 2 years.

Evaporated milk should also be stored in a cool, dry place. By mixing equal parts of water and evaporated milk, you have the equivalent of whole milk. Cans should be turned over every few months to discourage lumping. If this does occur, the milk is still usable; just shake the can vigorously.

Powdered buttermilk is also available now and is a tremendous storage item.

SUGAR AND/OR HONEY

Average yearly need per person: 30–50 pounds

This is an item of storage that is very important to calculate how much *you* use. It varies greatly from family to family. Also, make sure you store the type of sweetener your family prefers.

If you live in a high-humidity area, sugar tends to form a hard block when left in the original bags. I keep mine in a large, metal garbage can, emptying the bags right into the can. It is very easy to scoop out of, and I never have any trouble with lumps. Keep the lid on tight. (If you keep one small canister of sugar with a vanilla bean buried in it, you can use that sugar for baking and eliminate the need to add vanilla to your recipe. A vanilla bean will last a long, long time.)

Honey should always be stored in glass because of its moisture content. It draws moisture as well as gives off moisture, so it will eventually rust a metal container. If your storage area is exposed to light, wrap the glass jars in newspaper because light will destroy some of the honey's nutritive benefits. Honey has about 400 fewer calories per pound than sugar; it also tastes considerably sweeter, so less can be used. However, it is still a form of sugar and should be eaten in moderation.

To make a delicious honey butter, just whip together ½ cup of *real* butter and ¾ cup honey. Try this on some fresh, home-baked, whole wheat bread!

SALT

Average yearly need per person: 5 pounds

Salt is a must for storage since many foods would be very unappetizing without it. It also has many other uses: it can serve as a disinfectant, it melts ice, it controls the fermentation of yeast during baking, it is an aid in preparing ice cream and other frozen desserts, it can be used in curing meats, and it serves as a pickling agent. (By the way, never add salt to the water in which you dissolve the yeast when baking or it will inhibit the growth of the yeast plant.)

Salt can be stored indefinitely if it's in a dry area.

FATS OR OILS

Average yearly need per person: 20 pounds

Don't ever have the mistaken thought that you can totally do without fats of some form in your diet. We heard many sad stories in Europe of the agonies they suffered during the war because of the lack of any fat in their diet. There are essential ingredients we all need contained in this form of food.

If kept in a cool place, shortening may be stored in its original containers and will have a shelf life of 2–3 years.

Oils should not be exposed to light and will have a shelf life of 1 year.

Peanut butter is also a good source of fat or oil in our diet and is a good storage item.

Butter and margarine freeze well and can become part of your storage in this way.

DRIED LEGUMES

Average yearly amount per person: 50 pounds

Dried peas and beans make an excellent storage item. They are easy to store and are a powerhouse of nutrition. They are available in such a large variety that they provide many types of meals without monotony.

Kidney beans—a kidney-shaped red bean used in chili and Mexican dishes and salads.

Pinto beans—a smaller red bean also used in Mexican dishes such as refried beans.

Garbanzo beans—a tiny, nut-flavored round bean used mainly in salads.

Black beans—a heavy, dark bean used in Mediterranean thick soups and also turtle soup.

Black-eyed peas—a small white bean with a black spot on one side used in main dishes and soups. They are traditionally served in the South on New Year's Day for good luck.

Great Northern beans—also called navy beans and used for baked beans, salads, or casseroles. We like these cooked with ham hocks.

Lima beans—these come in two varieties: the large lima and the baby lima. They are a flat bean and tend to be dry and mealy and are used in soups and casseroles.

Mung beans—these are the little round green

beans that are used for sprouting and in Oriental dishes calling for bean sprouts.

Dried peas—come in green and yellow varieties. The yellow pea has a much milder flavor. These don't require a soaking time *or* long cooking as most dry beans do.

Lentils—these are little, round, flat, and brown and are delicious in soups. They also have a short cooking time.

WATER

Recommended amount for a 2-week period for an adult: 12 gallons.

We all could get along without food for a while, but water is a necessity we all must have. We have had several instances in our family where the water supply in the area in which we were living was cut off for several days. How thankful we (and our neighbors) were that we had some water on hand.

Water should be stored in unbreakable containers, if possible, in the event of an earthquake or tornado. I store mine in clean plastic milk jugs, adding 3 drops of Clorox to a gallon of water. To use, pour back and forth in two containers several times to put air back into it.

Boiling water vigorously for 3 minutes will also purify it.

Because water varies so much in every part of the country, it is hard to determine the shelf life, but if you have good, pure tap water, you can probably store it as is from the faucet in clean containers for up to 1 year. Since there is no expense involved, however, I rotate mine every 6 months.

It would be a good idea to begin today to train yourself and your family to conserve water. Repair all leaky faucets and learn to shut them off tightly. Showers take less water than tub baths. Never leave the tap running; fill a basin or pan and use it for washing or cleaning things. Use leftover sudsy dishwater to damp mop the kitchen floor. Run the dishwasher when you have a full load only. Keep a container of cold water in the refrigerator so you

don't have to let the water run to get it cold in the summertime.

Water purification tablets are a good item to have stored for an emergency.

SEEDS FOR SPROUTING

Since we all need a supply of fresh food each day, and this is virtually impossible to store, keep a good supply of seeds on hand for sprouting. These are very inexpensive and make a jar full of crisp salad "fixin's" in a couple of days, so you can always have fresh food at your finger tips. When seeds are sprouted, their nutritional value can increase as much as sixty times. They are loaded with vitamins, minerals, amino acids, and protein.

Sprouts are so quick and easy to do and are goofproof as well as free from any sprays or pests you may get from garden produce. They are highest in nutrition when eaten raw (we love them on salads, sandwiches, or even over cooked vegetables), but they can be added to cooked things such as meat loaves, omelettes, rice, muffins, pancakes, and breads. They are also very low in carbohydrates.

All you need is a quart jar, a piece of nylon net or old nylon stocking, and a jar ring or rubber band.

Put seeds in jar.
Rinse well with lukewarm water. (Some prefer to soak them overnight.)

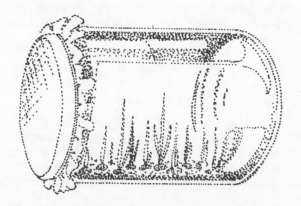

Pour off water. (The net will hold seeds in jar.)
Turn jar on its side so damp seeds cling to sides of jar.
Set jar on its side in a dark cupboard.
Rinse at least twice a day.

Sprouts should be at their peak in about 3–4 days, depending on variety used. After they are the length you desire, set them on a window sill in the sunlight for a day to turn green if you like. Then refrigerate and use within several days.

Some types that we especially like include:

Alfalfa: 1 tablespoon per quart jar
Cress: ¼ cup per quart jar
Lentils: ½ cup per quart jar
Radish: 2 tablespoons per quart jar
Mustard: 2 tablespoons per quart jar
      (This is real different. Try it!)
Wheat: ¼ cup per quart jar
      (Don't oversprout. Sprout should only be the length of the kernel. After that, it will be bitter.)

Never spout any seeds that have been treated with chemicals for planting. Tomato and potato seeds and sprouts are poisonous to humans.

VITAMINS

If you plan to store multivitamins, remember that no pill can supply you with all the nutrients your body needs. Only a variety of foods can do that. Vitamins have a shelf life of about a year if they are stored in a cool, dark place.

In purchasing the food items for your storage (especially fresh produce), why not form a group with a few of your friends and neighbors. It helps if some of you have a station wagon. Nearly any town or city has a wholesale produce supplier who supplies the local grocers. They are open all year and are usually very pleasant to work with provided you buy in crate lots, come early in the morning, and know what you want. (Don't take up too much of their time.) You'll be amazed how reasonable a head of lettuce figures out at when you buy a case of 24. By sharing with several others and taking turns driving to the warehouse, you will save many dollars in a hurry. An added bonus is that the produce is usually much fresher than you get at the grocery store.

Many other items, such as eggs, cheese, flour, spices, and so on, can be similarly purchased from wholesale suppliers. Check your Yellow Pages (especially the Business-to-Business volume if your city has it). By buying cinnamon, nutmeg, oregano, and so on, in 1-pound cans from a restaurant supplier, your savings will be phenomenal. Store them in containers in the freezer or split the larger sizes with your friends. You'll be astonished at the difference in price.

Now let's talk about the methods of preserving food necessary for filling our shelves. If you have never done any home canning, freezing, or dehydrating, you are in for a real thrill! I can't explain to you the joy that fills my being when I see all those pretty, gleaming bottles of fruits and vegetables neatly lined up on my pantry shelves.

CANNING

This is a simple method of preserving an abundance of fruits and vegetables to use in another season. The heating process inhibits the growth of the microorganisms that cause food to spoil, and at the same time all the air is driven out of the container to form a vacuum.

It is important to remember there are two types of foods, acid and low acid, and each requires a certain temperature to preserve them to ensure safe and edible food. The acid foods are fruits, berries, pickled products, and tomatoes. The low-acid types are vegetables, meats, poultry, seafood, and mixtures such as stews, and so forth.

Acid foods are processed in a boiling-water bath canner because the molds or bacteria commonly found in these foods are easily destroyed by the heat of the briskly boiling water in the time recommended. Low-acid foods can harbor certain bacteria that must be superheated to 240°. This can only be done in a pressure cooker for the prescribed time, which is why vegetables and meats *must* always be done in a pressure cooker. The "processing" time of both methods is very important because too short a time will not produce an adequately cooked and sealed food, while too much cooking time will give you mushy, overcooked food.

A boiling-water bath canner is inexpensive and very easy to use. Simply fill the canner with water so that the water level is 1 inch over the top of the jars when they are submerged in the rack into the water. Fill jars with produce; have lid "flats" simmering gently in a small saucepan of water. As you fill each jar with syrup, leave a head space of ½–1 inch, wipe off the rim of the jar, place hot flat on jar, and screw on ring securely. Fill seven jars, place in rack, submerge into the boiling water, replace canner lid, bring water back to boiling, and begin timing. It's important to maintain a rolling boil throughout the timing period but don't boil too briskly or some of the liquid may boil out of your jars. Have the next seven jars ready to add lids and process when the first batch is finished. Occasionally, between batches, you may have to add a little water to the canner as it boils away.

When you remove the jars from the canner, set them on a folded bath towel on the kitchen counter, away from drafts, to cool. The lid may not be concave when it comes from the canner, but as the jar cools, it will "pop" down, and your jar will be sealed. If by some chance one does not seal, refrigerate it and use within a few days. Avoid the temptation to push them down; let them pop down on their own. *Never* use flat lids over again!

For nearly all fruits, I use a thin syrup of 1 cup sugar to 3 cups water and keep it simmering to pour over my fruit just before I put on the lids. If you prefer a sweeter syrup, you can use a medium syrup of 2 cups sugar to 3 cups water or a heavy syrup of 3 cups sugar to 3 cups water.

The time processing chart I use, from the Blue Book Guide to Home Canning and Freezing, Edition 30, published by the Ball Corporation, is as follows:

Fruit	Minutes per quart
Apple slices, hot	20
Applesauce, hot	20
Apricots, raw	30
Berries, raw	20
Cherries, raw	25
Peaches, raw	30
Pears, hot	25
Plums, hot	25
Tomatoes, raw	45
Tomato juice, hot	15
Rhubarb sauce, hot	10

To peel the peaches, pears, or tomatoes for canning, I put a few in a square of nylon net, gather the corners up into my hand, and plunge them into boiling water for about 30 seconds. Then the skins slip right off.

If you are on a sugar-free diet, fruits can be canned very tastily by using unsweetened pineapple juice as your syrup or liquid. Peaches, pears, and apricots are delicious, and I have even sweetened applesauce with a little pineapple juice. It's great.

Never ever throw away all those apple peelings when you make applesauce or can pie slices. Put all the peels in a big kettle, add water (not quite covering peels), cover, and simmer for 10–20 minutes (or even longer, as it won't hurt). Strain off juice and you're ready to make apply jelly or can the juice to add to a punch or you can make apple syrup for pancakes. There's a lot of good nutrition and flavor in all those peels!

Here are a few other family favorites you've got to try:

GRANDMA SCHEEL'S VEGETABLE RELISH

Cut into large bite-size chunks:
1 head cauliflower
1 lb. carrots (6–8 large ones)
2 large green peppers
3 large yellow onions
6 stalks of celery

Mix well together in large bowl.

Pack vegetables into clean half pint or pint jars.

Heat pickling brine of:
1 qt. *white* vinegar (Use a good brand.)
2 qt. water
¾ cup pickling salt (not iodized)

Add *1 small dried red pepper to each jar.*

Pour *hot* brine into jars.

Add hot lids.

Process in boiling water bath for 10 min.

Makes 10 pt.

ROY'S MUSTARD PICKLES

In a large plastic or stainless steel container, combine:
5 cups sliced small cucumbers
4 cups skinned pickling onions
6 chopped green peppers
3 cups cauliflowerettes
1 cup chopped green tomatoes

Mix 1 cup salt in 4 qt. water.

Pour over vegetables. Refrigerate overnight.

The next day, drain and rinse.

Mix in a large saucepan: 1½ cups sugar
1 tbsp. turmeric
½ cup flour

Stir in: ½ cup water
½ cup mustard (table variety)
5 cups cider vinegar (brown)

Mix and cook until thick.

Stir in drained vegetables and simmer for 15 min.

Pack into jars and process for 10 min.

Makes 6–8 pt.

These are kind of a "pain" to make because it's a tedious job peeling them, but the love and appreciation Roy shows me when I serve them make it worthwhile.

ROY'S PICKLED ONIONS

Plunge 4 qt. of tiny white pearl onions into boiling water for 1–2 min.

Peel onions.

Sprinkle with 1 cup salt.

Cover onions with cold water and let stand 24 hr. in a cool place. (I put mine in the refrigerator.)

Drain and rinse well.

Combine: 2 cups sugar
           ¼ cup pickling spices (tied in a piece of cheesecloth)
           2 qt. cider vinegar

Simmer for about 15 min.

Put onions into ½ or 1 pt. jars.

Add 1 small dried red pepper to each jar.

Cover with hot liquid.

Process for 8–10 min.

Makes 8 pt.

Grandma always used carp in this recipe, but I'm sure most kinds of fish would work. I use whiting.

GRANDMA'S PICKLED FISH

Skin and fillet fish (about 2 lb.). (Do not cut in small pieces yet.)

Put fillets in a small crock.

Sprinkle with ⅝ cup pickling salt and enough white vinegar to cover fish.

Cover and refrigerate for 6 days.

Pour off liquid and cover with cold water. Refrigerate for 3 hr. (no more or the fish will soften).

Remove fish and cut in pieces.

Chop 2 onions.

For each cup of fish, you need:
           2 tsp. mustard seed
           8 bay leaves
           2 tsp. whole pepper
           8–10 little red chili peppers

Pack jar ¼ full of fish. (Make sure you pack it *firmly;* this will keep the fish firm.)

Add chopped onion and spices.

Then continue to fill jar with fish (packed firmly).

Combine: ⅔ cup water
           ⅓ cup white vinegar
           ¼ cup sugar

Bring to a boil and pour hot over fish.

Store in the refrigerator for 4 days. Then they're ready to eat and enjoy! Keep refrigerated.

I always like to have a few jars of Pink Cinnamon Apple Slices on hand. They look so pretty as a touch of color on the dinner plate and sure go well with pork chops and scalloped potatoes. They make a nice little Christmas or Valentine gift, also.

PINK CINNAMON APPLE SLICES

In a 6 qt. kettle combine: 2 cups water
4 cups sugar
½ cup cinnamon red hots

Bring to a boil, reduce heat, and keep simmering.

Peel and slice thickly (at least ½ inch) 20 apples. (A tart, firm cooking apple is best.)

Slice apples right into simmering liquid to prevent discoloring.

Let slices cook for about 5 min. after they are all in the pan.

Pack slices into half-pint jars and cover with liquid.

Process in boiling water bath for 15 min.

Makes 15 half pints.

Save those apple peels and simmer as I suggested; then make some delicious . . .

APPLE MINT JELLY

Combine: 3½ cups apple juice
1 cup cut-up mint leaves (firmly packed)

Bring to a boil and boil for 1 min.

Let stand to steep for 10 min.

Measure 4 cups sugar and put into mixing bowl.

In a saucepan, mix: 1 cup strained juice
1 package Sure-Jel

Bring to a full boil and add sugar all at once.

Boil rapidly for 1 full min.

Remove from heat.

Stir to cool and skim bubbles off with a metal spoon.

Pour into jelly jars.

Seal with paraffin.

To seal jellies with paraffin, fill jelly jars with hot jelly and *immediately* pour on a thin covering of melted paraffin (about ⅛ inch thick). Tilt jar slightly so the wax goes around the slides of the jar.

Always use regular canning jars when processing fruits and vegetables. Any type of cute little jars or glasses can be used as jelly containers (especially for gift giving). Jams and jellies are so easy to do, and I have never had a failure with any of the recipes or directions on the Sure-Jel package.

Many people ask me the difference between some of the terms when making jellies, and so on.

Jelly is a sparkling clear jellied fruit juice for spreading.

Jam is jellylike in consistency but contains small bits of crushed fruit.

Fruit butter is the pulp of the fruit cooked down with about half as much sugar and added spices until it becomes a buttery spread.

Preserves have less sugar than jam, are a little softer, and contain a fruit or combination of fruits. The fruit retains its shape more so than in jam.

Conserves are similar to preserves except they usually have raisins or nuts combined with the fruit or combination of fruits.

Marmalades are usually made of citrus fruits and contain bits of fruit throughout the clear, jellylike product.

I always can lots of tomatoes because they are so versatile and easy to do. Our all-time favorite is "Mom's Farm Tomato Soup." You've got to try this. It's the neatest thing in the world to have on the shelf for a cold, snowy winter day.

MOM'S FARM TOMATO SOUP

Combine: 14 qt. sliced tomatoes (not peeled)
14 bay leaves
14 sprigs of parsley
21 whole cloves
7 medium onions, chopped
3 stalks of celery, chopped

Boil all together until vegetables are tender.

Run through a mill.

Meanwhile, melt 1 lb. real butter and stir in:
14 tbsp. flour
14 tsp. salt
12 tbsp. sugar
¼ tsp. red pepper

Mix well and combine with tomato mixture.

Cook for 1½ hr., then put into pint or quart jars.

Process in boiling water bath for 15 min.

To serve, combine: ½ cup cream (half-and-half)
½ cup water
1 pt. soup mixture

If you use milk, sprinkle soda in tomato mixture while it's hot to prevent curdling.

When all the fresh garlic is available during pickling season, put up a supply for the winter months. Just peel 4 heads of garlic, place all the buds in a glass jar, and cover with salad oil. The oil is great for dressings, and the garlic cloves will keep for several months stored this way in the refrigerator.

To can vegetables and meats, use a pressure cooker. Don't be afraid to try this method. They are very safe now and simple to use if you accurately follow the manufacturer's instructions. Get out that direction booklet and enjoy all the bounties of your garden.

Be sure you always label every jar with the date and contents. Food that is canned properly can be stored for several years; after a year or so, however, it gradually starts to deteriorate to some degree, so it is best to use the oldest first.

FREEZING

Freezing is one of the easiest methods of food preservation, and it is also the process that keeps your produce the freshest. One of the most worthwhile investments you will ever make is a freezer. It can simplify your life so much if you use it properly.

Freezing is also one of the safest and quickest methods to store your food. Since there is a difference in the taste and texture of foods frozen, canned, or dried, you will need to determine how your family prefers each item. I usually choose to can most of my fruits, relishes, pickles, sauces, and jellies, while I freeze most of our meats and vegetables and fruit jams; then I always dry a supply of fruits, vegetables, *and* meats for emergencies and snacks.

In choosing a freezer, there are several things to consider. A chest type usually holds more food and costs less to run because less cool air escapes each time it is opened. Upright models are easier to use because the food is more convenient to get to. If you have back problems, this could be a consideration. An upright also takes up less space if that is a problem for you. The no-frost models are much more expensive initially and consume about 60 percent more electricity. They seem a little silly to me since you must empty and clean your freezer once a year whether it is self-defrosting or not, and if you are careful to not open it unnecessarily, the frost will not build up to require defrosting more often than that, anyway. Any freezer should maintain zero degrees or lower for fast freezing and to properly store your food.

In choosing the food to put in your freezer, remember that freezing will not *improve* the quality but *preserve* it; so select foods that are at their peak—young and tender, ripe but firm—and get them to the freezer as quickly as possible. Fruits and vegetables change rapidly after they are harvested. Many also lose considerable vitamin C if allowed to sit a day or two.

Be sure you use proper containers to prevent freezer burn. The secret is to get and keep as much air out of the package as possible. This is especially true if you have a self-defrosting refrigerator or freezer because the air is constantly circulating and drawing out all moisture. (Have you ever left a dish of something sitting uncovered in your frostless refrigerator, only to find it completely dried up in a day or two?)

Rigid containers such as plastic cartons with lids, freezer boxes, or canning jars may be used. Just be sure and allow at least a 2 inch head space for liquids and a 1 inch head space for loose pack to allow for expansion. This will prevent the contents from oozing out or your container breaking.

Wrapping materials such as freezer wrap or butcher paper work fine for meats provided they are moistureproof and your packages are wrapped skin tight.

Freezer, plastic, or sealing bags are the easiest and most flexible to use. Just check to see that they are heavy and strong enough to eliminate moisture *and* prevent breaking. When freezing fruits or vegetables in bags that you prefer to have "loose pack," such as peas, beans, blueberries, and so on, it is wise to freeze them first spread out on a cookie sheet and then, after they are completely frozen, transfer them to plastic bags.

As with canning, always label and date all packages. Then *promptly* place them in a single layer in the freezer so they will freeze quickly. Keep an inventory of all foods so that you can enjoy a variety in your meals and keep things rotated at the same time. No one wants to get stuck with eating peas 7 days a week because they were all at the bottom of the freezer shelf.

Vegetables should be blanched to stop the enzyme action that causes aging and loss of quality. Blanching also destroys harmful bacteria and keeps the color bright. This is done by plunging the cleaned and prepared vegetable into boiling water for the prescribed time or placing them in a steamer. I prefer to steam them because I feel there are less nutrients lost. As you steam your vegetables, you will find the water in the steamer does retain some color and flavor from the vegetables, so I pour this into containers and freeze to add to my soups. That way I don't lose a smidgen of nutrition, and I sure have some terrific soups!

As soon as the vegetable is steamed or blanched, it should be plunged into very cold water to halt the cooking action. Cool as quickly as possible, package, and freeze. A little speed here really pays off in fresh-tasting vegetables.

Here is my chart for timing.

Vegetable	Water Boiling	Steam	Amount	Yield (pt.)
Beans (green)	2 min.	3 min.	1 bu.	40
Broccoli	4 min.	5 min.	1 crate (25 lb.)	24
Brussels sprouts	3 min.	4–5 min.	4 qt.	6
Cabbage	1½ min.	2 min.		
Carrots	3 min.	3 min.	1 bu.	about 45
Cauliflower	3 min.	4 min.	1 head	1½
Celery	Cook until tender.			
Corn	4 min.	5 min.	1 bu.	15
Peas	1 min.	2 min.	1 bu.	15

Vegetable	Boiling	Steam	Amount	Yield (pt.)
Green peppers	Not necessary			
Summer squash	3 min.	4 min.		
Tomatoes	Cook up as stewed tomatoes.			

When I freeze yams or any type of winter squash, I bake the "whole shebang" (as many as I can cram into my oven) at 375° until they are tender. Then I scoop out the pulp and package in meal-sized bags and freeze. It is so simple to remove the bag and set it in a pie plate to reheat in the oven for a delicious meal. This also works great for pumpkin. Just cut it in pieces and bake them first.

Roy loves cucumbers and onions, so he is always happy when I prepare any extra cucumbers in this way for the freezer.

FROZEN "CUKE" SLICES

Combine: 2 qt. thinly sliced, peeled cucumbers
2 tbsp. salt
1 large onion, thinly sliced

Set aside for 2 hr., then squeeze out liquid.

Add: 1½ cups sugar
½ cup vinegar

Mix together, place in containers, and freeze.

I also keep containers of chopped green peppers, parsley, celery, and green onion tops frozen when we have an overabundance. They are sure handy for casseroles, soups, or stews.

Delicious fruit from the freezer can be a real joy in the winter. Most fruits taste better if some sugar or syrup is added; but they can also be dry packed if you wish to eat them raw. This works well with Bing cherries, green grapes, orange sections or slices, or banana slices. They will be at their best, however, if eaten when still slightly "icy." To pack fruits in syrups, we use the same proportions I gave you for canning. Again, we prefer the light syrup.

For a real taste treat, try this syrup over mixed fruit or peaches. It is out of this world!

FRUIT SYRUP

Combine: juice of 5 lemons
juice of 7 oranges
2 cups pineapple juice
4½ cups sugar

Mix well so sugar dissolves and pour over fruits.

If you have never made freezer jam, you just *have* to try some. It's a breeze to make and truly tastes like spreading fresh fruit on your toast. Our favorites are strawberry, raspberry, and peach.

SURE-JEL
RASPBERRY FREEZER JAM

Combine: 3 cups well-mashed raspberries
5¼ cups sugar

Let stand 10 min.

In a saucepan, combine: ¾ cup water
1 pkg. Sure-Jel

Bring to a full boil and *boil 1 min.*, stirring constantly.

Stir into bowl of fruit mixture and stir constantly for *3 min.*

Ladle into jars, cover, and let stand at room temperature for 24 hr., then freeze. Makes 6½ cups.

SURE-JEL
PEACH FREEZER JAM

Peel, pit, and smoosh peaches. Make 2¼ cups fruit.

Add: 2 tbsp. lemon juice
1 tsp. ascorbic acid

Add 5 cups sugar.

Mix well and let stand for 10 min.

In a saucepan, combine: ¾ cup water
1 pkg. Sure-Jel

Bring to a boil and *boil 1 min.*, stirring constantly.

Stir Sure-Jel mixture into bowl of fruit and sugar.

Stir constantly for *3 min. more.*

Ladle into containers and cover.

Let stand at room temperature for 24 hr. Then freeze.

Makes 6 cups.

SURE-JEL
STRAWBERRY FREEZER JAM

Combine 2 cups well-mashed strawberries and 4 cups sugar.

Let stand 10 min.

In a saucepan, combine: ¾ cup water
1 pkg. Sure-Jel

Bring to a full boil and *boil 1 min.*, stirring constantly.

Stir Sure-Jel mixture into bowl of fruit mixture and stir constantly for *3 min. more.*

Ladle into containers and cover.

Let stand at room temperature for 24 hr., then freeze.

Makes 5 cups.

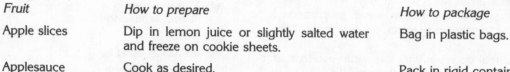

Fruit	How to prepare	How to package
Apple slices	Dip in lemon juice or slightly salted water and freeze on cookie sheets.	Bag in plastic bags.
Applesauce	Cook as desired.	Pack in rigid containers.
Apricots	These can be covered with light syrup with ascorbic acid added, but we prefer them "canned."	
Avocados	Puree with a fork and add 1 tbsp. lemon juice to each avocado.	Pack in rigid containers.
Bananas	Slice and place on a cookie sheet covered with plastic wrap and freeze until firm.	Put in plastic bags.
	Or	
	Puree with a fork and add 1 tbsp. lemon juice for 2 bananas.	Freeze in rigid containers for baking.
Blueberries	Freeze on cookie sheets until firm.	Transfer to plastic bags.
Strawberries	Toss whole or sliced berries with sugar (¾ cup sugar to 4 cups berries).	Freeze in containers.
	Or	
	For a short storage period, berries may be frozen whole without sugar.	Freeze in containers.
Cantaloupe	Cut in balls or cubes and cover with syrup, ginger ale, 7-Up, or orange juice.	Freeze in rigid containers.
Sweet cherries	Freeze whole on cookie sheets.	Transfer to plastic bags.
Coconut	Shred or grate the meat.	Freeze in plastic bags.

My Fruit Chart

Cranberries	Freeze whole on cookie sheets.	Transfer to bags or freeze in their original bags.
Grapefruit	Cut in half, scoop out sections, and squeeze extra juice over sections. Or Can be frozen whole. Peels wonderfully when thawed.	Freeze in rigid containers.
Grapes	Freeze whole for eating or add to fruit mixtures.	
Melons	The same as cantaloupe.	
Oranges	Peel and slice crosswise or peel and section. Freeze on cookie sheets covered with plastic wrap.	Transfer to plastic bags.
Peaches	Dip in boiling water for 15 sec., slip off skins, slice into containers, and cover with syrup to which you've added ascorbic acid.	Freeze in rigid containers. Be sure peaches are covered with syrup. I crumble a bit of plastic wrap on top to keep them immersed.
Pears	These darken quite easily; we prefer them canned or dried.	
Pineapple	Peel and cut up into slices or pieces.	Can be frozen as is or in its own juice. Do not use in gelatin desserts. They will not congeal.
Rhubarb	Clean and cut in 1 in. pieces and freeze on cookie sheets.	Transfer to plastic bags.

DRYING

Drying is one of the oldest and most exciting forms of preserving foods. I hope I have whetted your appetite through *A Family Raised on Sunshine* and *A Family Raised on Rainbows*. Many of your letters have asked that I give a complete list of basic directions, so here goes!

The practice of drying foods has been around for a long time. The Indians dried their corn and fish to maintain them through the winter; the early settlers hung beef and buffalo meat strips up to dry for jerky for nutrition during "lean" times; during the Civil War, dried fruits and vegetables were relied on heavily for nutrition for the troops; even in primitive times, fruits and leathers were dried in caves. In fact, mummies have been excavated with dried grains and other foodstuffs still intact.

To dry food properly, it must be done quickly. If the temperature is too high, it will destroy much of the food value; if it is too low, the food will spoil before drying. A certain amount of air must pass over the drying items, or a hard crust will form, and moisture will be trapped in the inner parts of the food. For these reasons, a dehydrator with temperature control and a fan provides the most satisfactory results. However, if you live in a very dry climate, foods can be dried successfully in the sun, or in a more humid area, an oven can be used with reasonable success. A controlled drying atmosphere will retain the most food value.

To dry foods in the oven, be sure the temperature does not exceed 150°. This is usually the "warm" setting. Place the food on nylon or poly racks and prop the oven door open slightly with a rolled hot pad to let the moisture escape. The timing will be longer because the air does not move, but I have had success with fruit leathers, apple slices, and banana slices by this method.

Select good-quality produce for any type of drying. If fruit is a little too ripe to dry successfully, use it in making leathers.

Vegetables should be blanched or steamed before drying. (Follow the procedure outlined in the freezing section.) Fruit does not need to be steamed. Because it has more sugar content, it is easier to preserve, and it also gives up water more freely than vegetables.

To keep fruit from discoloring, one of several methods may be used. (1) The sliced fruit can be dropped into salt water (4 tablespoons of salt to a gallon of water), then drained and dehydrated. (2) Fruit can be soaked in ascorbic acid solution (2 tablespoons of ascorbic acid to 1 gallon water). (3) Fruit can be soaked for 10 minutes in a solution of sodium bisulfite (1 tablespoon to a gallon of water). (4) Fruit can be sulphured outdoors. This method is a little complicated but pays off in beautiful fruit; it retards spoilage and reduces the loss of vitamins A and C. To sulphur fruit outdoors,

1. Put fruit on wooden trays (use no metal) with the skin side down, not touching.
2. Stack the trays about 2 inches apart.
3. Set the bottom tray on bricks about 10 inches off the ground.
4. Put the "flowers of sulphur" (available at the drug store) in a metal or aluminum pie pan, using 1 tablespoon of sulphur per pound of prepared fruit.
5. Set the pie pan into a little indentation in the dirt, in front of the trays, not under them.
6. Cover all with a large appliance box (from a stove or refrigerator).
7. Cut an 8-inch-square door in the front and on the top. Open these vents. Put dirt up around sides of box so that there are no air cracks.
8. Light the sulphur, *being very careful not to inhale fumes.* Do *not* leave the match stick in the sulphur.
9. Check in about 5 minutes to see if the sulphur is still burning, and when three quarters of it is consumed, shut the vents and leave the fruit in for the recommended time.

This must be done outside, preferably in a gravel or dirt area and never *around children or animals. Do not inhale the fumes!*

Timing for sulphuring fruit:

Apple slices—1 hour
Apricots—4 hours
Bananas—45 minutes
Peaches—45 minutes
Pears—45 minutes

I don't sulphur my apples or bananas, and I am pleased with them. If you want a snowy-white product, however, you should sulphur them. I do recommend sulphuring for peaches, pears, and apricots especially. Never dry fruits in your oven that have been sulphured. Use a dehydrator or the sun.

When drying any fruit halves with skins (apricots, plums, etc.), you will have much better success if you will "pop" the halves inside out before drying.

When drying in the sun, you may wish to cover the food with cheesecloth to prevent insects and bugs from getting on your produce. You may also want to turn the fruit once or twice to eliminate burning if it's awfully hot.

If you choose to make your own dryer, never use metal screening for the trays. It will discolor the food and give it a metallic taste.

Here is a general timetable for drying in a dehydrator, but check your food often because humidity and degree of moisture in the food can vary greatly, and this can only be a guideline. Be sure your room is well ventilated.

Food	Time (hr.)	Test
Apple slices	8	Pliable (like your earlobe) Soft but dry
Apricots	15	Leathery
Seedless grapes	10	Like raisins
Peaches	15	Leathery
Pears	16	Leathery
Plum halves	10	Leathery
Banana slices	8	Crisp
Broccoli	12	Brittle
Green beans	10	Brittle (I freeze mine for ½ hr. before drying.)

Food	Time (hr.)	Test
Cabbage	8	Brittle
Carrots	16	Very brittle
Cauliflower	12	Hard
Celery	10	Brittle
Corn	12	Dry
Mushrooms	10	Leathery
Onions	10	Brittle
Peas	12	Wrinkled and hard
Summer squash	15	Crisp
Cucumbers	15	Crisp
Tomatoes	15	Leathery to brittle (slice up and down, not sideways.)

Remember to dry all bits and pieces of leftover vegetables. They are great for adding to soups. Leftover bits of fruit or meat can be dried to use as snacks. Dried crisp vegetable slices make delicious chips served with a dip to accompany that sandwich at lunchtime.

To package any dried food, use air-tight plastic or glass containers. Freezing them in the container for 24 hours will eliminate any bugs, and then they can be stored on a shelf in a cool, dark, dry place for 1 year. If you are a novice at drying, watch your containers for any sign of moisture for a few days. If none appears, the food is sufficiently dry. If you do see some moisture, dry the food a little longer to avoid having any mold develop.

To cook dried fruits, cover with water, let stand 1 hour, simmer for 15 minutes, and add sugar to taste *after* cooking. (If you add sugar at the beginning of cooking, it will require more and also make the fruit fiber tough.) Dried fruits, of course, are also delicious eaten as is.

To cook dried vegetables, cover and soak in water for 2 hours. Leave the water on the vegetables that didn't absorb (at least enough to cover the bottom of the pan), cover with a lid, bring to a boil, turn down heat, and simmer until tender. Add salt *last!* It will also toughen vegetables and leach out important vitamins.

Jerky is a delicious *and* nutritious snack. We all love it. Here are our favorite recipes.

BEEF JERKY

Partially freeze a 3 lb. piece of lean beef for easier slicing.

Slice thin (¼ in. thick) in long strips.

Remove *all* fat as you slice. (It will taste rancid.)

Mix together: 1 tsp. salt
              ½ tsp. onion salt
              ½ tsp. garlic salt
              ¼ tsp. pepper
              ⅓ cup soy sauce
              ⅓ cup A-1 Steak Sauce

Mix the meat strips well in the marinade, cover, and refrigerate in the marinade for 24 hr., mixing several times.

Place meat strips on trays to dry.

Takes about 8 hr. until dry and brittle.

Store in a tightly covered glass jar.

I use white meat for this recipe.

TURKEY JERKY

Partially freeze for easier slicing.

Slice into ¼ in. slices or strips.

Soak in marinade of: 1½ tbsp. lemon juice
                    ¼ cup soy sauce
                    ⅛ tsp. onion powder
                    ⅛ tsp. garlic powder

Cover and marinate for 24 hr., stirring several times.

Dry on dehydrator trays for about 8 hr. until crisp.

Store in glass jars.

Ham jerky can be made by just drying thin strips of ham. No marinade is needed.

When making any type of jerky, meat sliced with the grain will be chewy; meat sliced across the grain will be tender and "snappy."

Fruit leathers are a delightful treat that your family won't be able to get enough of. Little or no sweetening is used, so it's great for children, diabetics, and for that matter, all of us.

Leathers can be made any time of year, and there is a never-ending source of fruits to make it from: home canned fruit that needs to be used up, overripe fruit, leftover pieces from canning and freezing, and an abundance of fruits in season. If you are using previously bottled or canned fruit, simply drain it well, mash it, or puree it in the blender to prepare it for leather. If using fresh fruit, simply mash or puree it in the same way.

Use a large 12 in. × 17 in. cookie sheet and line it with Handiwrap. (Other plastic wraps don't work as well.) Let the wrap extend over the ends and secure it underneath the pan with masking tape. Pour about 2 cups of fruit puree over the pan, making sure it is spread evenly with no lumps. Dry in a dehydrator until dry and leatherlike. While it is still warm, roll it up like a jelly roll. It should be stored in a cool, dark, dry place in air-tight containers. Glass jars work well, or it can be frozen. You'll find your family likes it so well you'll never have enough to store for a long time. Our favorites are apricot, peach, pear, plum, and applesauce. We don't add sweetener to any of these. You can be adventurous and experiment with spices, extracts, or flavorings, or even coconut, nuts, seeds, and so on, but we prefer the plain fruit flavors.

For a fancy treat or real splurge, spread the leather with one of the following, roll up, and slice in bite-sized pieces: cream cheese (great with apricot), melted chocolate, marshmallow cream, or peanut butter. These make pretty "candies" for the holidays.

Besides saving money, storing fruits, vegetables, and all your basic food needs will give you a wonderful feeling of security when the snow is blowing or unexpected bills bog down your budget. It's like having your own bank account in the pantry. You may never have a major disaster, but somehow blizzards, downed power lines, strikes, a broken water main, and illness have a way of touching all of us. You and your family can build a closeness you never thought possible by starting today to plan for your family's needs and carrying out those plans together. Work together on your family budget so that each one can see where the money goes. Flipping off that unneeded light or turning down the thermostat can become a lot more important if everyone has a working and active interest in it. Assign each family member a utility bill, and with the money they can save that month (compared to the same month last year), they can buy any items they choose toward the preparedness shelves.

In addition to the staples we need on our shelves to be prepared, it is also our responsibility to see that our family members are "prepared." Even if your pantry is full, can your family meet with emergencies or even everyday needs?

Does your 5-year-old know:

How to bathe and dress himself?
How to lock and unlock the house and car doors?
Where basic food items are kept?
His address and telephone number?
Can he see a list of emergency telephone numbers?
How to perform simple helping tasks (making his bed, and so on)?

Can your 10-year-old:

Use your standard appliances?
Sort laundry and use the washing machine?
Scrub a floor?
Prepare a simple meal?
Vacuum?
Know or find emergency telephone numbers?

Can your 15-year-old:

Do basic sewing?
Iron clothing?

Do weekly grocery shopping?
Handle upkeep and maintenance around the house and yard?

Do all the adults in your household:

Know the names and telephone numbers of family doctor, attorney, bank, hospital, and dentist?
Know how to operate the automobile and handle basics—fill with gasoline, change tires, and so on?
Have a working knowledge of insurance policies, bank accounts, wills, and obligations?
Understand outstanding bills and obligations and their method of payment?

In addition to family togetherness, this preparedness program may allow you to accomplish dreams and goals you never thought possible. Maybe you'd like to plan a vacation with the savings that you will be able to accumulate. How proud everyone will be when they know that they played an important part in this.

An older teenaged boy or father may enjoy preparing and being responsible for a car emergency kit. Some ideas for this might be

1. A first-aid kit, which should include basic items, such as:
      bandages
      adhesive tape
      petroleum jelly
      small tweezers and scissors
      safety pins
      Merthiolate or disinfectant
      tongue depressor
      small first-aid handbook
      aspirin
      a few sanitary napkins (These make excellent compresses for wounds.)
2. A can of tire inflator.
3. Flares.
4. A flashlight.
5. Jumper cables.
6. A good ice scraper.
7. A blanket.

8. Some small change taped in the glove compartment along with telephone numbers of:
    - police
    - towing service
    - three friends (including one neighbor close to your home in case you can't reach someone there or your line is busy)
9. A fluorescent vest to wear at night while changing a tire or if you must walk somewhere.
10. A small bag of kitty litter. (This is lightweight and excellent to sprinkle under tires to get traction in ice or snow.)
11. A box of 20 gallon garbage bags. (If you should get stranded in your car in subzero weather, it is imperative to trap the body heat while you are still warm. Step into one bag and bring it up around your waist; cut or tear a slit in the bottom of another bag to slip over your head and down to your waist. This method will keep you and your family warm until help arrives.)

This list was passed on to me some time ago by a friend, Kay Wadley, and I think it's invaluable. We sure feel better now that our car is equipped.

Peace of mind, happiness, security, contentment, and family togetherness can all be ours through a preparedness program that will truly be our sunshine on a rainy day. How long could *you* survive without going to the store? Do you know where your next meal is coming from?

5

LIVING HAPPILY WITH SPECIAL DIET NEEDS

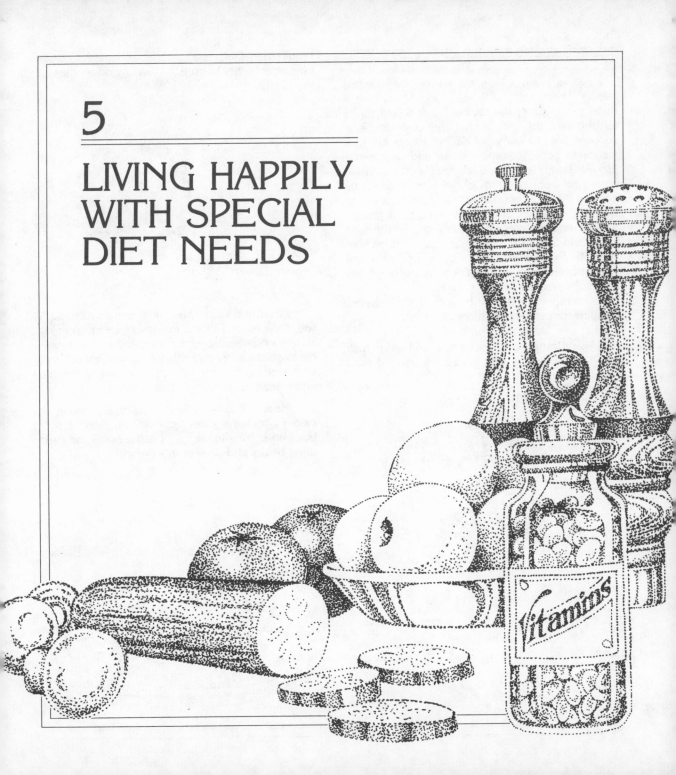

I get so many letters from you good friends asking for low-calorie dishes. It would be nice if there were "automatic recipes" that would make us thin, but the fact is that the best diet is a sensible one. It's really not difficult to eat wisely. It just takes some common sense and determination. And don't let anyone tell you it's an expensive way to eat because many of the best foods for us are also the most economical. Just begin today to eat small servings of the four basic food groups we discussed in chapter 3. Eliminate all the junk foods and those that are just empty calories with very little food value. Beware of all the "lite"- and "diet"-labeled foods and don't eliminate completely any of the necessary food groups.

If you're watching your budget as well as your waistline, remember these are "best buys":

Milk Group—cottage cheese and skim milk (or 2 percent milk). You get all the needed food requirements with less butterfat with these. Cottage cheese is higher in protein than any other cheese.

Fruits and Vegetables—just remember to stick with the produce that is in season. Learn to enjoy all the kinds available. Eat as many raw as possible to get the most nutrients for the smallest amount of calories and you will enjoy a variety for the entire year.

Meat Group—fish and poultry are lowest in calories and the most economical. Don't forget you can substitute an egg, peanut butter, or even dried beans and peas in this group.

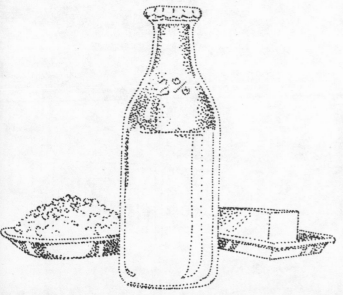

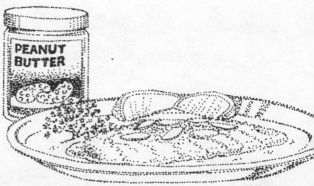

Cereal Group—this is the area where you can get a "powerhouse" of nutrition for a few pennies and also save calories. A small bowl of cooked whole grain cereal is very filling and supplies so many of the vitamins and minerals your body needs. They are very rich in niacin, iron, and thiamine.

If you eat a balanced diet, it eliminates the need for vitamins, thus saving you more money.

When you plan your three daily meals, keep in mind these things: *Variety* is important. Take advantage of specials in season. Consider color and attractiveness and also a variety of textures. *Moderation* is also a key. Too much of anything is not wise. I had a friend tell me once that even rabbits get fat on lettuce. Occasionally, a dessert is fine but not three times a day. Also, reduce the size of your portions; we all eat more than our bodies require. Finally, keep in mind the importance of *Attitude*. Enjoy this new way of eating. It should become a way of life.

None of us do our bodies any good by going on a fad diet or completely eliminating a necessary food or fuel for our systems. Think happy thoughts, enjoy shopping for good buys and preparing attractive meals, and leisurely appreciate the delicious flavor and texture of your healthful food. You'll like yourself so much better when you look in the mirror. *Keep that smile!*

Cut down but don't eliminate fats in your diet. We all need a small amount each day.

Don't avoid carbohydrates. Most people think of these foods as fattening, and this is not necessarily true. They have the same amount of calories as protein and provide many nutrients. Actually, they can help us lose weight by satisfying our need for bulk so that we don't want a lot of the "empty calorie" foods. Good carbohydrate foods include potatoes (eat them baked *with* the skins for the most satisfying, nutritious serving), whole grain breads and cereals, popcorn (a terrific low-calorie, high-fiber snack if all that butter is eliminated), and fruits and vegetables.

Experts tell us we all need fiber in our diets, but you must remember to drink lots of liquids. We should have at *least* 8 big glasses of water a day. Otherwise, fiber can be constipating. It is meant to stimulate our colon and lower intestinal tract but needs the liquids to provide this. (Please don't get your required liquid in the form of soda pop!)

We can all cut down on the sugar and salt in our diets with just a little conscious effort. Start gradually reducing the amount you use and you'll be surprised how quickly your taste buds change.

Here are just a few little hints that we have found to work in our family to cut down on calories and eat better.

1. Never butter your toast while it's hot. It takes twice as much butter.
2. Mineral water with a twist of lemon or lime is a very satisfying drink with virtually no calories. (Just watch the ones that are heavy in sodium.)
3. Use powdered milk in all cooking.
4. A glass of tomato juice with a lemon wedge or cucumber stick before dinner makes you feel elegant and takes the edge off your hunger.

5. Use a spoonful of yogurt in place of sour cream when serving foods.
6. Cook your own fruit sauces and baked goods. You can cut down on the sugar tremendously.
7. Think of yourself as a very special person and enjoy eating slowly. (I've found I only stuff myself when I don't like *me*!)
8. Learn to exercise that body. You'll be surprised how much better you feel with a little bit of movement, and, surprisingly, you eat less!
9. When you eat out, don't be afraid to ask for a substitute or something different. A lemon wedge over a salad can make a tasty addition instead of that heavy dressing. Ask for whole wheat bread instead of white or no gravy, and so on. The waiters are usually very cooperative. (I've even ordered a Big Mac without dressing and a bun!)
10. Teach your family and yourself to *sit down* and eat at the table. Never eat on the run, on the couch, or watching TV.
11. *Never* skip breakfast.
12. Always keep lots of fresh vegetables, cleaned and cut up, in the refrigerator ready for snacking.
13. Make all your gravies, and so on, with cornstarch instead of flour. It only takes half as much, so that's half the calories as well as giving you a pretty clear gravy instead of an opaque one.
14. Before eating a snack, ask yourself if it's worth the calories.
15. Don't weigh yourself too often. This can be discouraging. Once a week is enough to get an accurate picture of your progress.
16. Have confidence in yourself. *You can do it!*

These recipes are ones that we really enjoy, and I'm sure they'll become your favorites, too.

First, don't forget that delicious, easy banana ice cream with just the milk and frozen bananas that I told you about in chapter 2.

If you are trying to eliminate coffee or chocolate from your diet and still enjoy a hot drink, you'll love this. It is *so* good on a cold winter day!

HOT AND HEALTHY DRINK

Combine: ⅓ cup Postum
⅓ cup carob powder
1½ cups powdered milk
¼ cup nondairy creamer
2 tbsp. powdered sugar
1 tsp. cinnamon
1 tsp. dried orange peel

Use 3–4 tsp. mix in a cup of boiling water.

(Some carob powders don't dissolve as well as others, so you can blend it in the blender with the water and then heat in the microwave or saucepan if necessary.)

We love making nutritious drinks in the blender. My kids can't get enough of these:

BUNNY DELIGHT

Blend until smooth: 1 cup cut-up carrots
2 cups pineapple juice (unsweetened)
6 ice cubes

HAWAIIAN REFRESHER

Blend until smooth: 1 cup orange juice
1 cup cut-up cantaloupe (or honeydew)
1 tbsp. lime juice
6 ice cubes

Serve with a lime slice.

All the grandbabies are always asking for:

GRANDMA'S
HONEY BEAR DRINK

Blend until smooth: 2 cups milk
1 banana
4 squares graham crackers
2 tsp. carob powder
1 tbsp. honey
4 ice cubes

There's nothing like a pretty salad to make someone feel "special" while watching calories. I can't pick a favorite. These are all "top of the list." You'll think you're in heaven with this one!

FRUIT SPECIAL

Combine 2 cups each of: cut-up strawberries
green grapes
pineapple chunks
cut-up honeydew melon
cut-up cantaloupe
For the dressing, combine in blender:
1 banana
4 tbsp. yogurt
¼ tsp. nutmeg

You all know my family are great Mexican food lovers. This "main dish" salad is a summer favorite.

BEV'S TACO SALAD

Toss together: 1 head of lettuce, shredded or torn
1 can (15 oz.) kidney beans, drained and rinsed
1 cup sliced ripe olives
3 green onions, chopped (include *tops*)
1 tbsp. canned green chilies
2 chopped tomatoes
1 avocado, chopped
2 cups shredded cheese

Brown ¾ lb. hamburger with 2 tbsp. of my "Taco Seasoning Mix."

Just before serving, stir in the hamburger mixture and 2 cups Fritos.

Serve with a dollop of sour cream or yogurt.

Makes 6 *big* servings.

One of my special treats is avocado slices and grapefruit sections on a bed of shredded lettuce with "Poppy Seed Dressing" in *A Family Raised on Sunshine*.

And no one can pass up our

VITALITY SALAD

Shred or tear up 1 head lettuce.

Toss with: 2 chopped tomatoes
1 cup raw mushrooms
1 chopped avocado
1 small onion, chopped
2 boiled eggs, diced
½ cup crumbled bacon
1 cup alfalfa sprouts

Serve with your favorite dressing.

These two are fantastic for low-calorie varieties.

"THINK SKINNY" BLUE CHEESE

In blender combine: 1 cup cottage cheese
2 tbsp. lemon juice
¼ cup milk
dash of garlic powder, onion powder, and pepper
2 tbsp. blue cheese

Blend until smooth.

Let stand in the refrigerator several hours for flavors to blend.

ROY'S THOUSAND ISLAND

Combine: 1 container (8 oz.) plain yogurt
¼ cup tomato sauce or catsup
1 tsp. horseradish
1 tbsp. dried onion flakes
1 hard-boiled egg, diced
4 tbsp. chopped green olives, pickles, or relish (I use whatever I have on hand. Of course, dill pickles are lowest in calories.)

For an absolutely fabulous lunch or summer supper, try our—

VEGGIES FOR A KING

Put 1 tbsp. corn oil in a large skillet.

Heat and add: ½ green pepper, chopped
1 small onion, chopped
1 celery stalk, chopped (leaves and all)
1 cup broccoli buds
1 cup thin carrot slices
1 cup cauliflowerettes, sliced
1 cup mushrooms
1 tomato, chopped
1 cup zucchini slices

Stir and sauté over medium heat until lightly cooked but still a little crunchy (about 10 min.).

Beat well 4 eggs.

Pour over vegetables. Turn heat to low and stir slightly until eggs are set.

Sprinkle with: ¼ tsp. oregano
¼ tsp. basil
⅓ cup shredded cheese

Cover with lid for a minute or two until cheese melts.

Serves 4 nicely.

As an appetizer or main dish soup, you must try our gazpacho. This soup is served cold and is really good *and* good for you. With crackers and cheese, this is a real refreshing lunch.

GAZPACHO

Combine: 2 cups beef broth (I have used chicken broth.)
2 cups tomato juice
1 small onion, finely chopped
1 avocado, chopped
½ green pepper, chopped
2 chopped tomatoes
1 cucumber, shredded
1 tsp. lemon juice
¼ tsp. garlic powder
6–8 drops Tabasco

Sometimes I blend all the ingredients until *almost* smooth except the avocado, and then I add that last.

For those of you who would like some more good, healthy, high-in-fiber recipes, here are three super ones. The first two are from our daughter-in-law, Shelli.

SHELLI'S
WHOLE WHEAT WAFFLES

Beat 2 eggs.
Add and stir only until mixed:
1¾ cups water
½ cup Mazola oil
2 cups whole wheat flour
4 tsp. baking powder
2 tsp. honey
½ tsp. salt
Bake in waffle iron as directed.

These can be mixed up at night and refrigerated until morning, ready to cook for breakfast.

CHOCKFUL OF BRAN MUFFINS

Combine: 1½ cups unprocessed bran
1 cup milk
½ cup honey

Let stand 2 min.
Add: 1 egg
½ cup margarine

Beat well.
Add: 1½ cups whole wheat flour
1 tbsp. baking powder
1 tsp. salt
½ tsp. soda

Stir only until combined.
Stir in ½ cup raisins or currants.
Use paper muffin cups in cupcake pan.
Bake at 400° for about 20 min.
Makes 1½ dozen.

Even though this is technically a nut bread, it makes a wonderful dieter's "cake."

TERRIFIC APPLESAUCE LOAF

Cream together: ⅔ cup brown sugar
                1 stick margarine

Add: 2 eggs
      1 cup applesauce (I use unsweetened.)

Mix well and add: 1 cup all-purpose flour
                    ¾ cup whole wheat flour
                    ⅓ cup wheat germ
                    2 tsp. baking powder
                    ½ tsp. salt
                    ½ tsp. soda
                    1 tsp. cinnamon
                    ½ tsp. nutmeg

Mix just until smooth.

Stir in: ½ cup raisins
         ⅓ cup chopped nuts

Bake in 2 greased 7½ in. × 3½ in. (nut bread size) pans.

Bake at 350° for about 1 hr. or until done.

Let cool. Wrap and store overnight before slicing.

Many of you have also asked me for some microwave helps and recipes. Since this is a relatively new thing for me, too, our family has had lots of fun experimenting and learning more in this field. I don't claim to be an expert in this area, but it's exciting to learn more. I can't stress enough that you should study your individual owner's manual and cookbook thoroughly and then be adventuresome!

To begin—

1. Keep microwave clean; it is easy to wipe out. Boiled-over food spilled on the tray will burn and draw microwaves away from food in dishes, and food will not cook properly.
2. Standing time or resting time is needed for some foods to finish cooking. Do not eliminate this step; it prevents overcooking, which toughens food.
3. Pressure from steam builds quickly and causes foods to burst or spatter. Always pierce potatoes, fruits, and egg yolks to allow steam to escape.
4. For microwave ovens that do not have a rotating device, remember to turn dishes occasionally for best results.
5. For heating foods (not baking), use a plastic rack for sandwiches, pastries, and breads so the air can circulate around and prevent sogginess. Cover foods with a paper towel to absorb moisture.
6. Containers:
   a. Microwaves pass through seashells, so they are great for cooking seafoods.
   b. Some plastics will become deformed, so they should only be used to heat foods for short periods. Do not cook in them unless they are specially made for that purpose.
   c. When using pottery dishes, remember if the dish is extra thick, slightly more cooking time may be required.
   d. Wood and straw can be used for heating but *not* for cooking.

e. Paper plates and cartons are fine if they are not plastic coated.

f. *No* foil, Centura or Melamine dishes, or newspaper or recycled paper, should be used.

g. To test a dish for microwave cooking, place dish beside a glass that is half full of water and cook on full power for 1 minute. If dish gets hot, *do not* use it. If dish is just warm, it is OK for heating but not cooking. If dish remains room temperature, it is all right for cooking. In any case, if water does not get hot, *do not use the dish*. This means the dish is absorbing the microwaves. Remember, though, for *long* cooking periods, dishes may become hot. This does not mean they are unsafe; use hot pads to prevent burns.

h. Be sure there are no metal trims, which include metallic decorated dishes (gold- or silver-painted rims).

7. Always make a small slash in plastic bags or wrap to allow steam to escape when less moisture is desired.

8. It is wise to cover foods with paper towels or napkins, wax paper, or cotton or natural-fiber cloth napkins. (Don't use synthetic fibers such as nylon because they may melt.) They prevent spattering and promote more even heating. Use white, as colors may bleed. Plastic wrap is permissible, but *never* use plastic wrap in candy making. If it is in contact with the ingredients, it melts and disintegrates into the candy.

9. Three guidelines to follow in converting a standard recipe to microwave cooking are:

a. Reduce liquid to nearly one-half the amount as there is less evaporation in microwave cooking.

b. Reduce oils and fats or perhaps eliminate them entirely, as they tend to attract microwaves away from food.

c. Reduce cooking time to:
   one-quarter for full power cooking
   one-third for 70 percent power cooking
   one-half for 50 percent power cooking
   three-quarters for 30 percent power cooking
   (Check directions for your particular brand.)

10. If your microwave does not have a defrost setting, use low power (30 percent) to allow thorough defrosting without cooking outer edges. Cover foods for more even defrosting. Stir or rearrange pieces such as chicken, placing bony sections in center of dish and thicker ones on outer edges. For large amounts of ground meat, remove outer edges as they defrost to prevent them from cooking before the center meat is defrosted.

Always check the instruction booklet that comes with your microwave oven for special tips and charts that may apply to your brand oven only.

SURPRISE BRAN MUFFINS

Combine: 1½ cups bran
    ½ cup boiling water

Stir in ¼ cup shortening

Add: 1 cup buttermilk
    1 egg

Mix well.

Mix together: 1¼ cups flour
        ½ cup sugar
        ¾ tsp. baking powder
        ¾ tsp. soda
        ½ tsp. salt

Add dry ingredients all at once to first mixture and stir just until moist.

Put 2 tbsp. batter in paper muffin cups or container made especially for microwave oven muffins and bake on full power for:
    1 muffin—35 sec.
    2 muffins—50 sec.
    4 muffins—1½ min.
    6 muffins—2½ min.

Makes 24 muffins.

Batter can be stored in a covered container in the refrigerator up to 4 weeks.

Raisins, cut up dates, or any other dried fruit or nuts can be added. Even a teaspoon of jam can be added for a surprise, but with the added moisture, you need to allow a few seconds more baking time.

Put the paper muffin cups on the plastic rack to avoid moisture.

BREAKFAST RING

Combine in glass cup: ⅓ cup brown sugar
            3 tbsp. margarine
            1 tbsp. water

Heat on full power for 1 min.

Invert a custard cup in center of a 9 in. round baking dish. Sprinkle ⅓ cup chopped nuts around cup.

Mix together: 1¾ cups flour
        ¾ tsp. salt
        2½ tsp. baking powder

Cut in with a pastry blender ⅓ cup Crisco. (Be sure you mix until it's like fine meal.)

Add ¾ cup milk and stir lightly with a fork. (Don't overstir.)

Turn the dough out onto a lightly floured board. Gently knead dough (about 8–10 "flips"), then pat the dough out about ½ in. thick with hands. (Don't use rolling pin.)

Cut out 10 biscuits. (Save remaining dough in refrigerator to use later for biscuits and honey.)

Cut each biscuit in half and dip into sugar mixture to coat.

Arrange with flat edge down around custard cup to form ring.

Bake on 70 percent power for 5 min., turning halfway through cooking time.

Let stand 2 min.

Invert on serving platter and remove custard cup. Serve warm.

Makes 6 servings.

COOKED CORNMEAL CEREAL

In 2 qt. casserole combine: 2 cups hot water
⅓ tsp. salt
½ cup cornmeal

Cook uncovered on full power for 6 min., stirring often.

Cover and let stand for 5 min.

Stir once again and serve. Makes 3 servings.

General instructions for cooking cereals will be included in all microwave cookbooks.

Eggs are a delicate food and can become tough. Follow cookbook instructions *exactly* for your microwave.

LUNCH IDEAS

Serve this with a lettuce salad and milk. It's yummy!

TANGY BEAN SANDWICHES

Place 8 strips of bacon on plastic rack and cook on full power for 3 min. (If a more crisp bacon is desired, cook an extra minute or two.)

Spread 8 thick slices of your favorite bread with mustard.

Spoon on pork and beans (1 can (16 oz.) partially drained).

Arrange bacon strips on top of beans and cook for 3½–4 min. Do not exceed 4 min. or bread will get tough. Cover sandwiches with paper towel to prevent spattering.

This is great served with fruit and milk.

TUNA CHEESE'Y'

Combine: ¼ lb. cubed American cheese
3 chopped hard-boiled eggs
1 can tuna
1 tbsp. minced green pepper
3 tbsp. chopped olives
2 tbsp. pickle relish
½ cup Miracle Whip

Spoon mixture on bottom half of bun (6–8 buns); replace top of bun.

Place on plastic rack, cover with paper towel or cloth napkin, and cook on full power for 2½ min.

This recipe is especially good with carrot and pineapple Jell-O.

SLOPPY JOES

Crumble 1 lb. ground beef in 1½ qt. casserole. Cook on full power for 5 min. Drain off grease.

Add: 3 tbsp. chopped onion
½ cup catsup
1 tsp. chili powder
1 tsp. salt
¼ tsp. pepper
2 tbsp. sugar
1 tbsp. Worcestershire sauce
1 tbsp. mustard

Cover dish and cook on full power for 7–8 min., stirring several times.

Spoon mixture onto buns. Serves 4–5.

DRESSED FRANKS

Combine: ½ cup chopped celery
            ¼ cup chopped onion
            2 tbsp. margarine

Cover and cook on full power for 3 min.

Add: 3 cups bread crumbs
      ½ tsp. salt
      ⅛ tsp. pepper
      ⅛ tsp. poultry seasoning
      ½ cup milk

Split 10 wieners lengthwise and stuff with stuffing mixture.

Place 10 strips of bacon on plastic rack and cook on full power for 3½ min.

Wrap each wiener with a strip of bacon and secure with a toothpick.

Place wieners on rack, cover with a paper towel, and cook on full power for 6–7 min. Turn halfway through cooking time if necessary in your oven.

MAIN DISHES

GERMAN COUNTRY RIBS

Heat browning dish on full power for 4½ min.

Add 1½ lb. country ribs (pork) and cook on full power for 4 min. (Turn after 2 min.)

Salt and pepper to taste.

Arrange ribs in circle near outer edge of dish.

Fill with mixture of: 2 cups sliced apples
                    2 cups drained sauerkraut
                      (Reserve ¼ cup juice.)
                    ¼ cup raisins
                    2 tbsp. brown sugar
                    1 medium onion chopped
                    or 2 tbsp. minced

Add: ¼ cup reserved sauerkraut juice.

Cover with glass lid and cook on 50 percent power for 35 mins.

Turn dish halfway through cooking time if necessary.

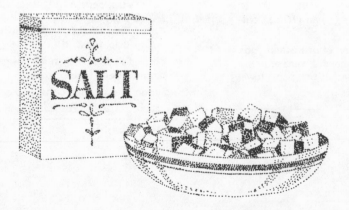

Serve this with corn chips and a tossed salad. Olé!

OUR MEXICAN CHEESE SOUP

In a 2 qt. casserole, put:
  3 tbsp. margarine or butter
  1 medium onion, finely chopped

Cover and cook on full power for 6 min.

Add: 1 qt. canned tomatoes
  1 can chopped green chilies
  ¼ tsp. chili powder
  dash of cumin
  2 minced garlic cloves

Mix well, cover, and cook on high for 8 min.

Stir in ¾ lb. shredded cheese (any variety) and continue cooking for another minute.

CHICKEN SOUP

In 4 qt. casserole, combine:
  bony chicken parts
    (approximately 4 ribs and 4 backs)
  3½ cups water

Cover and cook on full power for 30 min.

Remove chicken pieces and strain broth.

Return broth to dish and add:
  2 cups sliced carrots
  ½ cup dried onions
  3 sprigs parsley
  ½ cup chopped celery
  1 tsp. salt
  ¼ tsp. pepper

Cook on full power for 20 min.

Add chicken meat that has been picked off the bones.

DUMPLINGS

In 2 qt. casserole, combine: 1 cup water
                ½ cup margarine

Cook on full power for 2 min. (covered).

All at once add: 1 tsp. salt
                ¼ tsp. poultry seasoning
                1¼ cups flour

Beat in 3 eggs, one at a time.

Drop by spoonful into soup, cover with glass lid, and cook on full power for 7 min. (Turn dish several times for even cooking.)

After dumplings are cooked, stir gently and add 1 cup boiling water. (This must be added last to prevent soup from boiling over.)

Served over chow mein noodles or rice with a cottage cheese and pineapple salad, this is delicious!

PORK CHOW MEIN

In 2 qt. casserole, combine: 1 cup chopped celery
        1 cup chopped onion
        2 tbsp. margarine
        2 tbsp. water

Cover and cook on full power for 7 min.

Drain 1 can (16 oz.) bean sprouts.

Combine: 1 cup juice from sprouts (Add water if necessary.)
        2 tbsp. whole wheat flour

Add to celery and onion mixture:
    bean sprouts
    juice and flour mixture
    ¼ cup soy sauce
    2 cups cubed cooked pork roast

Cook on full power 11–13 min., stirring 4–5 times.

You may add pepper if desired, but no salt is needed.

Makes 4 servings.

RICE

In 2 qt. casserole, combine: ½ cup long-grain rice
        1¼ cups hot water
        ½ tsp. oil
        ½ tsp. salt

Cover and cook on full power for 5 min.

Let stand 5 min., then stir.

Continue cooking on 50 percent power for 8 min.

Do *not* stir again until ready to serve.

FRIED CHICKEN

2½–3 lb. chicken pieces

Mix in bag: ½ cup whole wheat flour
        ½ cup white flour
        1½ tsp. salt
        ¼ tsp. pepper
        ½ tsp. paprika
        ¼ tsp. dry mustard

Shake 2–3 pieces of chicken at a time in coating mixture.

Heat browning dish on full power for 4½ min.

Add 2 tbsp. margarine.

Place thickest meaty pieces of chicken around outer edge of dish, bonier parts in center, skin side down.

Cover with wax paper and cook on full power for 10 min.

Turn pieces and cook uncovered for another 10–15 min., depending on size of chicken.

CHICKEN BAR-B-QUE

In 1½ qt. dish, combine: ½ cup chopped onion
                          2 tbsp. oil

Cook on full power for 2½ min.

Add: ½ cup catsup
      2 tbsp. lemon juice
      2 tbsp. brown sugar
      1 tbsp. Worcestershire sauce
      1 tbsp. prepared mustard
      1 tsp. salt
      ¼ tsp. pepper

Cook on full power for 4 min., stirring several times.

Arrange 2½–3 lb. chicken pieces in a 2 qt. casserole (large pieces on outer edge, bony pieces in center) and cover with barbeque sauce.

Cover and cook on full power for 20 min. (Turn chicken pieces after first 10 min.)

Makes about 4 servings.

OVERNIGHT CASSEROLE

In 2 qt. casserole, combine:
    1 cup cooked meat (You can use chicken, ham, pork, or tuna.)
    1 cup milk
    1 cup uncooked macaroni
    1 can cream-type soup
    ¼ lb. diced cheese
    1 medium onion, chopped

Cover and refrigerate overnight. (The macaroni absorbs the milk and is softened during overnight refrigeration.)

Cook covered on full power for 15 min.

Top with croutons just before serving.

CROUTONS

In 4 qt. casserole, combine:
    ½ cup margarine
    ½ tsp. salt
    ½ tsp. celery leaves, crushed
    ¼ tsp. parsley leaves, crushed
    ¼ tsp. sweet basil leaves, crushed
    ⅛ tsp. oregano
    ⅛ tsp. garlic powder
    ⅛ tsp. pepper

Cook on full power for 1½–2 min.

Stir in 6 cups bread cubes and toss until well covered.

Spread on large glass platter and cook on full power for 4 min., stirring several times.

Immediately spread cubes onto paper towels to absorb any moisture.

Let set 5–10 min., then place on cookie sheet or platter to cool.

They will become crisper as they cool and can then be stored in a loosely covered container to use on salads and in casseroles.

SAUERBRATEN DELIGHT

In 2 qt. casserole, combine:
   2 cups cubed cooked roast beef
   ¾ cup water
   ¼ cup vinegar
   10 whole cloves
   ⅛ tsp. pepper
   1 tbsp. brown sugar
   4 crushed ginger snaps
   1 tbsp. minced dried onions

Cover and marinate in refrigerator for 6–8 hr.

Pick out whole cloves.

Blend: 1 tbsp. cornstarch
   ½ cup water

Stir into meat mixture and cook on 50 percent power for 10–12 min., stirring 2–3 times.

Serve over mashed potatoes. Makes about 4 servings.

MASHED POTATOES

In 1 qt. casserole, combine:
   4 potatoes, peeled and sliced
   ½ cup water
   ½ tsp. salt

Cook on full power for 10 min., stirring twice.

Drain and add: ¼ cup milk
   1 tbsp. butter

Whip and serve.

CHOCOLATE DELIGHT CAKE

Mix: 1½ cups boiling water
   1 cup quick rolled oats

Let stand 20 min.

In a covered dish, melt 6 oz. chocolate chips on 50 percent power for 4½ min., stirring halfway through.

Beat together: ⅓ cup shortening
   ⅓ cup granulated sugar
   ⅓ cup brown sugar

Add 2 eggs.

Add: oat mixture
   chocolate

Mix together and add to above mixture:
   1½ cups flour
   1 tsp. soda
   ½ tsp. salt

Line bottom of a 9 in. round casserole dish (at least 2 in. deep) with wax paper.

Grease a 1½ in. or 2 in. glass jigger and place in center of casserole.

Spoon cake batter evenly around jigger.

Bake on 70 percent power for 13 min., turning half-way through if necessary.

Use toothpick to test for doneness.

Let rest for 10 min.

Using a knife, remove jigger, place cake plate over dish, and invert. Peel paper off and let set in the air several minutes to dry.

COCONUT FROSTING

In 1 qt. casserole combine: 5 tbsp. margarine
½ cup brown sugar
1 tbsp. milk
⅓ cup chopped nuts
½ cup coconut

Cook on full power for 3½−4 min., stirring several times.

Spread gently over warm cake.

Another area that people ask for help in is cooking for one or two. Roy and I find ourselves in this situation now, and it certainly makes a difference, doesn't it? We find it really exciting because we can try lots of new and different things now that may not have appealed to the family, would have been too expensive for a large family, or may not have been filling enough for growing, hungry children. (Our appetites have diminished somewhat, believe it or not.) Nearly all the tried and true recipes from my books and newsletter can be cut in half or frozen, so that is a big help both in economy and time. As you know, my freezer is one of my most valuable appliances. I couldn't get along without it, and it saves me an awful lot of money.

If you find yourself cooking for yourself or for one other person, why not make and split a casserole with a neighbor one night a week and have them make and split a dessert with you; then reverse the process on another night. It's a big help and lots of fun.

The following hurry-up main dishes have become favorites of ours because they don't require a lot of *pre*cooking.

NOODLE SCRAMBLE

Brown ½ lb. ground beef.

Add: 1 tbsp. dried onion flakes
1 can cream of chicken soup (Sometimes I use cream of mushroom, cream of onion, or even tomato.)
½ cup milk
½ tsp. sage
1 cup uncooked noodles

Mix well, cover, and cook over low heat for about 30 min. until noodles are tender.

Leftover vegetables can even be added for color.

This dish has so much good nutrition because of combining the beans and rice with a small amount of meat. You'll love it with a small tossed salad.

LOUISIANA BAYOU BEANS AND RICE

Brown ¼ lb. ground beef.

Add: 1 tbsp. dried onion
dash of garlic salt
2 tsp. chili powder
½ tsp. cumin
1 can (15 oz.) kidney beans with liquid
¾ cup tomato juice
¼ cup long-grain old-fashioned rice (not "minute")
1 small tomato, cut up

Mix well, cover, and simmer on low about 30 min. until rice is cooked.

Cover with ½ cup cheese and return to heat until cheese melts.

Now this one is absolutely delicious!

FRENCH CHICKEN FOR ONE

In a small skillet, melt 1 tbsp. butter.

Sauté 1 tbsp. minced onion.

Stir in 1 tbsp. flour.

Add ½ cup chicken broth.

Stir until thickened and add: ½ tsp. dill seed
                                     dash of garlic pow-
                                     der

Add one breast of chicken.

Cover with lid and simmer for 45 min. or until chicken is tender.

Meanwhile, cook 1 cup noodles as directed.

When chicken is tender, stir in ½ cup yogurt and serve over noodles.

YUMMY GREEN BEANS

Cook 1 serving frozen or fresh green beans.

Crumble in 1 slice bacon (Fried crisp; reserve this in the morning when you're cooking breakfast.)

Add: 1 tsp. minced onion
       salt and pepper
       1 tsp. vinegar

Mix well and serve hot.

LUIGI'S ZUCCHINI

Melt 1 tbsp. butter.

Sauté: 1 tbsp. minced onion
         dash of garlic powder
         ¼ tsp. basil
         ¼ tsp. oregano
         salt and pepper

Slice 1 medium zucchini into pan.

Add 2 tbsp. water.

Cover and cook until tender. Don't overcook!

Serve with shredded cheese on top.

This is "the best" for an economical dessert guaranteed to soothe your troubles away.

LEMON POOF

Separate 1 egg.

Beat egg white until stiff. Set aside.

Combine: 1 egg yolk
           ½ cup sugar
           3 tbsp. lemon juice
           ⅓ tsp. lemon peel
           2 tbsp. flour

Stir in ½ cup milk.

Gently stir in beaten egg white but not until smooth.

Bake in 2 large custard cups; set in a pan of hot water about 1 in. deep.

Bake for 50 min. at 350°.

Serve warm.

With a scoop of ice cream on top, this is fit for a king—a great way to use up those odds and ends, too!

APPLE CRISP
FOR SOME "ONE" SPECIAL

Peel and chop 1 cooking apple. Place in a small baking dish.

In a saucepan, melt 1 tbsp. butter.

Stir in: ¼ cup quick oats
¼ cup fine bread crumbs
2 tbsp. brown sugar
¼ tsp. nutmeg
¼ tsp. cinnamon
1 tbsp. lemon juice

Spread mixture over apples.

Bake at 375° for 45 min.

No matter what your special dietary needs or how you cook your food, have fun with your meals. Start now to enjoy the really good foods available. Each day, eliminate one junk food item and add something new, exciting, and nutritious. Keep a food diary! You'll feel so proud of yourself and like what you see in the mirror as well!

6
THANKS, SUNBEAMS!

Sunbeams come in many shapes, sizes, and colors, and they have a magical way of affecting the things they touch. Remember that gloomy, cold day when you really felt like not getting up, and suddenly the sun broke through the clouds and a ray of sunlight streamed through your bedroom window and brightened up the whole room? You feel a sense of warmness from head to toe, and suddenly you're eager to start the day. At these times, there is nothing like the warmth of the sun to help you feel better inside and out. Or isn't it nice when you've finished a job like scrubbing the floor, polishing the furniture, or setting a pretty table to have the sun stream in the window and shine on your efforts as if to illuminate your works and compliment you on a job well done!

Friends can be sunbeams, too. They also come in many shapes, sizes, and colors, and they, too, have a magical effect on those they touch. They can brighten up a cold and gloomy day with a smile or kind word or come shining into our homes personally or by phone to help start the day off right. A friend's arm around your shoulder can be just the warmth you need when you are tired or achy, and a pat on the back and a complimentary word for a job well done can make you feel 10 feet tall.

My life has been filled with special "sunbeam" friends who have contributed a significant part of who I am. My interests, talents, and goals have been developed or discovered with the help of these beautiful people. Unfortunately, sometimes we take these friends for granted just as we do the sunbeams that shine on us each day. I would like to thank each one of my "sunbeams" now and let them know how vital they are to my life.

Let me introduce them to you because I'd like to share them with you.

First, you must meet my mom. Mom's life had many clouds along the way, but now that my own children are grown and married, I am constantly aware of how she conveyed sunshine to us through those clouds. My father passed away when I was a tiny baby, leaving mom with a family of four little children to raise. She worked very hard and did without even the necessities at times, but she was so full of love and dedication to her family that I always felt she could do anything. She had a way of making little things so special. Getting up on those freezing cold Nebraska mornings, she always had a crackling fire going in the potbelly stove with promises of some steaming hot chocolate and pancakes. Standing with my back to that fire felt like sunshine from heaven.

Even though many of our meals consisted only of potato soup or pancakes, she made them look *and* taste delicious and filled us up with compliments and praise concerning our school work or other jobs well done as we filled our stomachs.

I never heard mom say we were too poor for anything. If a need or desire for something arose, she just whipped out her ingenuity and made it! Many times I remember her sitting up late at night taking apart an old hand-me-down dress we were given to create a beautiful masterpiece of a formal or party dress for me. I never heard her say, "Impossible."

Neither did she ever condemn anyone. She always taught me that everyone has a reason for being as they are, and we should show understanding and love.

Yes, mom's life has been full of lots of clouds, but I will always love her for the sunshine she gave me. As I look at my children, I wonder if somewhere in their memories they will recall standing by my crackling fire and feeling the sunshine of heaven.

This recipe is guaranteed to soothe all your troubles away and was my favorite as a little girl.

MOM'S TAPIOCA PUDDING

Beat 1 egg white until fluffy.

Add 2 tbsp. sugar and beat until it holds a peak.

In a saucepan, beat slightly 1 egg yolk.

Add: 2 cups milk
     3 tbsp. sugar
     3 tbsp. quick-cooking tapioca
     dash of salt

Let this mixture stand for 5 min., then cook over medium heat until it comes to a full rolling boil.

Boil for 1 min.

Remove from heat.

Stir in: 4 tbsp. drained, crushed pineapple
         6–8 chopped maraschino cherries
         1 tsp. vanilla

Gradually add the hot mixture to the beaten egg white. Don't overstir. Can be served warm or cold.

LEMON SAUCE (FOR BREAD PUDDING)

Mix together: 1 tbsp. cornstarch
              ½ cup sugar
              ¼ tsp. salt

Add 1 cup hot water.

Cook until thick.

Add: 1 tsp. lemon peel (Fresh lemon peel is best.)
     3 tbsp. lemon juice (Again, fresh is best.)
     2 tbsp. margarine or butter (Butter is best.)

Serve warm over pudding.

This one is a man pleaser and gets raves every time!

SCALLOPED POTATOES AND PORK CHOPS

Trim a little fat from the pork chops and heat it in the fry pan for drippings.

Brown 4 pork chops well on both sides.

Remove pork chops from pan and stir 2 tbsp. flour into the drippings in the pan. Stir well for a minute or two over medium heat.

Stir in 2 cups milk and continue stirring until thickened. Season with salt and pepper.

Butter a 2 qt. casserole and layer in 6 nice-sized potatoes, sprinkling lightly with a little salt and pepper as you layer them.

Pour the sauce over the potatoes and lay the pork chops on top.

Bake at 350° for 1¼ hr. Halfway through cooking, turn pork chops over.

This is delicious served with fish and coleslaw.

MOM'S MACARONI AND CHEESE

Cook 2 cups macaroni according to directions on package. (This will give you 4 cups cooked.)

Then make a sauce:

In pan, melt 2 tbsp. margarine.

Stir in 2 tbsp. flour and cook for a minute or so.

Gradually stir in 2 cups milk and cook until thickened.

Season with 1 tsp. salt and dash of pepper.

Slowly add 2 cups shredded cheese (any kind you prefer). Stir until melted.

Mix sauce with cooked macaroni and put in an 8 in. × 8 in. buttered casserole.

Sprinkle ½ cup buttered crumbs on top and bake at 350° for about 20 min.

BUTTERSCOTCH PIE

In saucepan, melt 2 tbsp. butter or margarine.

Mix together: 1 cup brown sugar
2 tbsp. flour

Stir in: 1 cup milk
2 beaten egg yolks

Cook together over medium heat until thick.

Stir in 1 tsp. vanilla.

Cool and spoon into a small (8 in.) baked pie shell.

Cover with meringue and brown.

MOM'S SALMON LOAF

Mash 1 can pink or red salmon (do not drain) well with a fork.

Add: 1 beaten egg
2 tbsp. grated onion
2 tbsp. lemon juice
¼ tsp. salt
dash of pepper
2 tbsp. chopped parsley
½ cup fine bread crumbs
2 tbsp. flour

Mix well and then pack lightly into a small (7 in. × 3½ in.) greased loaf pan.

Top with buttered crumbs.

Bake at 350° for 1 hr.

DELICIOUS PRUNE CAKE

Bring 1 cup prunes in 1 cup water to a simmer and simmer 3–5 min. Save liquid.

Cream: 1 stick margarine
1 cup sugar

Add: 1 egg
2 egg yolks

Beat well.

Combine the 1 cup cut-up prunes with:
2½ cups flour
½ tsp. salt
½ tsp. cinnamon
¼ tsp. cloves

Add above to creamed mixture.

Then add ½ cup prune liquid mixed with 1 tsp. soda.

Bake in a greased 8 in. × 12 in. or 8 in. × 8 in. pan and 6 cupcakes. Bake at 350° for 30–40 min.

Frost and sprinkle with chopped nuts.

Grandma served this next recipe hot with creamed potatoes for supper or sliced, cold, on brown bread with pickled beets for a "smørrebrød."

GRANDMA'S DANISH FRIKADELLER

Mix well: ½ lb. ground beef
½ lb. ground pork
2 tbsp. grated onion
2 tbsp. flour
½ tsp. salt
dash of pepper
½ tsp. nutmeg
½ cup milk
1 beaten egg

Shape into oblong balls with a tablespoon.

Fry slowly in melted butter or margarine until done.

For another Danish treat, try her method of fixing a beef roast.

GRANDMA'S BEEF ROAST

In a heavy pan, brown a roast well on all sides, using a little suet in the pan for your drippings. After the roast is well browned, season with salt and pepper, and put 15–20 whole allspice berries on top and in the crevices of the roast. Cover tightly and cook on top of the stove on low heat for several hours. This is *so* good and makes delicious gravy.

My oldest sister, Maxine Haws, is truly that warmth of sunshine when she puts her arm around you. She has a loving, caring spirit that will always be an example to me. Through Maxine, I learned the principles of "cleanliness is next to godliness" and "whistle while you work." How well I remember her scrubbing our front door and saying, "That is the first impression people get of your home." No matter how much patching, mending, and making do she did, everything was always neat and shiny clean. (I even remember her *sewing* shoelaces together when we couldn't afford new ones. It sure looked nicer than a knot.) After she scrubbed the floor all shiny clean, she used to chase me out of the house with a broom so I didn't "track up" the floor. But Maxine could never bear to see anyone unhappy, so she would soon be outside to comfort me by reading me stories or pushing me around in her big wicker doll buggy. Many, many people's burdens have been lighter because of the love Maxine radiates.

There is a great way to make use of fats and drippings. Maxine insists homemade soap is better than commercial types because it has the glycerin removed. Homemade soap is such a pleasure to use. Nothing smells quite so clean. It can be used safely in automatic washers if you use a water softening agent; and you'll have the cleanest, whitest clothes ever. Just grate some of the bar soap into the washer with the water softener.

It takes a little practice to get the hang of making soap, and it is a little messy, but it will be an "art" you'll be proud to accomplish.

HOMEMADE SOAP

Save all your bacon grease, roast drippings, hamburger drippings, and all animal fat. Strain and keep in a covered container until you have 10 cups.

In a 3 gal. crock or enamel or stainless steel container (don't use aluminum, tin, or Teflon), mix well: 1 qt. water
            1 can (1 lb.) lye

Use a long wooden spoon or stick to stir and avoid getting fumes in your eyes.

Let mixture sit until cool.

(It is wise to make soap outdoors on a 70°–80° day.)

Carefully stir in: 10 cups melted down grease
               ½ cup Borax
               ½ cup sudsy ammonia

Stir slowly until all is well mixed and it is the consistency of thick pea soup.

Pour into a flat cardboard box lined with wax paper, foil, or a plastic garbage bag cut open. Let harden and cut in bars. Then let dry. The harder it dries, the longer it lasts.

CORN COB JELLY

Wash 12–14 large red dry corncobs.

Put in a large kettle and cover completely with water.

Boil for 30 min.

Strain off 3 cups juice.

Add 1 pkg. Sure-Jel (pectin).

Bring to a rolling boil and add 3 cups sugar, all at once.

Boil for 2 min.

Remove from heat, skim off bubbles, and let cool slightly.

Pour in sterilized jars and seal with paraffin.

BEET JELLY

Wash 6–8 beets thoroughly and boil until skins will slip off. Cool.

Cube beets and cover with 3½ cups water and bring to a rolling boil. (These beets can now be served as a vegetable with your next meal. All you need for the jelly is the juice.)

Mix 3½ cups beet juice and ½ cup lemon juice with 1 pkg. Sure-Jel pectin.

Bring to a hard boil and then add 5 cups sugar all at once.

Continue stirring; bring to a boil and boil for 1 min.

Remove from heat and stir in 1 pkg. (6 oz.) of strawberry, cherry, or raspberry Jell-O.

Stir for 3 min. to dissolve Jell-O.

Pour into jelly glasses and seal with paraffin.

Maxine's Fudge Topping is thick and rich and better than any commercial brand.

MAXINE'S FUDGE TOPPING

Melt together: 1 stick margarine
1 tbsp. butter
½ cup cocoa

Add 3 cups sugar (½ cup at a time, stirring well).

Have your heat on low and add 1 can (13 oz.) evaporated milk (slowly).

Bring to a good boil and boil 4–5 min., stirring often.

Remove from heat and add 1 tbsp. vanilla.

Makes 1 qt. Keep refrigerated.

My sister, Donna Haack, has brightened my life with the joys of organization. She is such an example of efficiency and determination. She has things so well organized that she truly never wastes a crumb. Every time I visit her, I come home with renewed determination to organize my home and life better. I think the reason she is so successful is that she is always receptive and ready to learn new ideas. This is a talent that pays off in many ways.

PERFECT CUSTARD PIE

Blend well: 4 beaten eggs
½ cup sugar
¼ tsp. salt
½ tsp. vanilla
½ tsp. almond extract

Gradually stir in 2½ cups scalded milk.

Set a 9 in. unbaked pie shell on oven rack and pour in filling. (This prevents spilling while carrying pie to the oven.)

Sprinkle top generously with nutmeg.

Bake at 400° for 25–30 min. After first 15 min., reduce heat to 350°.

This recipe sure goes great with a hot bowl of soup.

DELICIOUS DILLY BREAD

Dissolve 1 tbsp. yeast in ¼ cup warm water.

Add: 2 tbsp. sugar
    1 cup warm small curd cottage cheese
    1 tbsp. instant onion
    1 tsp. salt
    ¼ tsp. soda
    1 egg, slightly beaten
    2½–3 cups flour
    2 tsp. dill seed

Mix together well. Cover and let rise until double. Stir down and let rise until double again.

Place dough in greased loaf pan (9 in. × 5 in.) and let rise until double again.

Bake at 350° for 35–40 min.

This is a German drop doughnut that is really good.

FÜTEN (PRONOUNCED FIDDEN)

Beat: 2 eggs
    1 cup sugar

Add 2 tbsp. margarine.

Add ⅔ cup milk.

Add: 3 cups flour
    2 tsp. baking powder
    ½ tsp. nutmeg
    ½ tsp. salt

Then stir in: 1 tsp. vanilla
    ½ cup raisins

Drop by teaspoons into deep hot oil (375°) and fry until golden on both sides. Sprinkle with a little powdered sugar if desired.

Donna's freezer is never without a pan of this.

GORDON'S SPICE CAKE

Cream together: 2 cups sugar
    ½ cup shortening

Add 2 eggs.

Add alternately: 3 cups flour (She uses ½ whole wheat and ½ white flour.)
    1 tsp. cinnamon
    ½ tsp. cloves
    ½ tsp. allspice
    with 2 cups buttermilk with 2 tsp. soda in it.

Bake in a jelly roll pan at 350° for 30–35 min.

Frost with powdered sugar frosting and sprinkle with nuts.

YUMMY SUMMER SAUSAGE

Mix together well:
    2 lb. hamburger (Just use cheap hamburger—it works best.)
    1 cup cold water
    2 tbsp. Morton's Tenderquick
    1 tsp. garlic salt
    1 tsp. pepper (Coarse ground is best.)
    1 tsp. onion salt
    2 tsp. liquid smoke
    1 tsp. mustard seeds

The spices can be adjusted to suit your tastes.

Let this mixture stand in a covered bowl for 24 hr. in the refrigerator.

Roll in three equal rolls. Wrap each roll in foil. Poke holes with a fork along the bottom of the rolls for the grease to drip out.

Place the rolls on a broiler pan rack and bake at 325° for 1½ hr.

Let cool, unwrap, and store in plastic bags in the refrigerator. (It can be frozen.) Slice thinly for delicious sandwiches.

Marilyn Harroun, my niece, is a young mother, age 30, with five children ages 9, 6, 4, 2½, and 6 weeks. She has certainly been a sunbeam to me. Marilyn has taught me the valuable lesson that friendship has no age barrier. The young can learn from the old and vice versa. She is always eager to learn from others, yet willingly shares her skills and talents with those around her. She is a model homemaker, as she bakes all of her own bread. She gardens, preserves her fruits and vegetables and makes all of the family's clothing. She trains her children well and still manages to be a well-educated human being and interested in developing her own talents. I treasure the many things that Marilyn has shared with me.

MARILYN'S DELICIOUS DOUGHNUTS

Dissolve: 2 tbsp. dry yeast in ½ cup warm water
and
1 tbsp. sugar

Combine: 2 cups hot water
1 cup shortening
2 tsp. salt
1 cup sugar
4 slightly beaten eggs

Stir in 2 cups flour.

Add yeast mixture.

Gradually add 5½–6 cups more flour to make a soft dough.

Knead until light.

Let rise until double.

Roll out and cut. Let doughnuts rise until nearly double.

Fry in hot oil (375°) until nicely browned on both sides.

Glaze or shake in a bag of sugar.

Glaze: Add ⅓ cup boiling water to 2 cups powdered sugar. Mix well. Dip warm doughnuts and drain on a rack.

Everyone should have an Aunt Viola. Viola Ewoldt is the jolliest, most peppy and enthusiastic person you could meet, and she has a heart as pure as gold. She has a flair for cooking all the old German recipes that she acquired from my Grandma Scheel. Just the mention of her name brings to mind floods of good recipes. Be sure and give them a dash of love, as she does!

VIOLA'S "CUKES"

Peel cucumbers and slice very thinly. Put in salt water (2 tbsp. salt per quart of water). Push slices down in water (cover very well). Leave for 2–3 hr. or overnight.

Squeeze out all of the water with your hands very tightly.

Mix slices with Miracle Whip dressing until well coated and sprinkle with a little parsley or dill seed. (Dill is best.)

Keep covered and refrigerated.

FARM PEANUT COOKIES

Mix well: 1 cup white sugar
1 cup brown sugar
1 cup shortening

Add 3 eggs.

Add: 4 cups flour
1 tsp. soda
½ tsp. cinnamon

Stir in 2 cups ground peanuts.

Roll in balls the size of a walnut. Flatten with tines of a fork.

Bake on an ungreased cookie sheet at 375° for 10–12 min.

This is my favorite.

HOLIDAY RED CABBAGE

Slice or shred 1 head red cabbage.

Sauté 1 small chopped onion in 2 tbsp. butter until tender.

Add ¼ cup brown sugar and stir until onion is nice and brown.

Add: 1 tsp. caraway seed
     ½ clove of garlic, minced
     1 cup water

Add cut-up cabbage and simmer, covered, for 10 min.

Refrigerate overnight.

When ready to serve, heat and stir in 2 tbsp. flour.

At the very last, stir in 1 tsp. vinegar.

GRANDMA'S FAVORITE DINNER

Fried ham slices   Green beans
Boiled potatoes   Relish
Mustard gravy   Homemade bread
Vanilla pudding with fresh grated nutmeg and an apple slice on top.

To prepare ham:

Slice pieces from a precooked ham.

Melt *plenty* of margarine, butter, or shortening in pan; sauté a few onion slices and push onions to the side of the pan.

Dip each ham slice in a beaten egg and then in flour and fry until crispy in hot pan.

MUSTARD GRAVY

In saucepan combine: 2 tbsp. flour
     2 tbsp. sugar
     1 tsp. dry mustard
     dash of salt

Stir in 2 cups milk and cook until thick.

Add 1 tbsp. butter.

At the last, add ½ tbsp. vinegar.

Serve over boiled potatoes.

Aunt Verna Bailey has always been the "touch of class" in my list of sunbeams. She has taught me dignity and pride in my work. For many years, she did all the cooking for the ranch hands while my uncle ran a big sheep ranch. Despite the heavy work load and responsibilities, her appearance and actions were always "first-class." I always figured if she could stay looking that pretty while cooking for a crowd of ranch hands, I could manage, too. It takes work, but I am so thankful for her example.

You'll love this easy soup!

AUNT VERNA'S AUTUMN SOUP

In a large kettle combine:
    2 cups shredded cabbage
    2 cups shredded potatoes
    1 cup shredded carrots
    ¼ cup chopped onion
    2 tbsp. parsley

Cover with: 6 cups water
              2 tsp. salt
              ½ tsp. celery salt

Cook until vegetables are tender.

In a small saucepan, melt 2 tbsp. butter or margarine.

Stir in 2 tbsp. flour.

Add 2 cups milk. Cook until thickened.

Stir in 2 cups shredded cheese.

Add sauce to soup mixture and heat thoroughly.

Viola Knuth is a cousin who has the knack of making everyone feel important. She is always interested in everybody else and can make you feel so at home. When my mother married my stepfather and we moved to the farm, I'll never forget how welcome Viola always made me feel as a new member of that family. Sharing and caring are two of her special characteristics. Her mother, Aunt Martha, was famous in my eyes for the big "feeds" she put on for midnight "lunches" after a card game or birthday get-togethers. Of course, Viola was "first mate" in the kitchen.

After a big lunch of homemade breads (rye, graham, and white), mettwurst, egg salad, ring bologna, homemade liver sausage, sliced pork roast and ham, and homemade pickles of every kind, there would be a huge display of cakes and at least three kinds of pie. I remember the cakes being baked in pans as big as dish pans. They were *so* good!

POTATO CAKE

Cream together: ¾ cup shortening
                   2 cups sugar

Add 1 egg.

Add: 1 cup *hot* mashed-up potato
      2 squares of unsweetened baking chocolate (melted)

Add: 2 cups flour
      2 tsp. cinnamon
      1 tsp. nutmeg
      2 tsp. soda

Stir in ⅔ cup milk.

Add: 1 cup raisins
      1 cup chopped nuts

At the last, add 4 eggs, one at a time, beating well each time.

Bake in a slow oven (325°) in a 9 in. × 13 in. pan for 70 min.

BUTTERMILK CAKE

Cream: ½ cup shortening
      2 cups brown sugar

Add 5 egg yolks.

Add 1 cup buttermilk.

Add: 2 cups flour
     1 tsp. soda

Stir in: ½ tsp. vanilla
      ½ cup chopped raisins
      ½ cup chopped nuts

Bake at 350° in an 8 in. × 12 in. pan until done (35–40 min.).

Frost with powdered sugar frosting into which you stir: ½ cup chopped raisins
      ½ cup chopped nuts

Suzanne Paulsen is my closest childhood friend. We go back to the days of saddle oxfords, rolled bobby socks, sharing secrets and giggles, and just *having* to have matching pairs of bunny fur mittens with red leather palms. We always looked like Mutt and Jeff together because she was so tiny, but she has a spirit as big as her heart. She taught me what friendship is all about by sharing my hopes and dreams and accepting me for what I really was. Her father ran the local butcher shop in our town, and I loved to walk around in there with the sawdust on the floor smelling so fresh and clean and watch his expertise with the meat saw. I appreciate her sharing her dad's sausage recipe with me as well as some of her family's favorites.

SCHULTZ'S PORK SAUSAGE

Mix together: 20 lb. fresh pork, ground
      1 teacup coarse salt
      ¼ teacup sage
      ¼ teacup white pepper
      ½ teacup brown sugar
      1 tsp. cayenne pepper

Shape into patties and freeze until ready to fry.

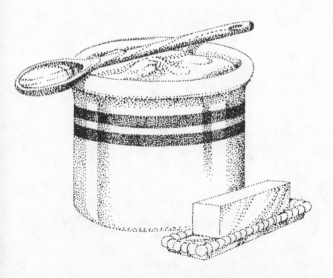

This one is a delicious casserole.

GRECO

Brown 1 lb. ground beef.

Add: 1 chopped onion
     ½ chopped green pepper

Add 1 small can of mushrooms, drained.

Cook 1 box (8 oz.) of shell macaroni as directed and add to meat mixture.

Add: 3 cans (8 oz.) of tomato sauce
     1 can (16 oz.) cream-style corn

Mix well and place in a 2 qt. casserole.

Cover with shredded cheese.

Bake at 300° for 1 hr.

Serves 6 generously. This can be made ahead and refrigerated until ready to bake.

VIENNESE HAMBURGER

Combine: 2 lb. ground beef
         1 egg
         ¼ cup milk
         2 tsp. salt
         ¼ cup dry bread crumbs

Shape into 24 balls.

Cook 1½ cups sliced onions in ½ cup margarine until tender.

Remove onions and add meatballs to pan and brown on all sides.

Remove meatballs and stir 3 tbsp. flour into drippings in pan.

Return onions to the pan and add 2 tbsp. tomato paste. Stir well.

Add 2 beef bouillon cubes dissolved in 2 cups boiling water.

Return meatballs to pan and cover and simmer for 20 min.

Just before serving stir in 1 cup sour cream.

Serve over broad noodles. This recipe will cover about ¾ lb. noodles. Serves 6.

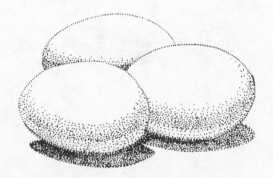

This is nice when it is frozen in individual servings (like margarine tubs) and then dropped into compotes for serving. Also it is good for a breakfast or brunch with a coffee cake. Keeps indefinitely when frozen.

FRUIT SLUSH

Mix together: 1 can (6 oz.) frozen orange juice
1 can (6 oz.) frozen lemonade
1 can (20 oz.) crushed pineapple and juice
1 pkg. frozen strawberries or 1 pt. fresh strawberries
2½ cups water
⅓ cup sugar
4 bananas, quartered and sliced crosswise

Freeze.

CRANBERRY SALAD

Grind coarsely 1 lb. pkg. cranberries. (Freeze the berries first and they aren't so messy to grind.)

Add 2 cups sugar and let stand awhile.

Drain 2 cups crushed pineapple and add to cranberry mixture.

Add 1 pkg. miniature marshmallows and mix well.

Let stand awhile.

Whip ½ pt. of cream and fold into mixture.

Keeps up to 4 days refrigerated and is best after it sits overnight.

MOM'S CHOCOLATE DROPS

Mash 1 boiled potato (medium sized).

Add: 4 tbsp. butter or margarine
4 oz. coconut
1 lb. powdered sugar (You may need more depending on the moisture of the potato.)

Mix to handling consistency.

Roll in balls, place on cookie sheet, and refrigerate.

Melt chunk chocolate.

Using a toothpick, dip each ball in chocolate and let set on waxed paper to harden.

Janet Twomey is that ray of sunshine in my life whom everyone needs at one time or another. She was a pillar of strength during my emotional growing-up years. I can always count on her to encourage me in whatever I try to accomplish. Janet's first love was popcorn, and I never see it without having warm thoughts and memories of my choice friend. I can't believe all the things you can do with popcorn.

Next time you buy popcorn to pop, remember there are two types available: the large yellow kernels and the smaller white ones. Please give them both a try. There is quite a delightful difference.

Instead of the usual hot, buttered popcorn, vary it with other seasonings like barbeque sauce or hot sauce, grated cheese, garlic powder, onion salt, taco seasoning, powdered chicken bouillon, oregano and basil, or a combination of any other herbs or spices. You'll be in for a taste treat, and you might make a delicious discovery on your own.

Did you know that popped corn can be ground in your blender or food processor? Just toss in a handful and blend until it's as fine as you wish. This ground popped corn has many uses—as a coating mixture for chicken, fish, or chops, sprinkled over a salad, or as a crumb topping for a casserole. It can also be added to casseroles and vegetable dishes as a meat extender. It really adds a nice flavorful touch. Use it in meat loaf, meatballs, stuffed peppers, macaroni and cheese, or tamale pie. When the popped corn is ground, it can be added to your flour mixture in making cookies, brownies, muffins, and even some candies.

Popcorn can even play an important part in the nutrition of your breakfast.

POPCORN CEREAL

Combine 2 cups popped corn and 2 cups boiling water.

Add a dash of salt.

Simmer together for 5 min., stirring often.

Cover the pan and let sit a few minutes.

Stir well and serve with milk.

Of course, if you're in a hurry, why not try a bowl of popped corn with a little milk and sugar and sliced fresh fruit. You'll be surprised!

Most of you already know my dear friend Marge Emery through her recipes in my other books, but I just want to share with you what a special person she is. Marge gave me so many guidelines while I was raising my young family and trying to be so much like her and other choice women I know. She counseled me to *"emulate not imitate"* all the good qualities I saw in others but to always remember that I was an individual. What a great help that was.

Since she lost her husband, she has also given me some wise advice. None of us should overlook the single person. When we are old enough to realize how important this is, it is often too late. Don't deprive them of doing a job or being involved; they need the activity and don't have families to go home to. Include them in your groups regardless of age. Widows often long to hear "man talk" like football games, weather, and politics again, and men like that feminine touch a woman adds to the evening. Touching is important to a single person. A handshake or pat on the shoulder can be worth millions. Now, a word to single people: enjoy sharing things—casseroles, desserts—learn how fun it is to give. Don't lose your knack of entertaining; enjoy people. Ask yourself, "Am I as happy as I can be? If not, what can I do about it?" Make it a point to get acquainted with your neighbors. Offer a helping hand to someone in need, volunteer to teach someone a skill that you have, and just learn to smile at everyone.

Marge often calls up a busy young family and asks, "How many are home for dinner? ... Five? Fine. I'll be right over," and then appears on their doorstep with apple dumplings or some treat for their mealtime.

In cooking for singles, don't limit yourself to cooking only small foods; you can cook a large roast and package in individual meals. Then make gravy, freeze it in cookie sheets, and cut it into squares and package. It takes up very little freezer space and heats quickly.

Marge is now remarried to a very special man, and I wish them a life full of sunshine. She is really a friend you can always count on, and you can count on her recipes being terrific, too!

This is so easy to do and it is inexpensive; serve a bunch or store in the freezer.

STRAWBERRY FLUFF

In *large* bowl combine: 2 egg whites
1 cup sugar
pinch of salt
1 small pkg. frozen strawberries

Beat with electric mixer for *20 min.*

Whip 1 cup whipping cream and fold into above mixture.

Line a 9 in. × 13 in. pan with vanilla wafer crumbs.
Pour on mixture and sprinkle the top with added crumbs and chopped nuts.

It will serve 18 people nicely.

This recipe is delicious served over rice.

HAWAIIAN MEATBALLS

Mix lightly: 1½ lb. ground beef
⅔ cup soda cracker crumbs
½ cup chopped onion
⅔ cup evaporated milk

Shape into about 40 balls.

Put about ½ cup flour in a plastic bowl and put about 5 balls at a time in the bowl. Cover and shake to cover the balls with flour.

Put balls on a cookie sheet and brown on both sides under the broiler. (This is really a fast, neat way.)

Make a sauce of:
1 can (13 oz.) pineapple chunks, drained
1 cup pineapple juice (Add water if necessary.)
2 tbsp. cornstarch
½ cup brown sugar
½ cup vinegar
2 tbsp. lemon juice
2 tbsp. soy sauce
1 cup coarsely chopped green peppers
1 tbsp. pimento

Cook together until thick.

Add browned meatballs, cover, and simmer about 15 min. Don't overcook or the peppers will lose their pretty green color.

I hope you have enjoyed meeting my friends and will enjoy using their recipes. We can gain so much from each other's talents and experiences. Don't wait until it's too late to say I love you and thanks for being my friend. Thanks, sunbeams!

7

"BUDDING" IDEAS FROM THE FAMILY TREE

Isn't it funny how one idea or suggestion can trigger another or how, out of necessity, we come up with money and energy-saving hints? (We always kept a box of old socks, and when the kids played in the snow, they wore these as mittens. There was always a dry change every now and then, and if one was "holey," they could double up and wear two on that hand. No more cold, wet hands!) These things just keep popping up like fresh buds on a tree in springtime if we nurture ourselves and our families with love. Love and happiness stimulate creativity. Here is a selection of ideas that are guaranteed to bring joy and smiles.

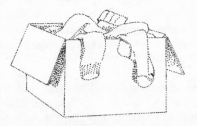

Frozen peas make a great snack for toddlers and tide them over until mealtime while you're busy cooking. Our little Jacob loves them.

A simple dip and fresh vegetable sticks are a good after-school snack that's nutritious for the older children as well as being a lot of fun to eat.

Don't overlook popcorn as a nutrition-packed snack, especially sprinkled with some grated cheese powder. (Check your Yellow Pages for national dairy distributors such as Borden's and Kraft. Many of them carry this delicious powder. It comes in large containers, but you could divide it with several friends. It's a terrific bargain for cooking and is delicious.)

A leftover sweet treat that my family always enjoyed was extra pie crust rolled out, cut in strips, and sprinkled with a mixture of cinnamon and sugar. Prick with a fork and bake at 425° until golden brown, about 10 minutes. Another treat was leftover pancakes spread with homemade jam and rolled up to make a "roly-poly." Another was leftover frosting spread between graham crackers to form sandwiches. (Heidi liked these so well, she thought I should make frosting just for this purpose.) Chocolate frosting with a "hint" of mint extract is yummy used this way.

When I'm baking, I always use my extra oven rack or a shelf from the refrigerator as a cooling rack on my kitchen counter. They are large enough to hold many things. If I am desperate for more cooling space, a muffin pan turned upside down works great, too.

That reminds me, *always* cool your pumpkin or custard-type pies on a cooling rack. *Never* set them directly on a cool, solid surface or your crust will get soggy.

To make a mock brick oven, get some unglazed

terra cotta tiles, soak in water for 24 hours, then preheat in oven for 30 minutes, and they are ready to use. Cover the oven rack with tiles and bake your bread or pizza on these. You'll have the best crust you ever tasted. It's not necessary to soak them after the first time. For a few cents, you'll get expert results.

To dust my cake tops, puddings, or cream puffs with powdered sugar, I just put a little powdered sugar in my strainer and shake it over the tops. It works beautifully.

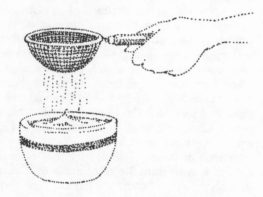

If you are making a cake or cookie recipe that calls for raisins, set the raisins in your preheating oven to warm through before adding to the batter. This will keep them from sinking to the bottom.

Remember a shiny pan is not a good baker. Things don't brown well.

When baking in glass, always lower the temperature 25°.

A little dash of nutmeg really adds a nice taste in chicken soup, and a dash of ginger in chocolate frosting will be a delightful change, too.

When making a recipe, I always read it clear through first and then assemble my ingredients before I start. This saves time *and* energy. It is nice if you can arrange your cupboards with all the baking needs in one area, the "lunch-making" necessities together, and so on. Mom always said, "Use your head and save your feet!"

A friend of mine color codes her recipe cards red for desserts, green for main dishes, blue for salads, and so on. She also sticks a color-coded star sticker by each recipe to indicate personal favorites. Yellow means Don's favorites, and silver is for Mary. I like that!

To save dirtying bowls when I make cookies, I cream my shortening and sugar together in a large bowl, push it to one side and beat the eggs on the other side in the same bowl, and then mix it all together and add the rest of my ingredients. I guess I'm lazy, but it sure works!

Also, when measuring my ingredients, I always put the eggs in the measuring cup first and then measure my shortening, molasses, or whatever, and they'll slip right out of the cup. It also works to rinse the measuring cup in real hot water before measuring the shortening. Again, it will slip right out.

One of the biggest helps to me when I was learning to cook was a list of substitutions and equivalents. Here are the ones I use most:

2 tablespoons flour = 1 tablespoon cornstarch
1 cup cake flour = 1 cup minus 2 tablespoons flour + 1 tablespoon cornstarch
1 square baking chocolate = 3 tablespoons cocoa + 1 tablespoon margarine or butter
1 cup sour milk or buttermilk = 1 cup regular milk + 1 tablespoon vinegar or lemon juice (Let stand a few minutes.)
2 mashed garlic cloves in a 1 pound box of salt = oodles of garlic salt
A vanilla bean in a canister of sugar eliminates the need to use vanilla when using that sugar in recipes.
1 regular marshmallow = 10 miniature marshmallows
1 cup sugar = ½ to ¾ cup honey (Adjust liquid in recipe.)
4 cups flour = 1 pound flour
2 cups sugar = 1 pound sugar
2 cups margarine or butter = 1 pound margarine or butter
10 graham cracker squares = 1 cup crumbs

1 cup uncooked regular rice = 3–4 cups cooked rice

1 orange = 6–8 tablespoons juice

1 lemon = 4 tablespoons juice

1 tablespoon = 3 teaspoons

¼ cup = 4 tablespoons

¾ cup whole wheat flour = 1 cup regular flour (in most recipes unless a light, fluffy texture is desired as in angel food cake)

Remember my delicious pancake syrup recipe I gave you in *A Family Raised on Sunshine*? If you don't use it up fast enough and find that it crystallizes in the bottom, next time you make a batch, add 2 tablespoons Karo corn syrup, and it will prevent that! Be sure and try it!

Frozen orange juice should not be thawed and mixed ahead of time and allowed to stand. As soon as it is thawed, it begins losing nutrients, so make it up fresh each morning. By the way, if you mix it in the blender, it returns some of the air to it, and it really tastes fresher.

A really fun and healthful breakfast for a cold winter morning is my apple surprise. Bake an apple ahead of time. (This can even be done the evening before when supper is cooking.) Heat the apple, fill the cavity with cooked oatmeal to which you have added a few raisins, and serve hot with milk or cream and brown sugar. You'll get raves from a healthy family.

Another delicious treat for breakfast is broiled grapefruit. Sprinkle a little brown sugar or honey on top of a half grapefruit and broil until browned and bubbly on top. This is so good with sausage and scrambled eggs.

SOME COOKING TIPS

Salt toughens eggs, so never add it until they are cooked.

Remember, as soon as you remove the food from any pan, fill it with hot water. That little step will save you lots of scrubbing later.

I keep a "casserole topping" bag in my freezer and toss into it any type cracker crumbs, chips, or bread crumbs. These crumbs add an interesting top to any type casserole dish. To make bread crumbs as "slick as a whistle," just toss ½ cup or so of broken-up bread in your blender and blend for a minute or two. Nothing to it and you'll be amazed at the beautiful crumbs.

Commercial gelatins are mostly all sugar, and it's so easy to make your own to eliminate the coloring, acids, and added sweeteners. Just sprinkle 1 tablespoon or 1 package of plain gelatin powder over ½ cup cold fruit juice. Stir over low heat until dissolved. Then remove from burner and add 1½ cup juice and ¼ cup sugar, if necessary. Fruits can be added in the usual way. Just remember never to add *fresh* pineapple to gelatins. Let stand until thickened in the refrigerator. You can make many exciting flavors and variations.

I'm surprised so many people don't know how to fry sausage properly. If you just try to "fry" it until it's done, you may have awfully crisp patties. Just put about ½ cup water along with your sausage in a skillet, cover, and steam it for about 15 minutes. Then remove the cover, drain off the liquid (*not* down the drain), and fry until lightly browned on each side. That way it will be well done without being overcooked and will be much better *for* you, also.

The principle of letting lost oxygen return is true with canned vegetables. They should be opened and allowed to stand in the saucepan at least 15–20 minutes before heating to regain the oxygen they lost in canning. I always open them and let them sit on the stove while I make my other meal preparations and then heat them through at the last minute. It really improves the flavor.

Be sure and develop the habit of turning the pan handles in or to the side when cooking at the range. Doing so will eliminate lots of spills and accidents.

Meat stocks are one of the most valuable items you can keep in your freezer. Then delicious soups, casseroles, and main dishes are a snap to make. *Never* throw a bone away. Cover that turkey carcass, pork roast bones, or whatever with water, onion, a little celery and carrots, salt and pepper, and let it simmer for a couple of hours. Then freeze in containers. You can make a rich beef stock by browning beef bones (the smaller the better—saw them up if you need to) on a cookie sheet in a 400° oven until dark brown and then proceed to make stock.

In Switzerland, a sweet little lady whom we stayed with showed me their secret of good soup. She took an onion, cut it in half, and set it cut side down on a *hot* stove until it was black (what a delicious aroma), then added it to the soup pot. I tried it on my electric burner, and it really works wonders; it adds color as well as flavor!

A couple of little tips will make lunch-box time easier for little ones. I split my cupcakes in the middle and frost sandwich style; it makes them

easier to eat. Also, draw arrows on the top of the thermos so they know which way to turn the lid. This can be a trying experience; I've watched many frustrated children trying to open their thermoses.

Four items I feel are invaluable in your kitchen drawer are scissors (for bacon, herbs, paper, string, etc.), a stapler (for lunches, chip bags, etc.), *sharp* knives, and a timer. I couldn't get along without these things. I think you'll find they are a big help to you, too.

I like cooking in cast-iron cookware. It does all the things manufacturers are trying to duplicate in modern-day cookware (nonstick, etc.), and chemists say we get valuable iron in the foods cooked in cast-iron utensils.

Whenever I open a bag or package of noodles, rice, coconut, popcorn, brown sugar, or anything, I always store the rest of the package in a glass jar in my cupboard. That way I can see what I have, and it saves the mess of spilled things all over the

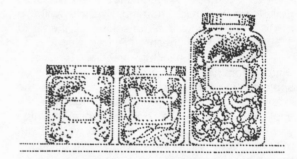

cupboard. I utilize any kind of jar—peanut butter, mayonnaise, and so on.

HOUSEHOLD HINTS

Since I buy most of my dry things in bulk and store them in large plastic containers, I save my bleach bottles, wash them well, let them sit in hot water about 15–20 minutes, and cut them for scoops. The hot water makes them easier to cut. The part you cut off is great for picnics or throwaway snack containers. They are neat sandbox toys, also.

In Germany, we were intrigued to see everyone have a small waste receptacle on the dining table.

This could be a little plastic bucket or basket. What an ingenious idea! It keeps the table neat and is great for those fish bones, corncobs, chicken bones, or peels that aren't eaten. We now use one at our house.

Save your little plastic berry boxes. They are so nice for a serving of potato chips or a nibbling snack.

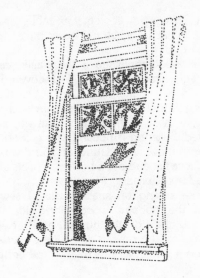

That extra iced-tea spoon works great in the jelly jar.

A cookie sheet covered with a finger-tip towel makes a handy TV or lap tray.

Keep a red and green magnet handy to indicate the status of your dishwasher—red for dirty, green for clean!

In the summer, never park your car in the sunshine if you can avoid it. The heat will cause your gas to evaporate, and the air conditioner will have to work lots harder to cool the car when you start driving.

To really save energy in the summer, open your doors and windows to let in the cool, shady morning air; then close the blinds and shades to the sun later in the day. This works in the reverse in the winter. Draw your blinds and shades to block out the cold and dark and open them to let in the sunshine. You'll be surprised what a difference this makes!

Before making a long distance call, I make a list of things I need to talk about and then set my timer. Our phone bill is never small, but this sure helps.

When I iron my tablecloths, I hang them over a pants hanger and hang them in my guest closet. They are easy to see, handy to use, and never wrinkled. (My girls think that's so clever!)

Setting up your ironing board and covering it with an oilcloth cover provides added serving room for patio parties and picnics. It also makes a great bedside table for an invalid since it's adjustable. Very roomy and useful!

A little body powder dusted on your hands makes it easier when doing needlework.

Sew a pocket in each corner of your picnic

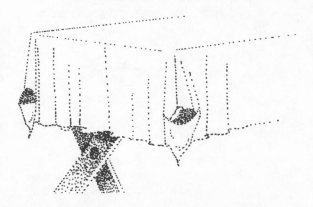

tablecloth. Then, when you set your table, you can put a rock in each pocket and never have a cloth blowing all over.

Heidi always complained if the elastic casing was too tight around sleeves. I discovered the simplest way is to make the casing, cut elastic the proper length, sew a hook and eye on each end, and thread it through the casing. That way it can be removed if altering is needed with growth, and it's great to remove when laundering, and you can iron the sleeve flat and put it back in. This is also a great idea for costumes.

To make sewing on snaps easier, I sew the halves with the "nubbin" on down one side of the material, rub chalk on the nubbin, and press the nubbins against the other side of the material so that there is a perfect mark where the other halves belong.

To fringe a fabric easier, make a long running machine stitch where desired. Then clip up to stitching every few inches. With a brush or needle, you can easily pull out the remaining threads.

I pin a safety pin through my last crochet stitch until I'm ready to start again. It keeps it from unraveling.

You can make a tiny embroidery hoop with a jar ring and a real tight rubber band.

Canvas work gloves trimmed with a cute appliqué on the back make nice gifts as hot pads. They work so well; I love mine.

When sewing and making crafts, don't forget the handicapped. Anyone with a physical impairment would appreciate an apron made from a

strip of fabric with a casing on top. Run a plastic waist hoop through the top and add some pockets. These are so easy to just clip on—no ties, buttons, or strings.

Begin now building a "gift drawer" or cupboard. In it, store gift wrap you buy *after* the holidays and used paper and ribbon you "iron" to use over. Pick up those little gifts when you see something "just right" on special and keep these tucked away. It sure saves time and money later when you run all over to find something like what you once saw!

When working on crafts, dampen your hands before using foam stuffing. It helps to keep it "under control."

Use an old empty ball-point pen to trace a pattern with tracing paper. It works so slick and leaves no ink marks.

A wallpaper sample book will provide many, many pretty placemats for a child or invalid. Just cut the edges with pinking shears.

One other thing that has been a big help to me many times is the definition chart of often-used prescription terms. It helps to understand the prescription your doctor gives you. Be sure and check when you have them filled to see if refrigeration is required and what foods you should and shouldn't eat with them. The doctor should tell you these things, but if he doesn't or you forget to ask, check with your pharmacist.

a.c.—before meals	dieb. alt.—every other day
agit.—shake	disp.—dispense
aq.—water	div.—divide
b.—twice	ex. aq.—without water
b.i.d.—twice a day	e.m.p.—as directed
c—with	gtt.—a drop
caps.—capsule	ad. lib.—as required for
d.—a day	preparation
d.—a dose	collyr.—eye wash

Enjoy your family and friends and entertain often. It doesn't have to be an elaborate dinner party. Just enjoy some companionship with easy entertainment and simple food.

FAMILY AND
GROUP ACTIVITIES

Why not have:

An old-fashioned ice cream party—make your own and have everyone bring toppings.
A pioneer taffy pull—assign each guest ingredients.
A sing along—everyone brings a favorite record.
A potluck dinner—be specific: a childhood favorite, family nationality dish, a dish beginning with the first letter of last name, and so on.
A game night—set up tables of old favorites: Chinese checkers, rook, dominoes, and maybe even a jigsaw puzzle. Every half hour or so, guests switch tables.
A "You're the Star" night—have each guest bring his twenty-five favorite slides. Serve popcorn and cold drinks.
A good mixer at any party is to have a "guest" scavenger hunt. Give each person a list as they arrive with questions like Who is a skilled artist? Who once fell into the Pacific Ocean? Who was the class valedictorian? Then have them mingle and get acquainted. Whoever has the most questions answered correctly by a certain time wins a prize.

One of our favorite mixers is to pin up many sheets of construction paper around the house, each one being numbered and having pictures on them depicting a guest's name. The guests have a numbered list and have to identify as many as possible by a given time. It is a real challenge to find pictures, and you may have to take liberties with some names, but it is really fun. Mary Brown may be depicted with a picture of a wedding for "Mary" and an item that is brown in color for "Brown." Sam Goldberg may be depicted with a picture of a *sand* pile for "Sam" and a watch for "Gold" and an iceberg for "berg." Give this one a try; you'll have many laughs, I promise you.

Here are some more family and group games we have had fun playing over the years.

This is my nose—everyone sits in a circle and the one who is "it" stands in the middle. He walks up to a player and, pointing to his ear, may say, "This is my eye," and quickly counts to ten. The player must then point to his *eye* and say, "This is my ear," before "it" counts to ten. If he goofs, he becomes "it." As this gets going fast, it can really be funny.

Chewing the raisin—tie a raisin exactly in the middle of a piece of string or thread 3 feet long. Then two people stand facing one another, and each puts one end of the string in his mouth. At the word "Go" they each chew as fast as they can, trying to get to the raisin first. Just warn them *not* to swallow the string!

Blow, wind, blow—divide players into two groups. Have the teams sit on the floor facing each other with a bed sheet between them. Taking the sheet in their hands, they each hold it stretched tightly under their chins. Someone drops a feather into the middle of the sheet. At the signal, the object is for everyone to blow as hard as they can and get the feather to blow off the opposite side of the sheet.

My cup runneth over—divide group into partners; players line up at one end of the room with their partners across from them at the opposite end. Each couple is given a full glass of water and a spoon. The partner must run across the room and feed his partner the water with the spoon without spilling any. The first couple with an empty glass wins.

Upset the fruit basket—everyone is seated on chairs in a circle. The player who is "it" stands in the middle. After whispering a different name of a fruit in each person's ear, he calls out two fruits. Those players must exchange chairs quickly without the person who is "it" getting a seat. The person who doesn't get a seat is "it." Occasionally, the person who is "it" may call out "upset the fruit basket," and everyone must change seats without "it" getting a chair.

Stack-up—each person is given twenty-five toothpicks; then, seated around a tall pop bottle, each person takes a turn laying one toothpick across the opening of the bottle. Continue in this manner until one person upsets the stack of toothpicks. He then must take all the toothpicks that fell. The object is to get rid of your toothpicks first.

Who am I?—sometimes in this busy world, our lives get so involved that we really don't know who our family members are and what they are all about. Set out a stack of old magazines, newspapers, and catalogues. Then give each person a sheet of construction paper, scissors, and glue. On the sheet of paper, list ten questions:

1. My favorite food
2. A type of place I like to go
3. My favorite color
4. A picture of my hobby
5. A job I would enjoy
6. Something I don't care for or am afraid of
7. Something I would like to own
8. Somebody I think is "special"
9. An animal I like
10. My favorite sound

Have family members paste corresponding pictures by the questions, and then try to discover whose page is whose. Then have each person explain his pictures and his reasons for choosing these. This is such a fun way to get reacquainted as a family and is an activity that can be adjusted to young or old members.

Be sure to keep a file card on each get-together so you remember which guests, which games, and which food. You'll be having so much good, old-fashioned fun enjoying your friends, you won't want to duplicate. It's amazing how enjoyable a simple evening can be when we turn off the TV.

I also keep a list of my menu pinned up in front of me while I'm preparing the meal for my guests. This serves as a constant reminder of what to do next and also helps me to remember a dish in the refrigerator that I made ahead and may forget to set out. (Guess I'm getting old; I need those lists!)

Socializing should be just that—having a pleasant, sociable time with friends and family. Elaborate entertaining is real work, so concentrate on socializing and enjoy. Don't worry about the faded rug, worn upholstery, dishes that don't match, or spoon handles dented by the disposal. We're all human beings with problems, but the burdens will be lighter and the smiles broader if we share a little love with one another.

A fun plan for a bridal shower is to have each guest bring her favorite recipe typed up and a package or can of the required spice. This gives the new bride a nice selection of spices to start out with. The hostess could supply a pretty recipe box.

At a shower for Shelli, our daughter-in-law, the hostess assigned each of the guests a time of day on the invitation, and we each brought a gift to coincide with that time. The gifts were so clever. She got a toaster for one of the morning hours, a popcorn popper for the eight o'clock evening time, and for the ten P.M. hour, she received a canister full of beans and a saucepan so she could put her beans on to soak at night! Everyone got a chuckle out of that.

Speaking of parties, we ran across the cutest idea and have started it for our grandchildren. We make a birthday banner each year on their birthdays from a 12 inch square of cream-colored canvas or duck-type fabric, hemmed, with a small dowel inserted across the top. This will resemble a child's building block. Then a large number (about

6 inches) is cut from bright-colored fabric and appliquéd on, signifying the birthday—1, 2, or 3, and so on. Each of the birthday guests signs the banner with a permanent magic marker, and a picture is taped along with the birthday child's height and weight on the back. These can be hung in his bedroom each year until he has a collection of every birthday past. Hung in a grouping, they form a stack of building blocks; later, they could even form a border around the room. What a treasure these will be as the child grows up.

When taking a gift to a baby, wrap it in a receiving blanket and pin with a new set of diaper pins. It makes such a pretty package.

I also purchase a newspaper on each birthday of my grandchildren and am keeping them in separate files to give them on their eighteenth birthday. Won't they be fun to read?

If you're stumped for a gift idea, why not give a "class" as a gift? Maybe your mother would like to learn how to paint, or your hubby might be interested in a foreign language. It will be a cherished gift, I'm sure.

You grandmothers who live far away from those little ones, get out your tape recorder and read a story book for them. Be sure and add personal comments as well as, "Now it's time to turn the page." Then package up the tape along with the book and make a child happy!

How about making a little grandma's comfort quilt for them—flannel on one side for warmth and coziness, and tricot on the other for a cool feeling on a hot or "trying" day. Using a layer of batting between, you could tie the quilt in an evening. (See instructions in *A Family Raised on Rainbows*.)

If your grandchildren come for a week or two to visit you, why not make them a scrapbook of activities, food you ate, things you saw, and record happenings and funny experiences. They will read and reread it, and it will be treasured as a special memory builder.

It is also fun to keep a grandmother's book on each child. Use it to collect their art work, letters, and pictures and add your feelings and thoughts occasionally. It will also be a treasure for them to have someday.

Many exciting and teaching toys can be made to give to children for just pennies, and they'll love them:

Finish a square of wood and pound in several rows of finishing nails part way. Accompanied by a box of colored rubber bands, give it to the child and he'll play for hours.

A roll of discontinued wallpaper and a box of crayons is a treat any little one will love.

A muffin pan with different-colored circles of felt pasted in the bottom of each cup along with a supply of pom-poms cut from pom-pom fringe in corresponding colors will be a great teaching aid and provide lots of enjoyment.

A square of pegboard and a bunch of colored golf tees can also keep little hands busy.

A magnifying glass or a magnet will be a gift any child will treasure.

A jar of big buttons and string to thread or a cardboard picture and a shoestring make a nice sewing card.

Learning as well as entertainment does not have to be costly, and children can be a joy. Let's take advantage of every minute. I'll always remember a picture of a little boy that I saw. He had on tattered pants and jam on his face, and hanging around his neck was a sign that read, "Please recognize me for what I am. My present appearance is deceiving!"

A bored child is a restless, unhappy child. Give him responsibility and he will soon be happier and learn a very valuable lesson. Even little 3-year-olds can pick up in their room, make their bed, empty wastebaskets, put silverware on the table, dust furniture, and scrub the tub. What a help to mommy and child.

Spend "one-on-one" time with your children; maybe a special hour each week with each child. Learn a new skill, sew, learn about nature, cook together, read aloud, or go to see something new and different.

Spend time building memories with your family. Make a family scrapbook, learn a new skill together, have a pioneer evening pulling taffy, or tell stories about ancestors, write a group letter to someone far away, have a hobby sharing night, or start a family project. Enjoy a special breakfast together and watch the sun rise. Do a good deed together now. Don't wait!

Plan a fun evening by giving each family member an invitation at breakfast to a "surprise supper." When they meet at the table, which you have previously set with a pretty centerpiece, give each one a designated amount of money and then go together to the grocery store. Each one can buy what he'd like for supper. When you come home, each one prepares his dish, and you all have fun enjoying your surprise meal. This is a great way to get to know each other better and learn skills at the same time.

Once a week, put a slip of paper under someone's plate with a subject listed on it and have them give an "after-dinner speech" about "My Happiest Day," "My Most Embarrassing Moment," "My Favorite Place," and so on. Or put a word on each person's plate and have them tell what they think about when they hear that word. Words might be wind, clouds, cat, music, airplane, and so on.

Why not record conversations on the cassette player? We keep picture records; why not voices? Think how much fun it would be to hear a loved one relate an incident 10 or 20 years from now.

With small children, when you are looking forward to an upcoming event, make a paper chain with links for the amount of days to wait. On each link, write a suggested activity or thought to do that day. This keeps them interested and involved without asking, "How many more days?"

Put rubber bathtub decals on seats of swings outdoors. This will save lots of slips and accidents.

It's fun to make personalized pillow cases for each young guest at a slumber party and have everyone autograph each other's with permanent marking pens.

Next time it snows, mix up some food coloring and water in containers and let your youngsters paint pictures in the snow with a small paint brush. They'll have a ball.

With toddlers, divide their toys in seven little boxes and get them a different box each day of the week. Everything will always seem new.

Save the daily comic strips for your children to color.

Let your children have the privilege of reading in bed for half an hour each night. It is a great relaxant, and they will develop a love of books.

A real cute "love me-teach me" quilt can be made on the same principle as the "Quiet Book" in *A Family Raised on Rainbows,* with each page being a quilt square.

Attractive food goes a long way in stimulating a child's appetite. Make that hot dog into a hot rod using the bun as the car, carrot slices for wheels, olives for headlights, and cheese and catsup for trimming. They'll love it.

As the kids and I used to travel a lot with Roy, we spent quite a bit of time sitting in the car waiting while he was at an appointment. I always tried to use this time as a learning experience. While we observed people walking by, we would discuss what kind of person he was—successful, happy, and so on. Through our little game, I hope the kids learned the value of a good image. How others see us *does* matter.

One of our friends has a bean jar for each child; a white bean stands for a good deed or special behavior, a brown bean for bad behavior. If a child gets all white beans in a week, he gets a special day of no chores. This is a cute idea with lots of possibilities. Let's start a bean jar for everyone today!

To keep a little one busy on a rainy day, give him various shapes of pasta and beans and let him divide and separate them in an egg carton or muffin tin.

Whispering will nearly always get a child's attention if he is upset or noisy. (This works for adults, too.)

Remember the family mail bag I told you about in *A Family Raised on Rainbows*? Why not have little red flags for each person; if they have had an upsetting day or are feeling "down in the dumps," they can put their flag on their mail pocket, and everyone will understand and show them a little extra love and consideration. You'd be surprised how well this works. We all need to cry help occasionally.

With children or teenagers, if there seems to be a problem, why not go on a walk or car talk. It's so much easier to discuss a problem as you walk or ride along one to one.

Occasionally, Roy used to take one of the kids out for breakfast on a Saturday morning. This gave them a chance to become closer and made it easier for me to get some work done.

Daddy-daughter dates and mother-son dates can be real special occasions, teaching social skills, sharing time and experiences, and helping the child to feel important.

Sincerely ask your children's opinions and then respect them. They are a somebody, too!

Teach your children to see. Too many people go through life missing all the beauties and pleasant things around them. Point out a dewdrop on a fresh rose, a new bud just opening, the design of a snowflake, a baby's precious smile, or a gentle old man's loving eyes.

Take a loved one or a friend on a "penny" hike. At each corner, flip the coin to see which direction to turn. You'll be amazed at the many things you see before you return home.

Spend an evening dancing as a family. You might want to invite another family to join you. Roll back the rugs and try everything from the old waltz to disco and rock. One of our favorite evening activities when the kids were all home was exercising to the "Chicken Fat" record by Robert Preston. If you can find a copy, give it a try. It is really terrific.

Read to your family. Even the youngest will gain from this. Help them to understand. Get them involved by making sounds or asking questions. Reading to the whole bunch doesn't take any longer. Choose things that are exciting and put yourself into it. Boredom and indifference will be just as catching as your enthusiasm!

Encourage children in art. They remember what they do far more than what they see or hear. Have the young ones draw pictures of their day's activities or for a grandma or holiday. Their art work can be slipped under a clear plastic tablecloth to be enjoyed at mealtime. Art can be done and enjoyed by all members of the family whether it's a "Welcome Home" sign strung across the front door for daddy, personalized Christmas and birthday cards, paintings, or needlework.

Before leaving on a vacation, let the children draw "bingo" cards with various objects in each square. They can then be used to play the game as you travel. It's much more meaningful if they made the cards themselves.

Sing together. You can even sing messages like "Put your toys away." Whistle, hum, or sing while you're working. It's contagious.

Play charades and act out favorite stories for a family activity. This does wonders for a child's confidence and self-esteem.

Build and create together, whether it's a bookcase, furniture, or a fence.

Encourage writing poetry, letters, stories, and so on, and have each family member keep a personal journal. Remember, you will be someone's ancestor someday, and how special it would be to have a handwritten journal of your life.

A special friend of mine has a loose-leaf notebook in which she puts all the letters she received from her family and friends. Her first one dates back many, many years. What a priceless possession!

All of these things bring about activities and traditions that bind families together and help us each to build a better world with happy, well-adjusted, and self-confident people.

If you live alone, why not plan a week of sunshine? On the first day, give the "hand" of sunshine to someone by writing a letter or making something for someone by hand. On the second day, give the "voice" of sunshine with a cheery phone call or visit in person. On the third day, give the "heart" of sunshine by doing a kind deed for someone in need. On the fourth day, give the "mind" of sunshine by sharing a book or helping someone with a skill to develop their intellect. On the fifth day, give the "taste" of sunshine by sharing a special casserole or dessert with someone. On the sixth day, give the "rays" of sunshine by smiling at everyone you meet. On the seventh day, give the "warmth and soul" of sunshine by giving love to someone who needs it most.

A most thoughtful gift, whether it's for the newlyweds, a wedding anniversary, a new baby, a birthday, or just for a shut-in, is a bunch of bulbs, some mulch, and a planting tool. Many, many months of enjoyment will come from a gift like this. Why not twenty-five tulip bulbs for that twenty-fifth anniversary or fifty for a fiftieth birthday?

Thoughts and sayings have always been a good source of learning for me. These things really stick in my mind, and hardly a day passes but one pops up and applies to something I'm doing. I'm sure you have your old favorites like:

Look before you leap.
Don't count your chickens before they're hatched.
A penny saved is a penny earned.

But here are some fun (and true) ones that aren't so common that I get a real chuckle out of:

The tongue, being in a wet place, is likely to slip when going fast.

You have what you save whether it's money or dirty dishes.
Every man knows where his own shoe pinches.
The biggest mistake is the fear that you will make one.
If you're at the end of your rope, tie a knot and hang on.
It is never wise to argue with a fool; bystanders won't know which is which.
There may be destiny shaping our end, but our middles are our own "chewsing."
Just think how happy you would be if you lost everything and then suddenly got it back.
A wise man has long ears, big eyes, and a short tongue.
A man who will never change his mind may not have a mind to change.
When obstacles get in your way, be like the wind; whistle and go around.
Ideas are like children; your own are wonderful.
Give some people an inch and they think they are rulers.
If you make your job important, it will return the favor.
You are doing your best only when you are trying to improve what you are doing.
A clear conscience makes a soft pillow.
Each day is the only one of its kind.

New ideas help us to learn, grow, and change. Life involves constant change, and when we are through changing, we are through! So feed your family and loved ones with encouragement, happiness, and love and your family tree will be full of buds of creativity and enthusiasm for life.

8
FROM CHAOS TO CONTENTMENT

Nothing can bring sunshine into your heart and a rainbow over your roof like a little organization. Some folks are natural-born organizers, and system and order come automatically to them. Others, however, have not developed this knack and become a bit discouraged by their shortcomings. They might even feel so inadequate compared to those who seem to accomplish things so easily that they don't even have the time to begin. Of course, the media leads us to believe that everyone is a bundle of energy, never tiring and always coping with every problem. This can be very disheartening, especially when you don't feel or look like the person on TV.

When our chores go undone—dishes piled up, house a mess, paperwork never finished—we find that the worse the situation gets, the worse we feel and vice versa. Then, usually out of desperation, we try to turn over a new leaf and get totally overwhelmed, realizing there is no way we can do everything. Herein lies the key! We *can't* do everything, but we can do *something*, and that's exactly the way to start. We are only human, but we are a "special" human being with needs, talents, and abilities.

My old philosophy of a positive attitude and wearing a smile is never more important than when your life needs some organization.

Begin by making a list to rid your mind of the old cobwebs and start building some self-esteem:

Column I—
things that really count in my life (If I had a week to live, how would I spend my time?)
Column II—
things I love to do (Have you ever asked someone what they would do if they could do anything they wanted? Their eyes light up, and a zest for living suddenly becomes contagious.)
Column III—
what special talents and abilities I have
Column IV—
my weaknesses
Column V—
what goals I want to accomplish in one year, in five years

After spending some time pondering these things, it's amazing how much better you'll feel about yourself. Whether you're a wife, a bachelor, a single parent, or a widow, you must begin getting your life in order by liking yourself. I'm sure you know the feeling; when you like yourself, *everything* seems terrific, even scrubbing the dirty kitchen floor. You feel as if you could conquer the world, even pass up that delicious hot apple strudel for dessert! You feel like throwing your shoulders back and smiling at everyone you meet. When you don't like yourself, life is yukky! You'd rather eat an extra piece of chocolate cake or take a nap than work. You don't want to talk to anyone or do anything, and soon you start worrying about trivial things or become cynical.

I'll never forget a story a good friend told me once. There was a man driving down a country road at night. As he drove along, he passed a house with a light on. A few miles down the road, he had a flat tire and realized he didn't have a jack in the trunk. Recalling the house with the burning light he'd passed down the road, he decided he

would walk back and borrow a jack. However, as he began walking, he started thinking and talking to himself. "Golly! By now," he said, "they may have already turned out the light." Worrying about this for a few minutes, he thought, *Oh, then I may awaken them, and they will be upset.* Farther down the road, he thought, *They will probably be very angry and not want me to borrow their jack.* And a little later, *They may even shout and scream at me for bothering them.* At this point, he reached the front door and hesitantly rang the bell. By the time someone answered the door, he was in such a state of mind he just stammered, "I don't want to borrow your old jack, anyway," and stormed off the porch! Isn't this exactly what we do by letting our imaginations run away with us when our self-esteem is low?

Concentrate on having days when you like yourself. Give yourself a pat on the back once in a while. You're a pretty neat person! Read and reread that list. As you go to bed at night, don't itemize the things you didn't get done; think of the good things you did. You'll have a peaceful sleep and awake refreshed.

Getting up an extra half hour early to spend that time just on yourself will pay dividends all day long and is worth so much more than that 30 minutes' sleep. For me, an ounce of morning is worth a pound of afternoon. Use the time to go for a brisk walk, do some reading, or spend it on a hobby. Then take the time to make yourself look nice and *you'll* like *you* all day long. When you care for yourself, you can think of others. Have you ever gone to a party when your slip was showing or maybe your shirt collar wouldn't lie flat? You are forever tugging and pulling, and your mind is on you and not on your activities or responsibilities. If you first take care to put yourself in order, then you can relax and truly think of others!

In taking care of yourself, besides eating balanced meals and regular exercise, keep that list in mind and concentrate on being a happy individual, accomplishing your goals.

In your new daily schedule, take a "2 minute break" once during each heavy task. If that doesn't sound like much, watch the clock and see how many pleasant things you can think of for those 2 minutes. You'll feel so refreshed. Touch up your makeup or comb your hair. If you've been sitting, stand up, or vice versa. A 2 minute change really helps. Make a quick "I love you" phone call. Whistle or sing a favorite tune. Fertilize and "mist" a plant. The nurturing will make you feel good inside.

Most of all, don't be too hard on yourself. If there are things about you that make you unhappy, you can change! *Do it* and be happy with who you are. Make a conscious effort to love life and it will be like that smile. Soon it will be there automatically.

Now we're ready to tackle the business at hand, organizing and scheduling time. My bulletin board contains my pattern for life, and I couldn't get along without it. If you find yourself jotting down notes on scraps of paper and misplacing them, making lists in notebooks and then losing the notebook, or having stacks of papers and clutter around or even trying to keep everything in your head, then I suggest it's time you get a bulletin board. Now everyone knows that before you can build a house or sew a dress, you need a pattern; so the bulletin board can do exactly that with structuring your life. You may want to have different types of paper or varicolored cards for each list or item because you can tell at a glance what you need to refer to. Keep one card or list of:

Long-range goals—
a craft you want to learn
a foreign language to master
weight to lose or gain
Weekly goals (or monthly if necessary)—
errands to run
meetings and appointments
projects to finish
deadlines to meet

I use a calendar with large squares for this one.

Daily chores—
clean the bathroom
mend shirts

weed the garden
scrub the floor
attend the meeting

I love this list because of the satisfaction I get as I cross things off when they are completed. I never make my daily list the night before, as some recommend. I find that I lie down and worry about the list at night if I do, so I prefer to check my weekly or monthly schedule and then make my daily list first thing in the morning. Sometimes I even write down a few fun things for added incentive. (Smell the fresh lilacs in the back yard or stop and listen to the birds singing.)

Fun things to do—
those books you'd like to read
scrapbooks to update
a movie you'd like to see

Just having these things spelled out in front of you will give you a real "together" feeling. And remember, the lists will change, so be flexible and update them often.

When planning your routine or schedule, remember it takes just that—some planning and thinking. These things don't happen by accident, so allow yourself the planning time to sit down with a pencil and paper. This can be done while you're waiting at the doctor's office, in the morning before the family gets up, while the iron is heating, or while the cake is baking.

To get on the right track, a few steps are required:

1. *Organize the necessary tasks.* Some things must be routinely done—like the meals, housework, laundry, and so forth.

   Plan your meals by the week or month in order to save trips to the grocery store and time on extra busy days.

   To keep your housework at a minimum, have a place for everything and *keep it there.* If you need an extra blanket in the dark, you'll be able to find it, and little Mary's shoes will be there when it's time to dress for school.

My publisher told me once that an efficient executive strives to only handle a piece of paper once. If this works for business, why not at home? When you finish with a dish, why not rinse it and put it in the dishwasher? When you take off your blouse, why not hang it in the closet immediately? When you change that diaper, why not rinse it and put it right in the diaper pail? It sure makes life simpler and frees up time in the long run. It takes much more energy and time to wipe up a spill that has dried and hardened. So do it now and save minutes for later!

2. *Outline each morning what* must *be done in order of importance.* They say work expands to fill the time available, and this is certainly true. It's surprising how two things on the list can take all day or an extra two or three things can be added and get finished, also. Remember how fast you cleaned through the house when you learned relatives were coming?

   By looking at your list of things to do, it will help you remember to stop at the cleaners on the way to the grocery store and save you an extra trip and valuable time. Those saved minutes become precious and treasured. The more careful we are with them, the more valuable and useful our time will be. These minutes actually make up our *lives.*

3. *Keep in mind that many hands make light work.* If you have a large family, laundry can be quite a chore. Why not have a box or basket for each person labeled with his name. These are kept in their rooms for dirty clothes. Then, on laundry day, all baskets are carried to the laundry area. After the clothes are washed and folded *immediately* from the dryer (this saves much ironing, keeps things looking nicer, and gives everyone more pride in their things), put the clothes back into each person's container for them to put away. Stuff from pockets can also go into their basket or box. If you do not have a table

nearby, remember to keep the dryer top free from clutter so that this space is available to fold clothes on. For those of you who are single or a couple, those stackable plastic vegetable bins are great to keep in the laundry area. I use them as load sorters, one basket for whites, one for darks, and one for coloreds. As I gather up laundry each morning, I just drop it into the appropriate basket, and I can easily see which load needs to be done. That way I can do a load every couple of days and always keep ahead of things.

All household members, no matter how small, can be a great help around the house. *However,* nothing is more important than making sure they know *how* to do a job well. Work along with them until they understand it. Once you teach them, you can delegate chores and feel comfortable knowing they will be done right. A small child can dust furniture, set the table, fold socks, and help put things away. If they grow up learning everything has its place, it will become a habit to put it there. If scattered toys are a frustration to you, why not make large drawstring bags out of fabric like denim or duck. Then use shortening cans or cottage cheese containers to hold the smaller pieces inside the bag. These bags are easy to fill and can be hung on a little hook in the playroom or bedroom. Of course, the one positive rule is that no second bag is opened until the first one is picked up and put away. This worked at our house.

After you teach the children how to do things, give them full responsibility. Give them specific instructions, answer all their questions, then *don't take over*! Relax, enjoy the help they give you, and be appreciative and flexible. Nothing deflates an ego and ruins incentive like criticism and lack of enthusiasm. (This goes for husbands and wives as well!)

Job charts are a terrific way to distribute work without fuss. One method is a chart with pockets (a pocket for each person).

Jobs are then outlined (or pictures drawn for little ones) to inform each one of their responsibilities. Another idea is a rotating wheel made from two circles of cardboard, the inside one with each person's name and the outer circle listing jobs to do. Our kids each had a little "job jar" with slips of paper listing things to be done. On the list, they would often find "free day" or "time for an ice cream cone." Little incentives never hurt!

As part of learning responsibility, children should know that there are rules that everyone needs to obey if there is to be order in our homes. A friend of mine had a rule that if anyone left his bed unmade, the next day he had to make everyone else's beds. Be careful of too many rules and not enough love, though; and be sure that the "punishment fits the crime."

Above all, be consistent. Set up a routine and schedule *with the whole family*. You'll find everyone more willing to do their work if they have a voice in the plan.

You may like to set up an incentive plan. Have a chart with each job worth a certain number of points: mowing the lawn, 25 points; dusting the furniture, 10 points; doing the dishes, 15 points; and so on. Then these points can be collected to use for a movie, a trip to the library, an afternoon at the swimming pool, or a new book. (Each requires a set number of points.) It's amazing how much all of us can do for a bonus! You'll find the children tackling jobs they never would have thought of. This plan works exceptionally well in the summer when everyone wants to enjoy lots of activities.

You'll soon discover that by enlisting everyone's help at home, the burden will be lighter for you, helping you to have more time for your hobbies and interests as well as teaching your family the proper use of time and money, learning skills, and most of all, pride in a job well done. Of course, the most beneficial underlying advantage is the sense of being needed, one of the most valuable gifts we can give our children!

4. *Be realistic in your goals.* Remember the little slogan above my kitchen sink. "You can only peel one potato at a time." Don't start several projects at once and finish none of them. Spread out big projects and pace your energies. Don't try to clean the oven and the refrigerator on the same day. Alternate big and small jobs.

Plan tasks for appropriate times. Don't scrub the kitchen on Friday if the boys will be doing the yard work and tracking grass clippings in on Saturday. Don't clean your oven and cabinets the day before your girls have a slumber and cookie-baking party.

Do the most difficult jobs or the ones you like the least when your energy level is the highest.

Don't try to do things too fast. As Mom says, "Haste makes waste."

Sit down when you can. You're not a machine, so rest while you work if you feel the need.

Eliminate that nervous strain. Don't fight it. If the drippy faucet bothers you, do something about it. If the rug continually slips, put a piece of foam rubber under it. Many times, our work seems twice as difficult because of annoying little things we could eliminate.

Dovetail your work. Curl your hair while the little ones are in the tub or clean the kitchen cupboard while supper is cooking.

5. *Get the jump on the job.* Plan ahead. Don't wait until suppertime to decide what you'll serve. Press the clothes when you wash them so you aren't trying to iron a blouse as you hurry to get ready for an important event. Have a "double" cooking or baking day to stock the freezer. Then you're prepared for those unexpected rush meals.

It's so much easier to keep working a little to stay on top than it is to work like the dickens to constantly try and climb up the heap.

Now the next step is to make a schedule. I have a regular "daily" routine. First, I make my list for the day, consulting my weekly calendar so that I'm prepared for any commitments. Then I "run" through the house and tidy up. A pair of old work socks are my favorite helpers. I put one on each hand as I zip through each room. One hand wipes off any obvious dust, and the other wipes off the chrome faucets, and so on. Since this one gets a little damp, it is great for wiping fingerprints off the woodwork or walls. I take my little squirt bottle with me so I can "mist" the plants in each room as I go. (They love it!) I also empty wastebaskets and sweep up where it's needed. I do a load of laundry as necessary. By doing this, the house is always fairly neat and gives us all a sense of well-being.

On Mondays, I also include any heavy ironing, mending, or general clothes repair that is necessary. Tuesday is my "errand and meetings" day. On Wednesdays, I try to include one major cleaning job such as washing windows, doing up curtains, waxing floors, cleaning a closet, or defrosting the refrigerator. Thursday is usually baking and cooking day, and I try to fill the freezer by doing things in quantity. If necessary, I do any grocery shopping for "specials" I need in the early morning. On Fridays, I clean through the house well. (When the children were small, they cleaned their rooms too, and any other area as needed when they came home from school. I miss those helpers now!) Saturday is "Family Fun Day." We always preferred working a little harder and faster on Friday afternoons to have everything shipshape so that we didn't have to work all day Saturday. However, Saturday mornings do include *some* yard work if needed. Sundays are a complete change of routine for me—attending church, reading, relaxing, and spending some time on a favorite hobby. Then I'm refreshed and ready to start a new week with enthusiasm.

To establish a daily and weekly schedule for your house, first remember, plan for *your* particular needs. Don't try to live by others' standards. Analyze your resources—number in family, budget, your energy and health, and your home and equipment. Ask yourself, "What is most important to accomplish for us?" and, "When do these things need to be done?" Then set up a simple schedule and follow it as closely as possible. If this is a new procedure for you, you may want to be specific at first:

Time	Plan	Memos
6:30–7:00	Take care of me. Make bed.	Check that scale!
7:00–9:00	Make, serve, and clean up breakfast. Do one load of laundry. Straighten main floor of house.	Take food from freezer for dinner.
9:00–11:00	Tidy upstairs of house. Do today's chore.	
11:00–11:15	Rest or relax and read.	
11:15–12:30	Prepare lunch, eat, and clean up.	
12:30–2:00	Have children take a nap. Do my special projects.	
2:00–4:00	Do weekly chores.	
4:00–4:45	Spend time with children.	Johnny needs some special attention this week!
4:45–7:00	Prepare dinner, eat, and clean up.	
7:00–8:30	Spend time with family.	
8:30–bedtime	Do special projects and take time for me.	

Weekly chores will be ironing, windows, menu planning and shopping, cleaning the oven and stove, cupboards, and so on. Monthly or seasonal chores will be cleaning closets, cleaning drapes and rugs, canning and freezing foods, and so on. You'll really be amazed at how simple everything is if you have a daily and weekly plan. Just don't allow yourself to get distracted on the way to a sink full of dishes or you'll spend all day at the sewing machine or whatever and never get caught up.

Here's some little tips that may help you on your daily routine.

KITCHEN

As you clean up after the dinner hour, set the table and make any necessary preparations for breakfast. If you pack lunches, utilize any leftovers from dinner (roast beef, chicken) and prepare sandwiches or package food and refrigerate, ready to pack in the morning.

Arrange your cupboards so that dishes are closest to the dishwasher, baking supplies are all in one place, pans close to the stove, and so on.

Keep all your appliance cords together in a drawer with an elastic band around each one or cover toilet tissue tubes with contact paper and store one cord in each tube. (Covering or decorating these tubes is a great rainy-day project for youngsters and a nice help to you.)

If you use soap-filled scouring pads, cut them in quarters. They work just as well, you stretch your budget, and a small one makes a lot less mess.

If you have a self-cleaning oven, turn it on to clean right after you have finished cooking in it. This really saves on the electricity since it is already hot.

When you need extra counter space, just pull out a drawer and place a cookie sheet on it.

I hate to waste money on disposable paper cups for drinking. It's more economical to have a mug rack hung near the sink with personalized or color-coded mugs for each person.

Always peel vegetables, husk corn, or do any messy job on a newspaper. It's so much easier to clean up. I always grate my cheese on a piece of Handiwrap for this reason, also.

Don't forget to clean all the crumbs out of the toaster every so often. It will work more efficiently, and you won't have those crumbs burning.

After a meal, we have a rule that each person is responsible for putting his dirty dishes in the dishwasher plus one other thing. That sure helps in clearing the table. (Guests don't mind this, either.)

Be sure you wipe off all bottles, jars, and containers before putting them away. That saves lots of hard cleaning and scrubbing later on.

Washable throw rugs are invaluable in helping to keep the floor clean. Keep them in front of the sinks and by each outside door especially.

One of my biggest kitchen time savers is my *long* telephone cord. Projects never have to stop for that phone call.

I never use dustpans; they are a frustration to me. I vacuum where I can, and when I sweep, I dampen a paper towel and gather up the dust and dirt and throw it all away.

Each time you bake a cake, cookies, or whatever, wrap up a few single servings and freeze. They are great to grab for lunches.

To really save time and energy and boost your spirits, why not trade dinner with a friend once a week. This is terrific whether you have a family to feed or live alone. It's just as easy to fix a double batch of something. Maybe you can have a break on Thursdays and return the favor on Mondays!

LAUNDRY

Anything with ties or sashes should be turned inside out to eliminate tangles.

I keep an old razor on my ironing board to "shave" the little "pills" or lint balls off wool or polyester clothing.

If you have little ones at your house, proper laundering of diapers is vital. Diapers should be thoroughly rinsed immediately after changing, then put in a covered diaper pail. Run through a complete *cold* rinse cycle and then launder with detergent or soap and a small amount of bleach. One-half cup of vinegar in the final rinse water will help eliminate diaper rashes. *Be sure* all soap is rinsed out. If there are still traces of soap in the final rinse water, you should rinse again and stop using as much soap.

Built-up soap is one of the biggest causes of dingy wash, so check your regular laundry loads occasionally to see if you are using too much detergent and not getting it all rinsed out.

Keep your laundry area as attractive as possible. Your time there should be enjoyable, too. Make sure you have adequate hooks and lines to hang things from the dryer. They will only cost a few cents and will save many dollars worth of valuable time.

SEWING AREA

While you are sewing or mending, why not have your tape recorder handy and listen to some educational tapes (you could learn that foreign language) or record a tape to a friend or relative. They are even more fun than letters, and you'll be making double use of your time.

I use small boxes and lids as compartments in my sewing drawers to hold zippers, tape, snaps, and so on. It's a real time saver.

I store my large pieces of fabric in big plastic garbage bags or new large trash cans and then tape sample swatches of each piece on the outside or lid. I can tell in a minute what I have.

Recycling clothes is a great saver, also. To make children's mittens from old sweaters, put the child's hand on heavy paper (I use a grocery bag) and trace around to make a pattern. Then cut out mittens using the bottom sweater ribbing as the mitten cuff. Put right sides together and sew a ½ inch seam using a close zigzag stitch. They are really neat. You could even use some scraps of yarn and embroider on them if you had time. Matching hats can also be made this way. Just use the bottom sweater ribbing for the band of the hat. Cut it as long as you want and gather up the top with a tassle or pom-pom.

Men's worn shirts make great sleep shirts for young teenagers. I remove the collar and trim the shirt with a little lace, eyelet, embroidery, or appliqué.

An easy, fast, and inexpensive way to appliqué is to put a piece of Handiwrap or bread bag over the area on which you're going to appliqué. Position appliqué, then cover *completely* with a brown paper bag. Iron with a hot iron. The plastic will stick to the bag and hold the appliqué in place. You are then ready to stitch around it without any slipping.

If your nightie is getting a little worn at the top, why not cut it off and make a half slip.

Before putting clothes in the rag bag when they are totally worn out, I always cut off all buttons, zippers, snaps, and trims. These have been reused *many, many* times.

Corduroy skirts and jumpers can be converted into cute little play clothes for toddlers because of the ample material.

BATHROOM

If you have more than one bathroom, it is just as economical and saves much time to have a supply of cleaning needs in each room.

Be sure you get *everyone* into the habit of wiping the shower down after *each* use. You may wash a few more towels, but you'll be absolutely amazed how much work you'll save cleaning that shower stall occasionally.

Before your shower curtain and rubber mat get too soiled or mildewed, toss them in the washer with a couple of old bath towels, some detergent, and ½ cup vinegar. They are a breeze to *keep* clean.

If keeping the towel hung up is a problem with your young children, simply use a couple of diaper pins and pin the towel, from the back, over the rod. Be sure towels are within their reach.

When there are several girls in the family, buy a full-length mirror and hang it crosswise above the sink. Sure saves frazzled nerves!

LIVING ROOM

Be sure and vacuum rugs and drapes often. It will eliminate lots of cleaning bills or elbow grease later on.

Don't be tempted to use carpet scraps as throw rugs over your carpeting; the coarse backing will wear on your carpeting. Use regular throw rugs where necessary. The best use for carpet scraps is to cover the basement steps. Boy, does that save a lot of tracking, and it looks nice, too.

My kids tell me that the thing they remember best when being taught about cleaning is that as you dust, work your way around the room in a circle and work from the top to the bottom. Dust and *then* vacuum the floor, and so on. This eliminates doing things twice.

BEDROOMS

Line children's drawers with white shelf paper and then draw pictures or write socks, underwear, shirts, and so on, so they can keep things in the right places. For young ones, you might even want to put pictures on the outside of each drawer. Children enjoy being neat, and if they have a proper place, they can manage easily.

I line my dresser drawers with leftover wallpaper to match the room. It looks so pretty.

Never throw away those old pillow cases. They sure make neat covers to slip over hangers storing out-of-season clothes. It just requires a small hole at the top.

I've found that my luggage also makes a great place to store out-of-season clothes when I'm short on drawer space.

Don't get in a rut and use the same sheets each week. As you launder them, put them at the bottom of the stack so you rotate the wear.

Use a quilt or comforter on beds to speed up bed making. This is especially easy for young children, although adults also appreciate the convenience. Roy and I bought a feather comforter in Europe and really enjoy saving time each morning. All it requires to make the bed is to flip it back and fold it over. (Feels great at night, too!)

Never store your blankets or comforters in a plastic bag unless you make a few small holes or slits in it. They need air.

A neat way to store baby blankets is to fold them over a hanger and hang them in a closet.

Remember to turn all mattresses often. This will prolong their life considerably.

Always have hooks and rods within reach of children to motivate neatness. And supply a wastebasket in each room!

When I clean a closet, I put an old sheet over the bed and then empty the closet, putting everything into three categories: discard, repair, and hang back in closet. Then I vacuum and dust the closet and wax the rod and put things back. It's always easier to keep neat if everything is kept up off the floor. Then the secret is to discard immediately and repair right away so your wardrobe is in good shape. I hang things in groups—all blouses, all skirts, dresses, nightgowns, and so forth—and remember to have all hanger hooks going the same way.

In general, the two rules that will help the most are: (1) use each room for its purpose (eat in the kitchen, dress in the bedrooms, etc.). This can soon become a family habit if the proper facilities are arranged. (2) Eliminate clutter. Don't hesitate to throw things away that are useless and dust collectors.

The heavy cleaning can be accomplished several ways. Some people like to do a room or two a month. I prefer to have a big cleaning spring and fall. I completely do one room at a time; it usually takes me two or three weeks to finish the house, allowing for other things in my schedule. The kids always looked forward to this time because this was when we rearranged furniture and added some new wallpaper, picture grouping, or other forms of new decor. It is always such a good feeling to have everything spanking clean and fresh!

I do the bedrooms first so that we all have a comfortable "retreat" as we clean the other rooms, and I leave the kitchen and laundry area until last so that is a working point while we clean the rest of the house.

HEAVY CLEANING

Bedrooms
First I clean the closet well, hanging all the clothes out on the clothes line to air so they go back in the closet smelling fresh.
Then wipe down all walls.
Clean each dresser, vacuuming out the drawers.
Turn the mattress and wash all bedding.
Clean all windows. Remember to wash the screens. (If you wash the glass sparkling clean and leave the screen full of dust and dirt, your window won't stay shiny very long.)
Wash, air, or clean curtains or drapes, as needed.
Polish furniture.
Clean and polish floor or shampoo carpet.

Bathrooms
Clean or dust walls.
Wash windows.
Wash rugs, shower curtain, mats, and curtains.
Clean out medicine cabinet.
Clean toilet well.
Clean sink and polish chrome.
Clean tub and shower.
Treat all drains.
Mop and wax floor.
Hang curtains.

Living Room and Family Room
Completely clean fireplace.
Dust walls.
Wash windows.
Wash, air, or clean draperies.
Clean pictures, ornaments, mirrors, and decorations.
Clean all bookcases, cabinets, and so on. Don't forget heat vents, registers, and light bulbs and fixtures.
Vacuum or clean upholstered furniture.
Polish furniture.
Wax floor or clean carpeting.

Kitchen

Empty and scrub cupboards.
Arrange cupboard contents for convenience.
Thoroughly clean range, oven, and refrigerator inside and out.
Clean all walls, woodwork, and vent or fan.
Wash windows and curtains.
Clean the sink and drain well.
Finish with the floors.

Those shining floors and sparkling windows will make you feel like royalty, and your home will truly be your castle.

Now that your house is in order, there are several things you may want to add to your list for organizing.

Record keeping can be a tremendous help. I prefer a small file cabinet. In it, I keep files for gardening ideas, decorating ideas, hobbies and crafts, warranties and guarantees, thoughts and ideas for speaking engagements, holiday ideas, house upkeep ideas, and so on. It's a good idea to keep a record of the name of the paint you used in the bedroom and how much it required, when you last changed the furnace filter, when the front yard was fertilized, and when you had the drapes cleaned. A health file is really beneficial for records of shots, diseases, medicines taken, accidents, and so forth. If you have a file for each of these things, it's so easy to just jot things down at the time. It frees your mind from trying to remember and saves literally hours of time later on.

A budget is absolutely crucial in every household. Allocate your money before you get it; don't just record what you spend and think you're managing your money. First, figure your actual "take home" pay, not your gross income. Then distribute this amount into categories such as housing, food, transportation, clothing, and so on, but always pay yourself something *first* in a savings account. After distributing your money into these areas, the key thing is to spend it wisely. I hope I have given you some ideas and helps. (When Roy and I were first starting out, we found the best way for us was to actually divide our money into envelopes for food, rent, gas, etc. It was good discipline for us.)

As a guideline in your purchases, you may like to keep in mind the best months to watch for sale items:

January—
white sales (all linens, towels, etc.)
furniture
coats
shoes

February—
housewares
electrical appliances
winter clothes
used cars

March—
tires
winter clothes
gardening supplies

April—
men's, women's, and children's clothing
shoes
fabrics
paints
garden supplies

May—
jewelry
lingerie
handbags
outdoor furniture
TVs
wallpaper and paint

June—
men's clothing and gift items
bridal gift items
bedding
women's shoes

July—
summer clothing
outdoor furniture
sportswear

August—
back-to-school clothes
new cars
camping equipment

September—
back-to-school needs
cars
bicycles
dishes and housewares

October—
coats
lamps
major appliances

November—
furniture
bedding
Christmas items

December—
clothing
toys
jewelry
after-Christmas items

After planning carefully and spending wisely, you will spend less than you earn and thus be rich in blessings and peace of mind. It just takes a little determination. As we learned in one of our church budgeting classes, "It depends on the chick whether you have a nest egg or a goose egg."

Begin getting organized with one step at a time and soon you'll be working wonders and will have that desired time to pursue a hobby. You may even have so much spare time you'll find yourself getting bored. Don't despair! I have a few solutions for that, too!

1. Send for something free.
2. Memorize the "Star Spangled Banner."
3. Learn all fifty states and their capitals.
4. Play a game with a child.
5. Pretend you're famous.
6. Learn the metric system.
7. Read the dictionary.
8. Invent a recipe.
9. Think of new names for the Seven Dwarfs.
10. Try eating a meal with chopsticks.
11. Really go fly a kite.
12. Sort out and throw away all your dried-up ball-point pens.
13. Practice smiling in the mirror.
14. Read your old love letters (out loud!).
15. Go buy a child the toy *you* most wanted as a child.
16. Plant a flower or a tree.
17. Hold hands and reminisce with someone.
18. Learn to say "I love you" in three foreign languages and practice on someone special.
19. Make a list of all your blessings that money can't buy.
20. Write a book (about your exciting life!).

Take a look at your life today, and if you feel you could improve toward reaching your goals, start now. The Lord provides us with the opportunities, but we must "do it!" An old Chinese proverb: Man who sits with mouth open waiting for roast goose to fly in has long hunger.

9
BUILD YOUR HOUSE UPON A ROCK

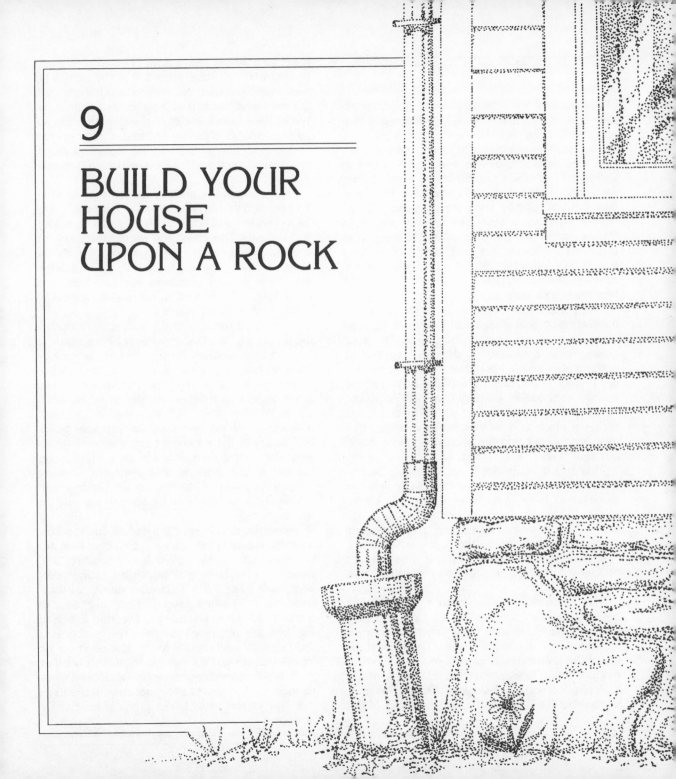

A long time ago, when our two sons, Stephen and Mark, were preschoolers, they learned a little song in Sunday school called "The Wise Man Builds His House Upon a Rock." After much practice, they were prepared to perform the number before a large crowd one Sunday evening. As we sat in the front row proudly watching these two little boys all slicked up in their "Sunday best" singing their hearts out, I saw the love radiate in their eyes, sensed the warmth and security they had, and felt the peace and contentment they knew. As I looked at Roy and saw tears of joy running down his cheeks, I knew then that our home was truly built on a rock.

This parable has always meant a lot to us, but the real and practical aspect of it came to us even more so when we were in Yugoslavia. Our tour guide, Mario, a handsome, dark-haired boy with flashing eyes, pointed out to us the many beautiful old houses in the hills. He explained that in their country earthquakes are very common, so all the wise people look for a solid foundation, or base of rock, on which to build their houses. Then, when the earthquakes come, the whole rock might shake, but their homes would stand.

How much this principle applies to our homes today! No matter where we live in the world, whether alone or in large families, rich or poor, "earthquakes" shake our home foundations through job loss, illness, loss of a loved one, peer pressure, inflation, or just the hectic day-to-day schedules. It is so important that we each have that solid haven or shelter to feel the security and contentment we need.

This foundation is much more than a physical base. Remember, home is not always a place; it's a feeling! We all have the responsibility to create it for ourselves and our loved ones. The first principle of the foundation is love. Love is made up of many actions. One is affection. Everyone needs both physical and psychological affection. No matter whether it's a pat on the back, a shake of the hand, or a tender kiss, it says, "I care." Tests with newborn babies have proved that the ones who were loved and caressed thrived much more than the ones who just had their basic needs cared for. We all have the capability of showing affection for others, and this is just as vital to our well-being as receiving it. Express to someone today how much they mean to you and it will come back a hundred-fold.

Understanding is another way to express love. To accomplish this, we really must care enough to try and understand how another person feels, thinks, and behaves. This can come about most easily by accepting people for what they are. We are all different, and by looking for the unique and different characteristics of others, we can learn and grow from them as well as serve as a magnet to draw out their good qualities.

Love also means listening, talking, and sacrificing for others. All of us, regardless of our status in life, can enrich others' lives as well as our own by showing love in this way. We have a little practice at our house of asking one another, at certain times of pent-up emotion, to "please be the whistle on my teakettle." We all know that when a teakettle is placed over heat, the pressure builds and builds. If the lid is kept on, there will be an explosion; but if there is a whistle provided over the spout, the pressure then becomes pleasant singing. Oh, what a listening ear and understanding heart can accomplish! Be someone's teakettle whistle today!

As we build our strong personal foundations, we must realize (1) we are each a child of God, (2) we are a part of His family (really brothers and sisters to everyone), and (3) we are unique persons, with talents and abilities to develop. I think too often people are caught up in their diets of foods, picking and choosing only quality things to eat, and are not nearly as selective in choosing their spiritual and mental food. How often do we sit in front of the TV set or flip through a book or magazine ingesting unwholesome or unclean mental food. (These things affect our mental health as that type of food affects our physical health.) Be selective in all phases of life. After all, you deserve the very best.

And don't forget that no one else can be "you." No one has the rights to your personality, talents, and characteristics. They are up to you to shape, mold, and use to the best of your ability. You might make a "funny" somebody else, but you are the best "you" in the world!

Nowhere is a good foundation more vital to success than in marriage. A happy marriage can truly be a heaven on earth, but happiness doesn't come by pushing a button or wishing. It is created by building one stone on top of the other—the stones of giving, caring, sharing, serving, sacrificing, and selflessness.

Marriages usually start in a state of bliss, but we soon realize our partners are human, too. They snore, leave the cap off the toothpaste, or forget to shut cupboard doors. But before you criticize, ask yourself, "I wonder what it's like to be married to me." You really wouldn't want a "perfect" mate, would you? I should think they would be awfully hard to live with. The number-one rule is to concentrate on the good things about one another. Differences just add a little spice to a marriage, and solutions *can* be worked out. At our house, Roy is the neat and tidy person, but sometimes I can be a little on the sloppy side. For 24 years, he used his shaving cream every morning, carefully wiped the spout off with the washcloth, replaced the cap, and placed the can on the second shelf on the right-hand side of the medicine cabinet. A short while after, I would go in, shave my legs, and leave the can sitting on the sink with foam dripping down the side. Invariably, I would hear him in the bathroom grumbling and muttering under his breath about the messy can. Well, believe it or not, after all those years, we finally discovered that all it took to eliminate the problem was *two* cans! Now, any morning of the year, you will find Roy's very neat can on the right-hand side of the second shelf, and *somewhere* in the bathroom is mine! Wouldn't life be dull if everything were perfect?

Marriage is a unity of oneness, not a couple or a partnership because that denotes two. It is genu-

inely a *one*ness. You must be united in efforts and purpose to accomplish the goals of a "forever union." I'll never forget how that principle became embedded in my mind. One snowy December morning in Omaha, Nebraska, Roy and I had a real doozy of an argument, and since he is stubborn, and so am I, it was one of those times when we slammed cupboard doors and banged drawers but wouldn't say a word. Roy slammed the front door, and the tires squealed down the driveway. He didn't apologize before leaving, and naturally I wasn't going to say anything because I certainly wasn't wrong! Feeling sorry for myself, I went into the bedroom thinking I would spend a fun day just doing what *I* wanted to do. So I reached in the closet and got out a box of sewing things that a friend had given me as she prepared to move. As I dumped the sewing remnants onto the bed, out fell a *half* pair of scissors from the bottom of the box. It was nicked and dented and absolutely useless. It's significance suddenly hit me. As I looked at that sad, old, rusty piece of metal, I could envision that at one time it was a beautiful, shiny, new pair of scissors capable of performing wonders, creating and assisting in making lovely clothes. But because someone *hadn't* cared enough to keep it well oiled, the screw tightened to hold it as secure as necessary, and used it for the purpose it was intended, it was now without its other half and unable to function. I thought, *This could be me a few years from now if I don't give my marriage the proper care and respect it deserves.* Believe me, I met Roy at the door that evening with a warm apology and lots of love and kisses and vowed that I would always keep the joints well oiled in our marriage. It becomes stronger, sharper, brighter, and shinier each year. This polishing and strengthening are an everyday thing and something we must work at constantly. Just as in any building, we go through phases, and each phase builds a memory to be tucked away in the foundation of a solid life together—the times of developing hobbies together (catching a fish or watching a bud), traveling together, raising a family, or gardening. Don't complain because you feel your mate isn't as involved in an activity as you are. Remember, we are all different, and each individual shows his enjoyment differently.

One of the best ways to learn to enjoy things together is to communicate. Nearly everyone manages to have "maintenance" communication, such as, "Did you take your suits to the cleaners?" "Will you pick up some milk?" "Did you iron my shirts?" "The bus is here." But do we really have any communication to help build personal relationships by discussing feelings, thoughts, interests, and goals? Ask open-ended questions, not ones that can just be answered with a yes or no. Try, "How are the teams lining up for the World Series?" instead of "Did the Reds win again?" or "I've noticed you look a little tired lately. Is there any way I can help lighten the load?" Then learn to *listen*. Give your mate your undivided attention and really care about what he says. Nothing stops communication colder than lack of attention in listening. Don't get impatient and answer your own questions. Relax and genuinely care about what they have to say.

Read and study together. New ideas can add enthusiasm to a relationship. Take classes together. Learn and grow. Never let monotony take over.

If you feel that your marriage is getting a little like "cold gravy," here are some ideas to "perk up" both of you:

WIVES

1. Buy a new nightie (flannel ones not allowed).
2. Determine to be an attractive wife.
3. Have his dinner ready when he comes home (at least have the dishes on the table).
4. Never criticize him in public.
5. Avoid those long phone calls when he's home.
6. Don't leave your stockings hanging in the bathroom.
7. Build him up in the eyes of your children and he'll strive to live up to those expectations.
8. Buy him a gift *he* wants, not what you want him to have.
9. Believe him when he tells you something.
10. Keep confidences he shares with you.
11. *Let* him be the leader in your home.
12. Keep your voice modulated. (Never raise your voice unless the house is on fire.)
13. Ask him sincerely for his advice and then take it!
14. Keep the house comfortable and let him enjoy it. Remember it's his home, too.
15. Don't be afraid to flirt with him and instigate a little romance once in a while.
16. Compliment him. Men love praise!
17. Learn about his occupation and hobbies and enjoy them with him.
18. Write him a love letter and send it to the office.
19. Be frugal and live within the budget. You'll both benefit in the long run.
20. Get up with him in the morning, fix his breakfast, and fill his heart with pleasant thoughts of you to last all day. Remember he is not deaf, dumb, and blind, and he'll probably be seeing lots of attractive women through the day!
21. Don't use his tools and forget to put them back.
22. Don't nag. After telling him twice, I'll bet his "turnoff" switch goes into action. (Believe me, he already knows his mistakes.)
23. Love and admire him for the man he is and give him a big romantic kiss right now!

HUSBANDS

1. When you come home from work, forget the little peck on the cheek. Give her a hug with both arms (not like two old grannies at the church picnic) and have a kiss you'll both remember.
2. Compliment her on how pretty she looks. Be specific: hair style, dress color, or the scent she is wearing.
3. Don't forget to tell her what you enjoyed at dinner.
4. Let her know her opinions matter.

5. Help her to find a little time for herself. You put the kids to bed, read them a story, or take them for a walk.
6. Surprise her with little things: a single flower, a candy bar, a book, or a poem you clipped from a magazine.
7. Share your frustrations and worries with her. You'll be surprised how much closer you'll become.
8. Don't be afraid to show feelings. Tears are a sign of tenderness and a very admirable male quality.
9. Avoid that forbidden question "Did you do anything today?"
10. Plan a special date with her and do something you enjoyed together when you were courting.
11. Never criticize her in public.
12. Let your children know you love her.
13. Instead of a client, take her to lunch sometime.
14. Help at home. She works, too, and it's your home together.
15. Hide a love note for her to find while she's doing housework.
16. Call her once during the day just to say, "I was thinking about you and wanted to say 'I love you.'"
17. Take care of your personal appearance. Be the man she fell in love with.
18. Learn about her hobbies and interests.
19. Learn to hear what she is *really* saying. When she says, "I feel ugly," she may really be saying, "Please tell me I'm pretty."
20. Let her know she's the light of your life and tell her so right now!

THINGS YOU CAN DO TOGETHER

1. Don't call each other mom or dad. Keep those romantic nicknames.
2. Develop a spiritual life together. (The strongest marriage in the world is the one striving for eternity together.)
3. Make your bedroom comfortable and attractive and use it as a haven from the world together!
4. Allow each other to develop their own talents and admire them for it.
5. Develop a hobby or sport interest together.
6. Have a long-range goal or project to look forward to but don't wait for the future to enjoy life together.
7. Work on your family scrapbooks and photo albums together.
8. Hold hands in the movies.
9. Make a list of each other's best features and positive qualities ("what I like about you").
10. Wink at each other now and then.
11. Make a list of "What I'd like you to know about me." This one can be very enlightening and lead to some new and exciting challenges.
12. Put your arms around each other and count your blessings.
P.S. No fair asking your mate to read a certain item on the list.

Start where you are with what you have. Be thankful for each other's good points and build on that with love and appreciation. Happiness is not having what you want but wanting what you have.

I can honestly say that for me the most fulfilling, exciting, and satisfying role I have had in my life has been that of a "wife." No other achievement or award could ever compensate for the rich feeling this role gives me. I meet a lot of women as I travel and speak to groups, and it soon becomes obvious that we wives fall into several categories. Faults and problems are always so easy to recognize on the other side of the fence. Maybe we can all learn from the types of wives I have talked with.

First, there's the competing wife. Those women not only see themselves as helpmates to their husbands but also feel they can do *anything* better. They soon become loud, overbearing, domineering, aggressive, and even masculine in their habits. When they find themselves taking over all the "avenues" of a marriage, they may soon be out in the "street."

The partnership wife is the one who tries hard to make everything "even" in the marriage—the fifty-fifty concept. They are so busy worrying if they are getting their fair share or doing more than they should that life becomes a constant game. When you get too caught up in the score, you miss out on all the exciting plays. In a successful marriage, each one gives his all.

Then there's the nagging wife. She's the one who is determined at the beginning to overhaul her husband and won't be happy until she has completely made him over. After constant nagging at him about his engine ("You need more exercise," "You don't read enough," "You're too slow," etc.), he may drive off to someone else.

How many of us become the "motherly" wife? She is the one who tries to become the ideal homemaker with never a speck of dust on the furniture, fussing over everyone, picking up after everyone, making all the decisions, gaining lots of weight, and forgetting she is a wife. It's easier and more practical to wear those double-knit pant suits and a simple, short haircut. (I once heard a fellow comment, "Can you imagine how sexy it is to run your hand up that bristly neck?") Her voice can soon sound like an army sergeant's, and she's *never* wrong. It sure wouldn't take long to find that husband in the arms of someone else who could give him the admiration he would appreciate.

I'm sure we've all met the disorganized wife. She flits from one thing to another, unable to say "no" to anyone, and then constantly complains because of the pressures that life forces on her. She never feels well and is mad at the world. She pushes herself night and day and still feels guilty about not doing enough. When her husband tries to help her organize, he just doesn't understand. These women hide their true light under a bushel of activities and constantly let things that matter least take precedence over those that matter most.

If we women could only realize the potential there is in lasting relationships, we might go about our lives a little differently.

We *are* feminine, and what a blessing! I love being treated like a queen by my husband. Let's feel, think, act, speak, move, and dress like the women we are. Let's smile and be beautiful. Put a little spark and creativity into these marriages and don't forget the sense of humor. Learn to laugh *at* yourself and then *with* one another.

We don't build a relationship by constantly tearing down our mate. Begin now to fall in love with your sweetheart all over again. Be loyal, truly care for each other, respect one another's differences, be best friends, be lovers, and most important, plan an eternity together.

If you're lucky enough to have children, an integral part of any home is a family. As parents, this can be a most challenging time, but how quickly the years fly by and will never come again. The best advice we ever received as parents was "take the time." How trite this can seem when you can hardly wait until they are out of diapers, starting school, or graduating. But I believe there is probably nothing in this life that will benefit you more, bring more happiness and peace of mind, or have as far-reaching effects as being a good parent. Take time for open arms, talking, reading, family prayer, building memories, teaching, and just plain caring. Don't brush your children off or turn all their care over to others. No one can take the place of mom and dad.

When Heidi was growing up, it became the "in" thing with the children in our neighborhood to call their parents by their first names. Since Roy and I were from the "old school" and believe this showed lack of respect, we taught our children that this was not proper. I'll always remember the day I took Heidi, then 4 years old, to the grocery store on a crowded Thursday afternoon. With her inquisitive nature, she wandered into another aisle and we got separated. I soon heard this timid little voice calling, "Beverly—Beverly." Embarrassed at her lack of respect, I immediately scolded her for calling me by my name. Then, in all sincerity and genuine love, she looked up at me and said, "But mommy, there are lots of moms in here. I wanted my own!" Every child feels that deep sense of "wanting my own," and this presents a responsibility but also a grand opportunity. Maybe we don't always recognize the opportunity because it goes around wearing an apron and work shoes.

Families, like marriages, do require a blueprint. First, we must realize that parents have a right (and a responsibility) to build the attitudes and behavior patterns of their children. The easiest and most direct way to do this is by example. You can't lead someone to a destination if you aren't going there, also. As parents we must *live* our convictions. Children don't care how much we know until they know how much we care. Establish guidelines and habits as a family. Just be careful that you are always headed in the right direction. Sometimes those habits can be hard to change. A road sign we saw out in Wyoming on a backwoods road read, "Choose your ruts carefully. You'll be in them for 8 miles."

Next, teach your family the principle of work. Home is the best place to learn the dignity of a job well done. This isn't easy in this day of modern convenience, travel, and leisure; but with a little ingenuity, scheduling, and discipline, it's amazing how much can be accomplished. Each person should have responsibilities in the home to fit their age and ability. What a help this can be to everyone. (Those schedules we discussed in chapter 8 won't work you to death, they'll work you toward living!)

As well as helping everyone involved, work also teaches. One summer afternoon, while we were remodeling and building a room on our home, Roy was working with the two little boys sawing, hammering, and measuring. Our neighbor came over and started telling Roy how he was wasting time using this method and how he could do things more efficiently. Roy very patiently listened and then said, "Thanks, Carl, but you see, we're not building a mansion here; we're building boys." How thankful I am for the patience and insight Roy has.

Sometimes we as parents hesitate to exert ourselves in our roles because we feel uncomfortable. This can be made simple by having a heart to heart talk with your child explaining you are new at this role of parenting and only have his interests at heart. You'll be surprised how understanding and forgiving a child can be if he knows none of us are perfect and we are all striving for the best for one another. It doesn't take a lot to give a child a sense of security. Gifts, money, and material things are not required, only time, patience, and a sense of caring. A magazine once carried an article in which college seniors expressed their wishes toward family:

1. I wish I could remember evenings when dad played or read with us instead of quietly reading his paper alone.
2. I wish I could remember one holiday when dad joined us in an activity instead of giving us money or equipment to do it while he stayed home and worked.
3. I wish I could remember one week, month, or day even that mom made purposeful work out of chores by planning them with us instead of merely announcing what our jobs were each morning.

Give them that time now. It will be much more valuable than the property or sum of money you may leave them later. Really enjoy each member of your family. Help them to feel special. Give them an opportunity to learn the skills that interest them. Work *with* them. (You may learn something, too!)

Children need physical, emotional, and mental caring from the time they are born and continuously throughout their lives. It doesn't stop when they become teenagers or even parents themselves. It's easy to hug, squeeze, and hold them physically when they are tiny babies, but as important are building snowmen together, walking hand in hand to catch a school bus, and later pulling weeds, playing catch, or wrestling on the living-room floor. Even later, a pat on the shoulder, a squeeze of the hand, or a good-night kiss is important.

Emotionally, we expect to comfort away the fears of the "gorilla in the closet" or the spider on the ceiling, but also there's the fear of going away to college, choosing that mate, and your calm reassurance with "Yes, dear, the baby is going to be all right." The most helpful way of nurturing our children emotionally is to accept their problems, fears, and worries without condemning them and to give them the opportunity to share yours. Let yourselves be "real people." Laugh, cry, and worry together. Have you ever felt closer to a child than when you were giggling together over a shared secret or laughing while you watched a new puppy playing?

Mental caring is the joy of helping a loved one grow. What a sense of satisfaction you both receive as the child labors to draw the "stick man" as you taught her, or to accomplish tying that shoe for the first time. Some of the sweetest words a parent can hear are "I'll always remember how much fun it was when you taught me to . . ."

Even when we are all adults, the mental learning never ceases. We continue to share thoughts, books, art, music, and ideas. Now the joy reverses, and the thrill comes in the statement "Here, mom, I thought you'd like to read this. Then let's talk about it. OK?"

Love yor children physically, emotionally, and mentally. Love them as persons, unique in every way. Love them in spite of their weaknesses and differences from you. Love them every day as a child *and* as an adult, through whatever stage you both are going. Give them the pride and honor in being who they are! *Tell* them you love them. Again, this is easy while they are cuddly, soft little babies, smelling sweet with talcum and with cute little smiles on their faces. But what about that teenager? Do your typical days sound like:

Are you going to be in that shower all day?
Don't gulp your food!
Those Levi's are too tight!
When are you going to clean your room?
Turn that stereo down!
You need a haircut.
Take your feet off the furniture.
Quit teasing her!
Get off the phone.
Clean up that mess.

Turn off that stereo and get to bed.
Don't bother me now. I don't have time.
The day is over, and I didn't have time—even for an "I love you."

It's easy to let trivial things cloud our vision, and we miss the important things in life. It pays to stop our busy, rushing pace once in a while and remember how much we love the ones we love.

When we lived in our "first" new little home in Sandy, Utah, I took great pride in having my house spanking clean and my floors spotless. I'll always remember the day I had just waxed my kitchen floor to look up and see Stephen walk in with a muddy hammer, some rocks, *and* muddy feet. Before he had a chance to speak, I raised my voice to the highest pitch possible and in no uncertain terms told him how hard I had been working and that because of him all my work had been in vain, and besides, he was naughty for getting the hammer all muddy! He turned and went back outside while I cleaned up the mud. I soon had a lump in my throat thinking of all the unkind things I had said to a loving, little, defenseless boy who was so tenderhearted he cried at the sight of a dead bird. I'm sure he just wanted the warmth and reassurance of my love. I dried my hands and went out to the field behind our house where he again sat cracking rocks (one of his favorite pastimes). I reached over and squeezed him and said, "Steve, I love you very much." With a smile on his face, he said, "I love you, too, mom, and I wanted you to see how the center of this rock sparkles just like your eyes do when you smile at me." I had seen the mud on the floor and missed the sparkle in my life.

As I talk with people in show business, they often use the term "on the road" in a negative way. I realized one day that Roy and I had raised our children "on the road." Not in the sense that show business people use it, but whenever a problem arose, a child was troubled, needed counsel or just cheering up, it seemed easiest to discuss these things while we drove to the gas station, dropped the books off at the library, or took the clothes to the cleaners. Whenever the kids asked if Roy or I had an errand to run and could they ride along, we knew a listening ear was needed. The security and privacy of a car can be very reassuring. Other times we took to the "road" on foot and solved our problems with long walks. Sharing time alone can mend many fences and heal heavy hearts. Kids raised "on the road" have a great advantage. But we must take advantage of the moment and not wait until "after the fact." This reminds me of one of Roy's favorite stories I'd like to share with you. It was written over a century ago by Joseph Malius and was retold by Harold B. Lee in his book *Youth and the Church*.

A FENCE OR AN AMBULANCE

Twas a dangerous cliff, as they freely confessed
Though to walk near its crest was so pleasant.
But over its terrible edge there had slipped
A duke and full many a peasant.
So the people said something would have to be done
But their projects did not at all tally.
Some said, "Put a fence round the edge of the cliff."
Some, "An ambulance down in the valley."

But the cry for the ambulance carried the day,
For it spread through the neighboring city.
A fence may be useful or not, it is true,
But each heart became brimful of pity
For those who slipped over that dangerous cliff;
And the dwellers in highway and alley
Gave pounds or gave pence, not to put up a fence,
But an ambulance down in the valley.

"For the cliff is all right if you're careful," they said,
"And if folks even slip or are dropping,
It isn't the slipping that hurts them so much,
As the shock down below when they're stopping."
So day after day, as these mishaps occurred,
Quick forth would their rescuers sally
To pick up the victims who fell off the cliff
With their ambulance down in the valley.

Then an old sage remarked, "It's a marvel to me
That people give far more attention
To repairing results than to stopping the cause
When they'd much better aim at prevention.
Let us stop at its source all the mischief," he cried,
"Come neighbors and friends let us rally.
If the cliff we will fence, we might almost dispense
With the ambulance down in the valley."

"Oh, he's a fanatic," the others rejoined,
"Dispense with the ambulance? Never.
He'd dispense with all charities, too, if he could,
No, No, we'll support them forever.
Aren't we picking up folks just as fast as they fall;
And shall this man dictate to us? Shall he?
Why should people of sense stop to put up a fence
While the ambulance works in the valley?"

But a sensible few who are practical, too,
Will not bear with such nonsense much longer.
They believe that prevention is better than cure;
And their party will still be the stronger.
Encourage them then with your purse, voice, and pen;
And while other philanthropists dally,
They will scorn all pretense and put up a fence
On the cliff that hangs over the valley.

Better guide well the young than reclaim them when old,
For the voice of true wisdom is calling.
To rescue the fallen is good, but 'tis best
To prevent other people from falling.
Better close up the source of temptation and crime,
Than deliver from dungeon and galley.
Better put a strong fence 'round the top of the cliff,
Than an ambulance down in the valley.

Many may say that raising a family is "no picnic," but I say it is! At a picnic, there are bound to be a few bugs to try your patience, sunburns that sting a little, some spilled beans, an overcooked hot dog, some limp potato chips, and even an occasional thundercloud, but the conclusion brings a full tummy, a happy heart, and peace and contentment.

Most of us start our lives seeing more sunshine than rain, but when the storms come, remember there will be rainbows. Everyone must experience rain showers to help them grow and develop and become stronger. Help yourselves and your family feel a sense of strength and unity by:

1. Building a "record" of your lives with albums, tapes, scrapbooks, and memory boxes. (What child wouldn't be thrilled to have her first school dress or his first baseball mitt?)
2. Helping a child write his personal history day by day.
3. Taping an interview with members of the family on their birthdays and recording their feelings and memories of the past year.
4. Starting a round-robin letter with members of your family. (Insist no one keep the letter longer than a week.) By pulling out your former letter each time around, you will have a diary of sorts of your happenings.
5. If your grandparents or favorite aunts and uncles live far away, why not have a birthday party for them, anyway. Serve their favorite dishes, talk about their lives, and look at pictures or keepsakes of theirs. (Did the children know Grandpa Jones was a blacksmith or that grandma won a national prize for her quilts?) This can be done with great-grandparents and relatives who are deceased, also. What better way for children to feel strength and unity in the family. By continuing to share these things through each generation, they will really become part of an eternal family.

As we build each day of our lives, mornings turn to afternoons, and soon we are in the evening of our life. But as someone once said, "Considering the alternative, I don't mind a bit!"

I learned a lot about growing old from my Grandma Benson, with whom I lived for part of my childhood. Grandma was never the grandmotherly type who resorted to rocking chairs, hair drawn back in a bun, and shoulders slumped in self-pity in her old age. Her face was bright with a smile, her walk quick with anticipation for each new step in life, and her clothes stylish in the trend of the day. After visiting with elderly acquaintances, she often commented to me, "He looked so grim and sour. He may get people to feel sorry for him, but he sure won't win friends." She felt posture played a key part in growing old. Even though her fingers were crooked with arthritis and her back wasn't as straight as a board, she kept stretching and exercising. I even remember her sitting in the evening "puffing" out her cheeks and smiling so when her face got wrinkles, "they'd be in the *right places!*"

Grandma always realized we were impressed with her knowledge and experience, but she never belabored the fact by telling us countless times about her past. Instead, she realized that younger people are living *now,* and she kept herself up to date on current things. She lived and talked in the present.

She accepted the fact that age brings aches and pains, and she always knew how to look on the bright side. As she looked on her bottle of pills and read what ailments they were good for, she said, "Well, I'll really get my money's worth. I've got them all!"

I suppose it's OK to collect salt and pepper shakers or sit and play cards all day, but grandma preferred to be sewing new dresses for the girls, taking care of the yard, painting a wall, or tending the great-grandbabies. Not having much wealth was never a problem for grandma. Her philosophy was soap and water are cheap, creativity can make something from nothing, so laugh a little, sing a lot, and never take your teeth out in public.

In thinking of grandma's life, I think of the lines from Jack London, "I would rather be ashes than dust." It is sad to see someone sitting and waiting for the days to pass by. The number of days is not important but how we live them, and not just the physical accomplishments but the treasures we store up in our minds and the attitudes we have toward living. Our responsibility is to live and not just exist.

If you have reached retirement age, may I urge you not to also retire your spirit and mind. You have so much to give, *now,* so share it with the world. Marion G. Romney once said, "You can tell a man's age by the amount he suffers when he hears a new idea." Keep alert and active. Write or visit friends, read good books, attend lectures and cultural events, travel. If you are physically unable, don't let that stop you. Study about other countries and places. Eat regular meals and do suitable exercises, teach a skill to a youngster, enjoy and learn about a new type of music. Old age is not for quitters, so throw back those shoulders and "live" a life full of love.

A HOUSE BECOMES A HOME
by Wells and Lorraine Wilkinson

A house becomes a home when there's love inside,

When you let your love be as a guide,
When there's joy and sweet understanding,
When you're handing out a compliment or two.
A house becomes a home when you do your part,
And when all your heart is wrapped in those around.
Life can be just like a symphony
When you see a house become a home.

A house becomes a home when it's peaceful there,
When for every one, there is a care,
When each one is kind and forgiving,
When you're living for some happiness to share.
A house becomes a home when it's full of life,
When there is no strife among its very own.
Life can be so sweet and heavenly
When you see a house become a home.

Begin now to build your house on a "rock." Create the walls with love, warmth, and unity and then crown it with a roof shingled with memories, experiences, peace of mind, and contentment. I promise you, yours will be a house full of sunshine.

INDEX

INDEX TO RECIPES

*indicates use of microwave oven

ABOUT THE AUTHOR

Beverly K. Nye is a homemaker first—she insists on it. Television audiences and people who meet her warm immediately to her low-keyed personality. Her comfortable manner makes things seem not only possible, but almost easy.

She was raised on farm in Nebraska and that, coupled with her Mormon upbringing, provided much of her background for the homemaking skills she possesses.

Beverly and her husband, Roy, an insurance executive, are the parents of four children, all of whom are married. The Nyes now have seven grandchildren.

Practicing creativity, economy, and old-fashioned nutrition, the Nyes raised their family while living in ten different locations in the United States. Frequent moving has given Beverly Nye an appreciation of various ways of life—and has also contributed to the wide assortment of recipes she has collected over the years. Interested in sharing her many hints and ideas, Beverly Nye has taught homemaking classes for over 20 years in various church, community, and school groups. She appears frequently on radio and television shows, and for several years she has been a regular on The Bob Braun Show, a syndicated program produced in Cincinnati, Ohio. She lectures throughout the country and feels her biggest rewards are building confidence in others and seeing others motivated to enjoy their roles as homemakers.

Beverly Nye's belief in the importance of the family is summed up in the quote, "No success on earth can compensate for failure in the home."

Get the
latest tips & recipes
from Beverly Nye:
Subscribe to
Sunshine Notes

Sunshine Notes is a monthly newsletter from Beverly Nye, packed with good ideas for saving time and money in the home. Beverly Nye discusses:

- Best supermarket buys of the month
- New recipes
- Gardening indoors and out
- Food storage tips
- Information on new home products
- Plus other items that will add to your family's enjoyment and pocketbook.

It's like a monthly visit with Beverly Nye. Don't miss an issue. Subscribe now with the order form below.

Order Form

Please send me *Sunshine Notes* for one year (12 issues) for $15. My payment is enclosed.

Name

Address

City   State   Zip

Make checks payable to Sunshine Notes.

Mail to:
SUNSHINE NOTES
P.O. Box 42309
Cincinnati, Ohio 45242

GUARANTEE: If you are not satisfied with *Sunshine Notes* you may cancel at any time for any reason and receive a full refund for all copies still due you.

A home full of love for everyone

Beverly Nye, one of America's leading homemaking authorities, believes in a strong, vital family unit as the source of happiness and well-being. She comes by this philosophy quite naturally, having been born and raised on a farm near Grand Island, Nebraska and having nurtured her husband, four children and seven grandchildren. Now she shares the wisdom of her experience with hundreds of ideas for making your own family life richer and more enjoyable. For everyone who has ever tried to create a haven of their own, Beverly Nye shows how to make homemaking easier and more rewarding. It's all here: delectable new recipes (including low-calorie feasts), a wealth of supermarketing know-how, from best buys in food to seasonal sales of household necessities; all about freezing, drying, canning and storing foods; timesaving sewing and needlework hints; imaginative party games, family activities and more. On every page she shares her secrets for a happy home and a joyous, healthy, loving life.

LOOK FOR
Beverly Nye's
A Family Raised on Sunshine
AND
A Family Raised on Rainbows